Some Appreciation for

This is not so much a book as a compelling encyclopaedic excursion informed by the fertile, creative and committed scholarship of Jock Stein. While firmly grounded in the biblical Psalms, new light is thrown on their texts not only by reference to the work of scriptural experts but also to the perspectives of such diverse writers as the French deconstructionist philosopher Jacques Derrida, the celebrated Canadian literary critic Northrop Frye and the Scottish conservationist and explorer John Muir.

While *Temple and Tartan* explores ancient poems and cites celebrated intellectuals of previous centuries, its insights are not wedded to the past. Allusions to contemporary issues and current politicians and theorists abound, and issues of Scottish civic life and nationhood are ever present. What is distinctly original are the poems which Jock himself has written, often taking their subject matter from the biblical texts, but pursuing highly imaginative thought lines. Take, for example, the opening verses of the poem based on Psalm 13:

> I'm beating, God, upon your door.
> I screw my eyes to read your lips
> but I am shaken to the core
>
> by covid, climate, and what's more
> you've morphed into a God who sleeps
> when I would worship and adore.

Or this Scots vernacular musing on Psalm 94 entitled *Rage*

> Cum oan, ma Goad, ableeze wi wrath,
> wha kens the hairts ill-cleckit airts,
> jist gie the prood yins thair awmous,
> ding them doon tae chow the stour.

The scholarship, intellectual dexterity, range of subject matter, and all-pervasive faith and creativity of the author cannot be underestimated. My only regret is that Jock Stein was born too late. Had he been around in 1647 when Presbyterian rhymers were tinkering with the metrical psalms, we might have had more spirited paraphrases of the sacred texts.

John Bell, Minister and Hymn-writer

Writing books imitating the Psalms, whether on the whole psalm or on just a single verse, has been a popular initiative undertaken in Judaism, Christianity (and also in Islam) for well over a thousand years, perhaps reaching its zenith in English literature during the Elizabethan period.

This has continued up to the present day: indeed, only in the last two years two seminal works of this nature have appeared and have each had excellent reviews. The poets, Ed Clarke and Malcolm Guite, each show that imitations of psalmody, which play as much on the *poetry* as on the psalm, are perhaps bringing in a new literary approach to studies of the Psalms. But why another work, by Jock Stein, using the same literary engagement with the Psalms ? One of the key differences is this work focuses not only on the Psalms, and not only on poetry in general, but on Scottish poetry and Scottish Psalms and indeed on Scottish history and literature. So this work continues a literary tradition of poetry imitating psalmody.

There are therefore places when those without this Scottish background cannot fully appreciate the nuances of interpretation. But there are many more places with original and indeed moving insights: for example, the poems in Book Three, on migration, are particularly memorable, not least for the way in which they touch on a good deal of Scottish history. And other poems by Stein are similarly accessible and provocative. I'm thinking here of, for example, one on Psalm 13: 'I'm beating, God, upon your door'; or on Psalm 20:

> 'God save the king – or maybe queen.'
> Have we no republican psalms,
> no hint that what's aye been
> might be a changing scene?'

> Susan Gillingham, Professor Emeritus of
> Hebrew Bible at Oxford University

The Psalms are the spiritual well of our nationhood from their daily recital in the Border monasteries of the medieval Kirk to their sung recital by a Gaelic choir from the land of the Free Kirk at the opening of the Scottish Parliament. *Temple and Tartan* magnificently shows the creativity of the Psalms to illumine our common life in all its complexity and challenge. The well of the Psalmist overflows in its poems for the renewing of the nation today.

> William Storrar, Director, Center
> for Theological Inquiry, Princeton

Jock Stein's poems in *Temple and Tartan* are the culmination of many years of tense, attentive thought about the meaning of the Old Testament Psalms, throughout history and in the immediate present, in Scotland and for humanity at large. They have arisen from a lifetime's deep immersion and slow marinading in the Bible and a long enquiry into the toughest questions of theology and Christian practice.

Their immediate drive towards a structured form is the result of Jock Stein's eident work of self-conscious organisation of research undertaken for a PhD in creative practice at the University of Glasgow but any trace of the merely academic is blown away by the immediacy of the poetry, the storytelling, the imagery and the political application they deliver. Their power is striking and sustained. This grand, epic sequence ranges through history, confronting both the independence of thought struggling for clear presence through Medieval Scotland, and the Calvinist inheritance at work in the Highlands and Islands.

The whole work is leavened by good humour, sharp wit and generous sympathy but these are matched by a sense of unanswered questions, irredeemable loss and despair. A particularly tough and compassionate episode engages with the tragedy of the loss of the men of the *Iolaire* early in New Year's morning, 1919. Throughout the sequence the focus is consistently sharp, clean and clear. So many different poetic forms are fluently and engagingly at work in Jock Stein's poems that the broad, sweeping canvas seems almost effortlessly covered and makes for constantly compelling, gripping, page-turning reading. Yet the poems not only prompt but command deep contemplation.

This is an extraordinary work, leaving no room for any doubt that the Psalms have much to tell us today of the big contemporary questions that society, politics and human experience bring upon us. They remind us of the virtues of the faith in a Christian culture which made possible Chartres, and Bach's B minor mass. They do not shirk from counting the cost but ultimately, they are poems of affirmation, never more needed than now.

Alan Riach, Professor of Scottish Literature,
University of Glasgow

Many years ago, in my first proper job, Jock Stein was kind and trusting enough to allow me to work from and along with the church. His support and understanding of my early adventures in youth work gave me an apprenticeship like no other. I listened, learned, chopped and changed direction a thousand ways and for the whole time I enjoyed the patient oversight of my friend and mentor, Jock.

In trying to make sense of my own faith in those early days I would read the Psalms. They seemed to offer consolation, energy and occasionally some inspiration. They were songs and I was trying to be a songwriter. They were written when people felt happy, or scared, triumphant or defeated, hopeful or desolate. They became a place to go, a shelter from the chaos that reigned in and around our small flat in the early days of the youth project we'd started with the help and inspiration of Jock and the people of the Steeple Parish Church.

So, forty years later, I find myself reading my old mentor's reflections on these psalms. His knowledge is boundless and though his focus is on Scotland, there is much to learn and understand for any culture. If there is one take-away, spend time with the psalms of exile and Jock's own, characteristic compassion for the migrants and the outsiders.

His poem on Psalm 73. Prescient and urgent:

> Alan Kurdi, toddler, drowned en route to Kos,
> island of healing and some hope of passage;
> a photo speeded evolution, changing migrant
> cockroaches to human casualties in hours;

Then on Psalm 81, on the horror of the forgotten Morecambe cockle pickers:

> How many migrants die in lorries,
> in the desert, on the mountains,
> in the dangerous sea? How long
> before a cockled world takes notice?

There's much to reflect on in *Temple and Tartan*. Perhaps the book itself might act as an appropriate prompt to his own Church of Scotland which, Jock reflects, is the only one of the major denominations not to guarantee a Psalm reading within every congregation's weekly worship.

I'm grateful to Jock for so much. On reflection too, I'm grateful that, in Scotland, there is still the intellectual, theological and artistic space afforded to allow his learning and imagination to take flight.

Ricky Ross, Deacon Blue

APPRECIATION

Temple and Tartan is a joy of a book. It combines good scholarship (which it wears lightly) and wide reading, with the rich fruits of a seasoned imagination, both poetic and political. Some may be surprised that a book by a retired kirk meenister has some 'piss and vinegar', but that reflects the earthiness of the Psalms which provide rich literary and spiritual inspiration for this work. Don't mistake this for a book only of interest to religious people, it makes an acute, sensitive and thoughtful contribution to contemporary Scottish Studies and to our national self-understanding. And the poems are terrific. Highly recommended.

Doug Gay
Glasgow University

Underpinned by wide reading and a depth of scholarship, Jock Stein's poems have a freshness and an urgency, tapping ancient springs so that they flow once more and 're-enchant the universe'.

Roger Garfitt,
Poet and erstwhile Editor of *Poetry Review*

It was a privilege to have early sight of this remarkable work which is a signal contribution to Scotland's literary heritage, and also of the reflection on the Psalms of the Hebrew Bible. It is unashamedly one man's reading of the book of Psalms and of Scottish history, but what an informed, curious and articulate reading. A panoply of conversation partners from past and present are brought into the mix. For those to whom the Psalms are scripture, it is well to be reminded that their power comes from their humanity, their fractiousness and their contradictions.

Jock Stein's intensely personal and human reflections embody the paradox that what is most universally true about us is our particularity, a paradox which is at the heart of the psalms. The language of these poems combines familiarity with originality in a way that is consistently fresh. Its ease and communicativeness conceal the masterly deftness with which formal devices are deployed. These are poems for the tongue and ear, not just for the eye. Read them aloud and let them tease your palate with the complexity of a really good whisky.

Hugh Pyper, Professor of Biblical Studies,
Sheffield University

Other books by the author
may be found on the Handsel Press website,
www.handselpress.co.uk

A CD of the author reading poems on the first book of Psalms
is normally included with this book, recorded on the Scotsoun label.

Copies of this, and of later CDs of poems on books 2-3, 4-5
will be available through the website

Poetry on Book 4 of the Psalms, found on page 174 of this book, has
been published along with a Gaelic translation by Maoilios Caimbeul
as a separate booklet, *The Iolaire*

TEMPLE and TARTAN

Psalms, Poetry and Scotland

Jock Stein

British Library Cataloguing in Publication Data:
a catalogue record for this publication
is available from the British Library

ISBN: 978-1-912052-74-5

Typeset in 11.5pt Minion Pro at Haddington, Scotland

Printed by West Port Print & Design, St Andrews

Contents

Thanks   x

Invitation   xi

Chapter One   The Magic Carpet   1

Book 1 Poetry   *CARPET*   22

Chapter Two   Ballads and Bridges   59

Book 2 Poetry   *JOURNEY*   83

Chapter Three   Migration and Identity   106

Book 3 Poetry   *MIGRANTS*   129

Chapter Four   Music and Beyond   150

Book 4 Poetry   *PIBROCH*   174

Chapter Five   Protest and Praise   184

Book 5 Poetry   *TAPESTRY*   229

Chapter Notes   265

Acknowledgments   292

Bibliography   294

Thanks

To John Bell, Susan Gillingham, Iain Provan and Will Storrar in particular for advice and encouragement on writing and re-writing this book.

To Stewart (Jay) Brown, Edward Clarke, John Davies, Malcolm Guite, Colin Herd, Tom Hubbard, Kerry Magruder, James McGonigal, Alastair McIntosh, David Mitchell, Angus Morrison, John Purser, Jamie Reid-Baxter, Michael Symmons Roberts, Harry Smart and other academics, clergy and poets who shared their wisdom and knowledge with me – and especially to my PhD supervisors Doug Gay and Alan Riach.

To Ian White, who now leads the Inspiration Orchestra, but who himself wrote and performed musical versions of all the Psalms in the 1980s, and was a role model for my project of writing poetry on all the Psalms.

To others who have read and commented on this book, in particular Roger Garfitt whose Poetry Masterclasses at Madingley Hall kept me on the right road, Tom Gordon whose own daily blog is full of wisdom and encouragement, Hugh Pyper, whose translations of Old Testament Hebrew poetry into Scots are a wonder, and Ricky Ross, who many years ago in Dundee's Steeple Church, showed me what music and drama, youth and commitment could offer the world.

To George Watt and Scotsoun for recording the poems read aloud.

To my wife Margaret whose love, encouragement and household care has given me so much freedom of body, mind and spirit.

The faults and lacunae remain my own, and I will be happy to continue learning about the book of Psalms with others who have been touched by these inspired and inspiring writings.

Invitation

Welcome to this quick tour of a book which is a bit unusual.

- It's about the Psalms – but it's ancient *and* modern.

- It's about Scotland – yet for people of other nations too.

- It includes history, politics, philosophy, theology – but it's written in a fairly popular style.

- It has some serious poetry – yet I think it's accessible.

The subtitle indicates three axes which I am proud to grind, but I really mean axes in the other sense, which will keep crossing: the book of Psalms, poetry, and Scotland. This is certainly true of the poems I have written on Books 1 to 5 of the Old Testament Psalms.

These poems (numbers and title in italics, e.g. *3 Chin on Chest*) are responses to the Psalms, not versions of them. They pick up ideas, but may then dispute them. They can be read without opening a Bible, though good to have one handy. They use a variety of forms, old and new, simple and complex. Two long poems have been written for Books 2 and 4 of the Psalms, which have a particular focus on Scottish history, and short poems for Books 1, 3 and 5.

Before each set of poems there is a chapter introducing the Psalms and the poetry. The American poet William Carlos Williams once said to Harvard students, 'You should never explain a poem – but it always helps!'

Each chapter-and-poem has a different thread (which also goes through the whole book). You could read the chapters without the poetry, you could read the poetry without the chapters, you could read them as they are, one after the other . . . but they are placed where they are for a reason: to try and make connections, in the spirit of George Davie's *Democratic Intellect*. That's what the world needs today, not the quick links of the internet but the deep links of the mind. The algorithms used to feed social media accounts often push people towards extremes and into silos. This book is a protest, and a modest spinning of threads which can be used to join up rather than drive apart.

The poems themselves make up what I call *a poetry of enquiry*. The five chapter-and-poem threads weave a plaid which I hope the reader will enjoy wearing. Of course, being tartan, there are another five threads running the other way, describing what poets are actually doing, but to keep life simple I won't draw them together till the start of Chapter Five.

One last thing which is unusual. Some readers enjoy skipping – you read a bit, then you jump on. I have tried to anticipate this, and make it easy. Chapters have two parts, and you can read Part 1 to get a handle on the poetry which follows, missing out Part 2 which is generally more academic. These second parts are more detailed – though if that makes them dull, that's my fault. To help you with this, there is a summary of each part at the start of each chapter. Other than that, I have put references and some detailed argument in endnotes (easier than footnotes for the general reader), and occasionally used smaller indented type for more scholarly material. I use 'Psalms' for individual psalms and for the whole book of Psalms, 'psalms' otherwise, though it is hard to be consistent.

The connections in the book arise from a combination of standard academic research with the more controversial 'research through creative practice', which is, I suppose, much what poets and other craftspeople do anyway.

Welcome now to the book itself.

Jock Stein
Haddington
August 2022

Chapter One
The Magic Carpet

To enquire in his temple (Psalm 27:4)

Part 1

1 Temple Travel

2 The Psalms

3 Five Books

4 Temple and Tartan

Part 2

5 Genesis and the Psalms

6 More on 'Temple'

7 The First Two Psalms: Poem 1 'Temple Garden'; Poem 2 'Irony Redeemed'

8 Enquiry: The Jewish Way of Interpretation; the Democratic Intellect in Scotland

Part 1

1 Temple Travel

Not many people enter the world a few centuries ago, as in the *Outlander* films. Not many people enter a cathedral and find themselves looking down on the world from the other side of the planet. But that is what cathedrals, and stories, and poetry are for – space and time travel, in the temple of the imagination. Wallace Stevens wrote, 'We say God and the imagination are one,'[1] which makes a temple an appropriate place for take off, since whatever Stevens himself meant or did not mean by that, it allows imagination a key role in the mind of God, and invites God to take a special place in the human imagination.

1

To enter the temple of God is to stand on a carpet. A carpet of welcome, since it is soft underfoot, and brightly coloured, perhaps even like tartan, which will feature later in the book. A carpet of judgment, since to be 'on the carpet' before God is to see things as God sees them, in ourselves and in the world, and that is uncomfortable as well as purifying: but to get things (even a little) sorted out is the gift of the temple, whether for poet or peasant or prelate. True, if you hear 'I'll sort ye oot' in some parts of Scotland, you'd be advised to run, and run fast – but to be judged, or 'sorted out' by God is to be made clean and ready for the kind of journey I am speaking of.

Beyond welcome, beyond judgment, lies the journey which the temple offers us. A journey of the imagination, yes, but a journey occupied by real people and places. A journey on a magic carpet, with those two gifts of welcome and judgment on offer to every situation we encounter.

For this journey, the Psalms are a wonderful, if unexpected guide. That is what I found writing poems on them all. I didn't try to copy what was in a psalm, nor did I usually explain what I came across, though I did a fair bit of study on them. I let them steer the carpet, through my own memories, through other books I was reading, through current events . . . but it's time I said something about the Psalms themselves. Not that much – there are plenty other books about them – but enough to prepare you for the journey.

2 The Psalms

The Old Testament Psalms are a series of one-sided conversations, some quite heated, on the joys and sorrows of life in Israel, and (to our surprise) on life in the 21st century. They are an enquiry into the meaning of life, sometimes affirming they know what it is, other times complaining that they don't. The conversation partner is sometimes God, sometimes friends and family, sometimes enemies, sometimes the writer himself (it's generally been assumed not *herself*).

The language is not the language of science, which is descriptive and precise. It is the language of art, which invites the participant to bring themselves into the picture. When the Psalm writer floods his bed with tears, it is the person, not the mattress, who is soaked with grief. Not so different from poetry in many times and many languages, except for two words.

God has dropped out of serious speech in many parts of Europe today, even though religion remains a major factor in the rest of the world. And where this is not the case, as in Russia, Poland and Hungary, countries which do not suffer from public atheism, commentators shake their heads over their politics and by association their religion. Strange that, you would expect that when the welcome and judgment of God is taken seriously it would change so many things, but we humans have a terrible habit of domesticating God to suit our own inclinations. The current misuse of the 'Holy Rus' myth to support Russia's war on Ukraine is an awful example.[2]

The other word – **Israel** – is another subject of controversy, due to its 20th century revival as a modern nation, and the complexity of Middle East politics. As far back as the time of Charlemagne, the Jews were presented as the only proof of God's existence. They certainly are distinctive – they punch 500 times their population weight in earning Nobel prizes.

They are not the only people to suffer genocide, but they have survived – just as they survived without a homeland for nearly two millennia after the Romans bulldozed capital and country in 70 CE. I recognise this in a short poem on the shortest Psalm 117, '*Nae Hairm*', one of a few poems written in Scots:

> Wee psalm, nae hairm intendit.
> Jist the scandal o particularitie.

The Psalms, like the people, are particular, even peculiar. Some of their sentiments irritate and challenge us, just as they did those who wrote and collected them. And yet, as the poem on Psalm 128 has it, the fifteen notes of the Psalms of Ascent (120 – 134)

> make a symphony for Israel,
> an orchestra of horticulture
> seeded in a thousand lands.

Scotland also is a particular nation, and has been deeply affected by this collection of writings. Its history and people have in turn influenced other countries, not least America. As *Poem 82 'Clearance'* puts it:

> Scots and powerful doctrine
> cleared the ocean

and turned up in many lands. 'Powerful' can also be dangerous – think of two ideas: 'the white man's burden' which fuelled British Colonialism, and 'American exceptionalism' which may have died only recently when the last serviceman left Afghanistan.

However, any nation can apply the Psalms to their own life. The Psalms are not just for people of a particular religion, or a particular race. 'All human life is found within the Psalms', as the Church Father and theologian Athanasius put it in a famous book on the incarnation.[3] The Psalms are arranged in five books, and while my poems on Book 2 and 4 are focused more on Scotland, the poems on Books 1,3 and 5 are universal.

3 Five Books

Book 1	Psalms 1 – 41
Book 2	Psalms 42 – 72
Book 3	Psalms 73 – 89
Book 4	Psalms 90 – 106
Book 5	Psalms 107 – 150

Judging from the headings to some psalms, perhaps added later on, there are three smaller collections of 'David Psalms' within the whole (3 – 41, 51 – 72, 138 – 145). Until the 19th century the Psalms were generally assumed to be written by David, Asaph and others given in the headings,[4] and there is a long tradition of seeing them all as 'Psalms of David'. In the last two centuries, three things in particular have impacted how we understand the Psalms:

(1) People have noticed **the different types of psalm**, like royal psalms, wisdom psalms, temple psalms, psalms of lament or complaint, psalms of praise or thanksgiving; Walter Brueggemann, for example, talks of psalms of orientation, disorientation, new orientation. Yet psalms like 72 combine several categories, and

some like 31 have a mixed genre, so the psalms themselves resist being tidied up too much.

(2)   The Ras Shamra Ugaritic texts were discovered in Syria in 1928. Some of the language is very like the language of e.g. Psalms 29 and 96, indicating that **some of the psalms had Canaanite antecedents**. They didn't just drop out of heaven into the mind of the psalmist – though there is nothing wrong with a bit of borrowing, which all writers do, consciously or unconsciously. This and other discoveries opened up a dialogue with Ancient Near East texts, which is picked up in *Poem 29 'Mind Map'*:

> . . . five lasting steps to bury Baal,
> that chancy god, for good and all.

(3)   Did the final editor(s) of the Psalms put them **in a particular order**? Why *five* books, like the first five books of the Old Testament, Genesis to Deuteronomy (known as the *Torah*)? Psalms which 'frame' the start and finish of each book are now reckoned to have been placed there on purpose. If we take Psalm 1 as an introduction to the whole Psalter, and put Books 1 and 2 together because they conclude with 'the prayers of David the son of Jesse are ended', then at the two seams there is a 'royal' psalm (Psalms 2 and 72). Book 3 has many psalms which lament the loss of David's kingdom, but again concludes with a 'royal' psalm (89). Then Books 4 and 5 respond to the loss of the Davidic kingship by proclaiming the reign of God. That is why on a Book 1 psalm, *Poem 20 'Royal Rule'*, I ask,

> Have we no republican psalms,
> no hint that what's aye been
> might be a changing scene?

Individual psalms even in the same book were composed at different times. But there is no consensus on dating the collection as a whole, and the *Oxford Handbook of the Psalms* avoids giving any date. Psalm 137 obviously reflects the experience of exile in Babylon. Others are less clear: Psalm 61 has been dated to the 10th century BCE, just after Absalom's rebellion, to Jehoiachin's captivity in Babylon after 597 BCE, and to 315 BCE following the death of Alexander the Great!

Eugene Peterson says the Psalms 'have the *Torah* for their mother, the Prophets for their father . . .' and that the five books of Moses are matched by five books of Psalms 'like two hands clasped in prayer'.[5] It is likely that the five books of Psalms were arranged in parallel with the five books of Torah – not the only such arrangement, since the English historian Bede compares the five languages in Britain, including Irish which at that time was allied with Gaelic, to the five books of the divine law. In any case, the Psalms share an understanding of the world with Genesis 1 and 2, and that is partly where the 'temple' in the title of this book comes from. When I wrote poems for Book 1 of the Psalms, my inspiration was Psalm 27:4,

> One thing I have asked of the Lord, that will I seek after;
> to live in the house of the Lord all the days of my life,
> to behold the beauty of the Lord, *and to enquire in his temple.*

If you asked someone today what that meant, they might say it means 'ask the minister or priest', or they might get as far as saying it's about prayer – which it is, but it is much more than that.

4 Temple and Tartan

Temples are more naturally linked with robes than with tartan. If you think it takes a bit of imagination to put them together, I hope this book will put a bit of culture into temple and bit of wonder into tartan. Tartan is rich, not kitsch, and temples are big enough to embrace history and politics as well as spirituality. The magic carpet I imagine leaves with a full reference library, or if you prefer, modern internet search facilities.

For many today, a temple is where Hindus and Mormons worship. Occasionally you find a place of Christian worship like the City Temple or Kensington Temple in London, but people in Scotland are more likely to think of ancient Druid temples, as in the remains at Clava on Culloden Moor;[6] or the Egyptian and Greek temples which inspired architects like Alexander 'Greek' Thomson of Glasgow, who cited Psalm 111:2 ('Great are the works of the Lord') in his lectures. Or even the Stag Ballroom at Mar Lodge, described as a temple for the red deer.[7]

'Temple' is a key idea in the Old Testament. Not just because of the 'first temple' built by Solomon, or the 'second temple' built when Israel returned from exile, but because temples had a vital symbolic role in Ancient Near East society. Psalm 78:69 affirms this ancient view that an earthly temple was supposed to be a symbol of the whole cosmos which is a heavenly temple:

> [God] built his sanctuary like the high heavens,
> like the earth, which he has founded forever.

In 1903 the explorer John Muir took President Roosevelt camping in the Sierra Nevada, and made him a conservationist. Muir is on record as saying that the Yosemite Valley was a glorious temple. If anyone had challenged him, Muir, who knew his Bible, would have quoted that Psalm 78, which says that God's temple (and therefore Yosemite) is like the high heavens, where God is at home. The poems here enquire in God's temple, and therefore explore God's presence everywhere,

> somehow befriending
> these strange temples, this new world,
> riding pillion with a God far bigger
> than the one we used to know . . .[8]

Muir might also have cited Psalm 29, where the voice of the Lord breaks the cedars, shakes the wilderness, whirls the oaks, and although his Bible version followed that by saying a little tamely, 'in his temple doth every one speak of [God's] glory', the Hebrew in Bagster's version says, 'in his temple all of it is saying glory'!

Temple is a universal concept, and poetry a universal practice, but some poetry at least has national characteristics, or at least is concerned with the culture, history and politics of one nation among others. It's said that English cabinet ministers, when they want to introduce a policy to a Scottish audience, will try to find some way to 'put a kilt on it' – an expression which really amounts to giving policy no more than a Scottish tweak.

That is not how 'tartan' is used in this book. While many of the poems deal with human nature in general, the long poems on Books 2 and 4 of the Psalms have a distinct reference to Scottish history and culture. Later chapters will look at how the poet is an interpreter of events. But tartan can be used as a metaphor going far beyond one particular culture.

Tartan is a woven fabric, and a weave with two fabrics at right angles is a straightforward analogy for the 'horizontal' and 'vertical' dimensions of human life, with one another and with God. Or for two themes, two melodies, two aspects. Further, tartan is used as a dress, and poetry is a way of 'dressing' culture, in order to address it in a particular way. Again, tartan is a dress which was outlawed for a considerable period, and while for many today it is just a fashion accessory, it used to function as a symbol of rebellion – closet rebellion, you might want to say.

'Tartan' will feature later on, but now it's time to explore 'temple' a bit further. I hope you will find what follows as interesting as I do – and it goes on to explain what lies behind my approach – but if not, **leave out Part 2** and start reading the poetry in the next chapter, **'Carpet'**. These poems flit between different parts of the cosmos of place and history, as if on that carpet, linked by the theme of enquiry. There is a significant common word carried forward between all the poems of Book 1; for example, *Poem 1* and *Poem 2* share the verb 'plant'. Readers are left to spot the rest if they wish.

Part 2

5 Genesis and the Psalms

If the five books of Psalms are linked with the five books of the Pentateuch, then they share with Genesis and Ancient Near East (ANE for short) religion a common understanding of the world as sacred: and this sacred nature of the cosmos is signalled in Genesis 1 and 2 through the metaphor of the temple. As soon as you use a word like 'metaphor', you invite imagination, which Rowan Williams calls 'a vision that escapes control.'[9] Come to that, all our biggest words, like 'God', 'universe', 'humankind' need imagination as we can't put any of them neatly on a table and look at them. 'Temple' is just the same.

Temples in the ANE were residences for the gods, more than places of worship.[10] They were the centre of the cosmos and of social good. The principal temple of Babylon was called 'the temple of the foundation of heaven and earth', representing the primordial hill that first emerged from the waters covering the earth in creation. So all that can be said about sacred mountains can be said about temples.

You get the same ideas in Africa. The Kenyan novelist Ngũgĩ wa Thiong'o wrote (in Kikuyu and English) *The Perfect Nine*, a story about origins which features Mt Kenya as the primeval mountain. He introduced the book at the 2021 Edinburgh Book Festival.

On the ANE mountain there is a spring of the water of life, found both in the Garden of Eden (Genesis 2:10) and in Ezekiel's ideal temple; in Ezekiel 31:9, the prophet describes Eden as 'the garden of God'. In Psalm 36:8, 'They feast on the abundance of your house, and you give them drink from the river of your delights.'

The temple is associated with a sacred river, and with the tree of life, and is oriented to the cardinal directions and to stars like the polar star.[11] In the form of ziggurats, temples express the idea of an ascent towards heaven. The temple is the central unifying institution of a nation, and God's word is revealed in the temple, whose symbolism relates in turn to the creation story in Genesis 1. The daily offering in the temple is like the rainbow, says *The Wisdom of Jesus Ben Sira* (a Hebrew text), and the high priest is like the sun, moon and a star of light – the very celestial bodies which Psalm 148:3 commands to praise God because God 'has made them stand for ever and ever'.[12]

The construction of the Israelite tent or 'tabernacle' in the wilderness runs parallel to the account of creation in Genesis 1.[13] In Genesis 1 humans are rulers of creation, in Genesis 2 humans are priests, looking after the garden of creation. The vocabulary is like that of the book of Numbers, where priests are there to serve the temple – and the entrance to the garden is on the east side, as in the temple. Priests were sometimes referred to as gardeners. Adam, the gardener, is a servant priest and king. Maybe the New Testament has an unconscious reference to the risen Christ as a new Adam, when Mary confuses him with 'the gardener' in John 20:15.

6 More on 'Temple'

Michael Morales has commented that the temple cult is now the literary centre for the discipline of biblical theology.[14] The word he uses is *omphalos*, which means navel, and he chooses that word I think because in Jewish mystical writings it's a word for 'the centre of everything', as when Jerusalem is said to be at the navel of the world. But 'temple' is more than just a cult – it stands for the presence of God in all the cosmos:

> The Old Testament tabernacle and temples were symbolically designed to point to the cosmic eschatological reality that God's tabernacling presence, formerly limited to the holy of holies, was to be extended throughout the whole earth.[15]

Stripped of the jargon, that means that God is present everywhere, and the point of having a temple (or a church) is not to remove people from the world, but to give them such a taste of God and for God that they will recognise God in their lives outside the temple.

> A word for 'everywhere' is universe. 'Cosmos' today speaks of the vast scale of the universe, but 'universe' is closer to the Hebrew ʿôlām than the original Greek kosmos which had the sense of 'something tidy, something reasonable'.[16] The universe is God's greater temple, in which God 'rests' – as God rested when the work of creation was completed (Genesis 2:3, Exodus 31:17, the only two occurrences of šābat with God as subject).[17] 'Rest' in the OT (and as picked up in Hebrews 3 and 4) is not a state of relaxation. It is a state of peace where things can now proceed to happen, properly ordered.[18] In Psalm 132:1-8, the temple is not only where God dwells, but where he rests, called 'Zion' in 132:13-14. Divine rest in temples in the ANE was a condition for God to rule over all things: 'The temple was the command centre of the cosmos.'[19] For a simple overview, visit https://bibleproject.com/bible-studies/temple/
>
> Chapter 1 (and *Poem 1*) introduced Eden as a temple garden. Judaism identified Eden not only with Mt Zion but with Mt Sinai: 'The three of these were created as holy places, one facing the other.'[20] So we find in Psalm 18 that God comes from his temple mountain with the same kind of language as we have around Sinai in Exodus 19; and in Psalm 68:
>
> With mighty chariotry, twice ten thousand,
> . . . thousands upon thousands
> . . . the Lord came from Sinai into the holy place.[21]
> You ascended the high mount . . .
>
> which is followed later by a description of worship in the earthly temple.[22]

Temple is a great image because it spans three worlds: science (as it refers to the cosmos), liturgy and public worship (as it refers to a place of worship, a cathedral), personal experience (as it refers to the human heart). But when the augmented Second Temple built by Herod the Great was destroyed, the Jewish rabbis were left with a problem. From the time of exile in Babylon, the local synagogue had developed, so it was not hard to set up places of worship in their new exile after the destruction of Jerusalem. But how could they hold on to the meaning of temple without a physical temple?

One way might have been to have kept the temple as some kind of 'big idea'. The prophet Ezekiel, for example, linked his vision of a new temple back into ANE 'cosmic religion' by locating it on a high mountain (the physical temple in Jerusalem was never on a high mountain). Cosmic does not mean heavenly in the sense of 'detached from the world', it means everywhere. But they had a better plan.

Donald Akenson wrote a book called *Surpassing Wonder*, with a subtitle 'The Invention of the Bible and the Talmuds'. What the rabbis did, says Akenson, was to 'move the temple into every home' by the Mishnah, a set of texts which functions a bit like the New Testament does for Christians.[23] The idea of temple became something for the heart and the home as well as the heavens. He also suggested that for Christians it became an other-worldly idea, a 'heaven' distinct from 'the heavens', but that seems a little misleading, since for Christians heaven and earth are firmly joined together in the person of Jesus, who is quoted as claiming the word temple for his own body (John 2:19).

> The New Testament itself illustrates this nuance between a literal and imaginative meaning of temple. In John 3:18-21 'temple' is a symbol for the human body of Jesus, to be raised from death. In Mark 14:58, in the mind of other (antagonistic) witnesses it has become a temple 'not made with hands', which is easily taken, as by Leslie Weatherhead and others in a positive sense, as a 'temple of the imagination'.[24]

Christians see Jesus as the Messiah who fulfils the Psalms and the meaning of temple; Jews generally have a broad view of Messiah which might stand for the people of Israel as well as an individual figure to come; there is a well known story of how a failing monastic community revived when they were given a secret message, 'the Messiah is among you', which led to them treating every member as a potential Messiah.[25]

7 The First Two Psalms

Psalms 1 and 2 set the scene for the rest of the Psalter, calling individuals and nations to the obedience which will mark God's rule and human well-being. Unlike the David collection which Psalm 3 begins, they have no heading. Psalm 1 is about wisdom and the personal, Psalm 2 is about authority and the political, but they each call out good and bad behaviour.

Psalm 1 is focused on a book and a tree (found in temple and sacred garden, of course), while in Psalm 2:6, the king is set on God's holy mountain. These themes signal that the Psalms are not just about 'Jewish religion', but about cosmos and humanity. Later, in Psalm 24, 'the earth is the Lord's', and God ascends to a heavenly temple when he enters a temple in Jerusalem.

World religions all have ways of relating the individual, the ruler and the cosmos. However, Israel went further than other ANE religions. The Old Testament stories have no other gods and goddesses – only one God, creator of heaven and earth. Other religions had temples in which were placed the images of their gods; for Israel, the only image of God in the cosmos was man and woman.[26] This affected their style of worship, which allowed no images. But the temple remained a place where God met with humans, whether with sacrifices as in Psalm 51:19 or with festival as in Psalm 42:4. In any case God had to 'come down' as well as 'go up':

> I guess Mount Zion comes and goes
> like that, somewhere above our woes:
> it leaves us hoping that the Lord our God
> might ski or leg it down, meet us roughshod.[27]

Poem 1 'Temple Garden'

With Psalm 1, the 'before and after' of the story of 'the Fall' in Genesis 3 is flattened into 'the righteous' and 'the wicked', as in later wisdom literature. The poem hints that there is good and bad in all of us, that our choices are influenced by our genes, and this 'complicates the rhythm / of a temple garden house'. But the psalms are there to 'penetrate our dusty skin'. The poem begins with 'illuminated manuscript' because this first psalm was often copied artistically, without a number, as standing for all the Psalms. The line endings are all half-rhymes to symbolise how outside of Eden we live somewhere between order and chaos.

Poem 2 'Irony Redeemed'

Like the two Psalms, *Poem 1* addresses the person, *Poem 2* addresses politics; it invites God to 'plant your questions', 'refine your iron work', but 'in a human frame' with Zion 'somewhere in our hearts'. *Poem 1*, like the psalm, is about understanding and obedience in situations where our freedom may be limited, *Poem 2* is about questioning the status quo with some hope of change – the personal and the political.

All this signals a number of themes which appear in the Psalms and in later poems:

- You can question God and leaders (as God questions us)
- The work of God proves helpful and hopeful in real human situations
- 'Zion' is a link between universe, building and person, with God present in all

Both Psalms picture God as watching over the world, in Psalm 1 with more emphasis on care, in Psalm 2 more emphasis on judgment – in fact here God is like a ruler sneering at his enemies, a ruler whose feet should be kissed by other rulers. We meet this kind of language, God with feelings, God with hands and feet and so on, often in the Old Testament. The modern tendency is to dismiss it as myth as well as metaphor, or at least to say, 'Well, that is how they thought in those days.' A better approach is to say, 'Given that all our language about God – today's as well as yesterday's – is bound to fall short, what is this pointing to, where might it take us?'

8 Enquiry

Long ago, poetry was called the language of the gods. In a strange way, modern agnosticism has taken us back to this position, ever since the American poet Wallace Stevens saw poetry filling the void left by the loss of religious faith. 'The gods' now stand for anything and everything. Many contemporary poems would expect to give the reader a sense of 'something' that transcends everyday experience, even when 'the everyday' is being explored in all its grittiness.

Without denying this intention, I write poetry on the Psalms from a different angle. I start by recognising that the Psalms themselves take us, through the experience of the writers, to a new understanding and experience of God and of ourselves – as all good religious writing should. As a believer, I bring to my study of the Psalms a wider framework of belief, but I allow the Psalms themselves to question that framework, which is why I think they work for agnostics too.

I also wonder whether the Psalms can take us to a new understanding and experience of the world as it is today, as well as perhaps how the world always has been. Naturally, I bring to the Psalms my own 20th and 21st century experience of life, so that when I use the word 'smelt' in *Poem 2*, or compare Israel to a melting shop in *Poem 78*, I am recalling a time when I worked in the English steel industry. And the poetry has something in common with two rather different traditions, Jewish and Scottish, described below.

Two other poets, Edward Clarke of Oxford and Malcolm Guite of Cambridge, have also recently written poems on all the Psalms, but in more consistent styles.[28] I have allowed the magic carpet to take me through a wide variety of forms, though I describe it overall simply as 'a poetry of enquiry', letting the poems seek or suggest insight into matters triggered by the Psalms, and it is this insight which (along with the language of the poem) I hope will take the reader to 'somewhere new'.

This introductory chapter is followed by Book 1 Psalm poems. I suggested that Israel (and humankind) are 'on the carpet' before God. This reverses European practice of the last two centuries, where the Bible has been 'on the carpet' before academics, and its relevance to public life marginalised. Later chapters will illustrate the part the Psalms have played in Scottish public life as well as personal life, but the purpose of the poetry is to create a work of art showing how the Psalms touch the outer as well as the inner worlds of today.

Psalm 139 affirms that there is nowhere God cannot be found, even if as the poet R.S. Thomas used to say, it is sometimes like coming on a patch of grass still warm, although the creature has left.[29] Preachers and writers take up the challenge to explain why and how the invisible God warms the grass, and I think of the rather ambitious prayer of Duns Scotus in the 13th century:

> Lord our God
> may I also be able somehow to expound
> the totality of your real primal unique being.[30]

This opens up the Psalms in all kinds of directions, and the poems themselves reach into the past as well as contemporary life, using a variety of poetic forms, and styles ranging from whimsy to satire. Like the Psalms themselves, the poems do not follow an obvious sequence, but (as mentioned) every poem is connected with the next by (at least) one significant word. The word 'psalms' completes the circle from *Poem 41* back to *Poem 1*.

The Jewish Way of Interpretation

Older Jewish interpretation of the *Tanakh* (Old Testament) was carried out in two forms:

(1) **Haggadah** took the form of dramatic narrative, such as the Passover *Haggadah* (comprising poems, prayer hymns and prose commentary).

(2) **Halakah** was concerned with the interpretation of Torah, ethical and theoretical, to which was later added allegory, under Greek influence. The important centre for the latter was Alexandria, which reached its height with Philo in the 1st century CE.

> Philo distinguished the literal external meaning (the body) and the inner meaning (the soul). Midrash searches the biblical text for meaning beyond the surface sense, but does not necessarily follow the neoplatonism of Philo. It is 'oral Torah', filling in the gaps of the written Torah.

Barry Holz says that Jewish tradition shows how the Torah remains a living thing, calling for a dynamic response.[31] He links this with contemporary trends in interpretation, which give the reader a significant place, but this has been a longstanding way of understanding the Psalms: in Hebrews 4:12, part of Psalm 95 is quoted as 'living and active'.

The rabbis saw how scripture linked temple and universe. They said that the navel of the world was located at Zion from Psalm 50:2. In Ezekiel 38:12, those who are gathered from the nations live at the navel (ṭabbûr) of the world. The world proceeds from Zion in the same way that a fetus proceeds from the navel.[32] In ways like this, rabbinic thought joins 'temple' with God and creation, people and worship, past and present and future in a network or tapestry of understanding to which the Psalms make their own contribution. Here for example is the mission statement of Psalm 65:

> Praise is due to you, O God, in Zion . . .
> To you all flesh shall come . . .
> We shall be satisfied with the goodness of your house,
>   your holy temple . . .
> You are the hope of all the ends of the earth
>   and of the farthest seas . . .
> The river of God is full of water . . .
> You crown the year with your bounty.

Josephus said of the Mosaic tabernacle, that 'every one of these objects is intended to recall and represent the universe . . .' for example, the 12 loaves of the bread of the presence represent the 12 months of the year.[33] Josephus and Philo discuss a number of ways that the temple or parts of it symbolically reflect the cosmos, such as:

- The outer and inner court, and the holy of holies represent earth, sea and heaven

- The seven lamps represent the seven (visible) planets

- The outer veil and curtains represent the four elements of the cosmos (earth, air, water and fire)

- The jewels on the breast-piece represent the twelve constellations[34]

Richard Middleton points out how Jewish commentators compare the sevens of Genesis 1 with Solomon's building of the temple during the seven day Feast of Tabernacles (which is in the seventh month).[35] There are similarities with the earlier tabernacle – in Genesis 1 the sun and moon are described as *mĕorot*, lights, the same word as for the sanctuary lights. The end of the creation account in Genesis 2:2 (God finished the work) is like Exodus 40:33 (Moses finished the work).[36]

The links are complex, not unlike the branches of the vine referred to in Psalm 80:8: 'You brought a vine out of Egypt.' A *targum* (Aramaic version of a Bible text) of early Judaism identified the vineyard of Isaiah 5:2 as Israel's 'sanctuary' (i.e. temple).[37] But in these ways people and temple are both identified with cosmos and creation, as in *Poems 24, 27, 28 and 41*.

The 'Democratic Intellect' in Scotland

Early psalms celebrate David as king, but the later psalms show how people in Israel had to readjust to loss of independence, and reckon with God alone as their king. The experience of exile in Babylon was the key to this dramatic change, and one of the things which made Jewish education and life democratic, at least for boys and men.

Scottish history never saw quite such a dramatic shift of fortune, but – as George Davie was to put it – if the achievement of the Renaissance was to have restored poetry to a place of honour along with science, one achievement of the Reformation was to bring at least some aspects of democracy to a place of honour in Scottish education and worship.[38]

Poem 116, 'Common Cup', describes two elders, a Provost and an MSP, serving bread and wine to the congregation of St Mary's in Haddington today. While the people no longer literally sit at tables, the equality is preserved:

> . . . and here the Provost of a Council ranked
> no higher than the least of other men
> and women. Clasping hands around the cup,
> we drink a portion rooted in a psalm . . .

The Scottish reformers were clear about the equality of all before God. James Cameron refers to the Reformers' 'splendid notion of equality of all men in the sight of God', but it was men rather than women and children – though this did not prevent them wanting education for girls as well as boys.[39] This inspired their view of education,[40] even if a primary motive was their desire that each child should be able to read and understand the Bible. The use of a catechism alongside it was to help children hold together image and idea. The history of Israel, often referred to in the Psalms, shaped 'the tools that the mind requires'.[41]

John Knox wanted a school in every parish. Although it was not till the 1686 Education Act that this vision became anything like reality, it was a democratic recognition that people deserved equal access to learning; even if for the Scottish Reformers a major concern was biblical literacy, the schools were to provide 'Logic and Rhetoric and Tongues', and even rural schools should teach Latin.[42]

The Reformers were not democratic in a modern political sense, although Knox used to extract political theory from the Hebrew prophets.[43] But their belief in our equality before God certainly nourished what was later to be called the 'democratic intellect'.[44] George Davie argued that a priority for education should be enabling people who will pursue different disciplines to share common knowledge, before later specialisation.[45] When C.P. Snow reviewed Davie's book in 1961, he said that he and Davie shared the same concern to bridge the gulf between the arts and the sciences.

This breadth of vision for education was not confined to Judaism and Presbyterianism. A later Catholic writer shared this common vision for a university as a place where people would make connections with one another, and with all subjects. Cardinal Henry Newman gave a number of lectures in Dublin which paved the way for a new Catholic University, published as a book in 1873.[46] Without excluding vocational studies or specialisation, Newman argued for a liberal education which would explore relationships between subjects.[47]

The founder of the Scottish Poetry Library, Tessa Ransford, in an interview before she died in 2015 spoke about this:

> We need cultural ecology to allow the variety of genres to grow and interact beneficially with each other and with all aspects of life. Literature shouldn't be in a bubble unconnected with daily life.[48]

Connections – connections between subjects, between minds, between people. And so to the 'democratic intellect'.

This is a horizontal cord which runs through the intellectual history of Scotland. David Daiches writes of 'a deep democratic trend in Scottish Calvinism'.[49] It can be traced back at least as far as Andrew Melville, who was Principal of Glasgow University in 1577 when it was remodelled in the *Nova Erectio*, which 'established the broad 'democratic intellect' pattern of the Scottish university curriculum followed for the next 300 years or so.[50]

It has three strands – equality, 'common sense philosophy', and generalism.

The Scottish bent for argument about first principles meant that what Davie calls 'the common sense of subjects' was put before questions of detail. It is in this sense that Davie uses the idea of 'democratic intellectualism' to characterise the Scottish mind. For 'in discussing these general, fundamental issues . . . professors and students, specialists and laity can meet on more or less equal terms . . .'[51]

Scotland had a different educational tradition from England, and the established system of schooling was 'the chief asset of a poor country whose wealth to an unusual extent depended on the export of educated men.'[52] The Presbyterian context and history of education not only gave opportunities to the poor 'lad o' pairts', but promoted the ideal of equality over privilege, which was more strongly established in England with the Church of England's hold on the Universities. The purpose of the Catechisms used in Scotland, shared by high and lowborn, was not only to give people 'information', but to shape their thinking so that the ploughman could discuss morality with the professor.[53]

The parish school was also seen as the cradle of the 'democratic intellect', where, it was said, the children of lairds rubbed shoulders with the offspring of the poor. This equality extended to the seminars held after lectures.

The idea was given some intellectual shape by Thomas Reid's 'common sense philosophy'. Reid (1710-1796) succeeded Adam Smith as Professor of Moral Philosophy at Glasgow University in 1764 and noted a number of 'Principles of Common Sense', which are 'universal among humankind – apart from lunatics and philosophers', and included:

- The things we perceive with our senses really do exist

- What we remember really did happen

- There is life and intelligence in our fellows with whom we converse

- These principles are 'found in us antecedently to any instruction we receive'[54]

Of course philosophy has taken various directions since then, not least concerning how we know things, without reducing this to what is happening within the human brain. Michael Polanyi, for example, discussed how the mind makes an intuitive leap which results in 'tacit knowledge'; T.F. Torrance extended this idea from the experimental sciences to theological science, or more simply how we know God. And Alister McGrath later explained how a realist philosophy applies to theology as well as science.[55] The relevance of this to a 'poetry of enquiry' is that the poet, like the preacher though in a much more oblique way, is inviting others to discover something which is known as well as felt, but cannot be reduced to the words themselves.

Davie was influenced by David Hume's contemporary Thomas Reid. Two particular things followed from Reid's 'Principles':

(1) People deserve respect whatever their level of education.

(2) Education should be general enough to help people communicate with one another.

Thomas Reid had noted that philosophers often seemed to depart from common sense, and he did not wish philosophy to become esoteric, or education proud. 'Everyone possesses and applies the Principles, whereas by contrast only some people are skilled in mathematics or natural science . . . where it is most important, we are cognitive equals.'[56]

While science was to become a byword for specialisation, in the 19th century great scientists like David Brewster and James Clerk Maxwell looked on academic philosophers as allies. Davie commends Maxwell when he argues from the *differences* between the sciences that the object of knowledge is *relation*. The human mind is not just a set of conditioned responses; the laws of nature are not a mere series of equations. Davie's point here is that a knowledge of philosophy *matters*,[57] and philosophy is part of the generalist Scottish tradition.[58] He lauds the European continental tradition which postpones specialisation, and cites a review of the Scottish philosopher John Ferrier's book *Institutes of Metaphysic* by the French De Rémusat, who wrote:

> The unusual combination of instruction and entertainment in Scott, the paradoxical position of Reid as the plain man's Plato, perhaps typify what is most distinctive about Scotland . . . if you speak to a Scottish peasant you speak to your equal; he, as well as you, knows what it is to be genuinely human . . .[59]

A poet in this tradition is therefore engaging in a broad enquiry, which specialises in bringing together things normally separate. We know that land, culture and people are deeply connected – as Alan Riach points out so clearly in his recent book, *Scottish Literature: an introduction*. In *Temple and Tartan* I try to spell this out in unexpected ways. Some of the connections in this book are made to my knowledge for the first time.

In Davie's thinking, such connections are typically to be made between different disciplines, to help people in different walks of life have a common understanding, but another form of connection lies in the threads that run through one or many societies over a period of time. In using a phrase like 'the democratic intellect' Davie is speaking of democracy as one such thread in the carpet that Scots (and others) walk on.[60]

Book 1 Poems: Carpet

1 Temple Garden

Illuminated manuscript,
unnumbered, naming no and yes,
by some anonymous lyricist
who introduces all the rest
with contrast and with chiasm,
two parallel lines that never kiss
but cross and complicate the rhythm
of a temple garden house.

The righteous prosper, trim and trig,
manicured by God's own hand,
nourished, watered, planted snug
and safe, quite sure they know the plan.
Outside Eden, sour soiled farms
make cultivation toil and pain,
yet still enlightened by the psalms
that penetrate our dusty skin.

How simple seem God's garden themes
for daily work and sabbath rest;
but underground, deep hidden genes,
our subway roots, in battle dress
keep us alive, write up our files,
assess the truth of war and peace,
press our buttons, tell us tales,
feed our choice of ant or louse.

2 Irony Redeemed

You make them look ridiculous,
these tin pot gods, this pompous lot
of presidents. So plant your questions,
smelt, refine your iron work,
but craft it in a human frame,
with hands and feet we recognise,
and Zion somewhere in our hearts.

3 Chin on Chest

'You, O Lord, are . . . the one who lifts up my head.' *v. 3*

Chin on chest, dream walking,
still I carry disappointment.
Lord, cup my face within your palm
and lift it, so I see another
pair of feet besides my own.

My skin bleeds from the cruelty
of those who fight me or forget me.
Lord, draw a circle close around
my fraying edges, so I find your
cross-shaped failure hides my own.

4 Bedtime Sonnet

'When you are disturbed . . . ponder it upon your beds.' *v. 4*

Bad lands for the sleepless face
fetched flat, mind grounded, stoppered,
shaken with a poisoned word;
jeremiad days, without a trace
of laughter oxy-bubbling fertile chatter
through that shame pool: there it learns
to surf its own dissatisfaction, churns
dark cream which never turns to butter.

Lord, turn my squat into a sanctuary,
show your face, and smile upon my sleep
to make my bedtime better brain time, deep
with surge and flow; a nest up high,
a restful REM sleep, dreams
from God who hears those silent screams.

5 Daily Routine

'In the morning you hear my voice.' *v. 3*

A turtle wakes and waits, a little shy,
a lizard wakes and tongues a passing fly,
a warrior wakes and checks his blade is true,
an infant wakes, and all the world is new.

Lord, I am many things, and many people,
so each morning smiles a welcome
– and then hits me somewhere deep;
wake up is a new-staked claim on life
– and then a count of more than I can do.

But if you listen, while those turtles crawl,
while lizards laze, and warriors take a fall;
then I will talk, and take this infant chance
you like me, and my complicated dance.

6 Honest Tears

'My bones are shaking with terror . . .
I flood my bed with tears.' *vv. 2, 6*

When he fell into my arms,
I held him tight, remembering
that awful night, the rift
torn through his tender gut,
and somewhere deep, nudged into me,
how God is good with tears.

Unlike the hypocrite crocodile,
third eyelid brimming cheerfully
while jaws are full of meat,
we source our butchered sorrow
soulfully; with aching bones
and breaking hearts we sob our grief.

His pain racked three of us,
if God be counted, counter
to earth's bald arithmetic.
I count on God, with Jesus
putting skin and hair on God
who spots the tiniest teardrop.

7 Shiggaion

'On their own heads their violence descends.' *v. 16*

We cannot harmonise this song,
this hurt and angry 'shiggaion';
for sure we often get it wrong
when thinking with our gut.

We do not recognise this God
who fires his arrows on the nod
to pierce the tongue of each poor sod
who disagrees with us.

Yet God is not so soft a touch
that evil keeps on winning. Such
an absent God is far too much
a non-theology.

The mills of God grind slow but sure,
fed by our dull revenge. If you're
God's target, let him score
a bull's eye, drill the heart.

8 Old and Young Newscasters

'Out of the mouths of babes and infants
you have founded a bulwark.' *v. 2*

They say the Americans never
made that full moon landing,
they call it fake news, filmed
by old and frightened men
to boost a President scowling
up the back of a Russian bear,
down in the polls, prevent
his legacy pop into thin air.

They say that climate change
is just a Leftie game call,
something we can handle.
So the children strike, all
resolute to raise a flag
of inconvenience, rattle
politician's cages, join
this dark green battle.

May the mouths of infants
build a tower, provide
a slit for awkward arrows
fired to pierce the hide
of backward leaders
mouthing *ichabod.*   *the glory has departed (Heb.)*
Curse those lame excuses,
cast the majesty of God.

9 Forgetting

'The very memory of them has perished.' *v. 6*

An appointment, a face, a nation, a race;
a garden, a country, a moon or a cosmos;
things blur, they say, get vague as we age
and edge into forgetfulness,
unlike the Lord who's busy, busy
turning page on complex page
of evolution. Memory loss,
for God, is choice to take our sins
and bin them, off the cosmic stage.

A brother, a mother, a dance with a lover,
a flourish, a foul up, a flower will fade
as neurons falter in our brains
and leave us strangers to ourselves.
Can we believe God will remember
how we lived, if our remains
are burned or buried? When our faith
has vanished off the scene, forgotten,
is there ought a poor saint gains?

A coat, a prayer mat, a favourite cat;
a diary, a smile, a shadow, a sundial;
no stars in the grave, it's lonely down there.
A prayer: 'God, while my twitching nose
can smell a clue to human life,
made to be raised from death, somewhere,
somehow, re-membered – help me find
some traveller who has lost the scent
and needs a whiff of praise, and care.'

10 Hard Questions

'Some questions are too good to spoil with answers.'

Nahum in the red corner, walks out tough:
'Belt those Ninevites, knock them dead,
God is a word you'll come to dread.'

Jonah in the blue corner, off to sea:
'They'll get no word of God from me,
God better find someone willing instead.'

Jonah in the belly of a fish came round
to target Nineveh, launch a career,
put citizens down on their knees in fear.

God saw change and switched his view,
Jonah whinged as he fought the clue
that God likes love more than sword or spear.

No easy answers in psalms are found,
if the cry, 'God, why?' just calls God's bluff,
and despairs of justice when times are rough.

Choose bully or wimp and you banish belief,
so stay with the psalmist and feel the grief
till you meet with a God you can trust enough.

11 Exam Time

'The Lord tests the righteous and the wicked.' v. 5

Essays, orals, surveys, morals,
pushy tweets 'we want the best!'
Instant soup in a public cauldron
stirred by winners, losers, sinners
learning lines that fail God's test.

Academics, civil servants,
priests unfrocked and in disgrace;
'Wicked' spins, since relativity
shocked us, rocked amoral waves
through brains as well as time and space.

Those who fear foundations knocked out
lose the plot. Gear up the program
for the gaze of God, rejig the lot
to get some temple target practice,
daily assessment God's exam.

12 Watch God's Lips

'Yetser hatov, yetser harach' – a Rabbinic antinomy

Binary systems
serve more
than laptops.

Each pair
of lips –
open goal
for love,
open tap
for truth
or flattery,
open space
for things
that matter,
open market
to exchange
who knows
what kind
of words?

Each pair
speak of
two hearts,
two rivers
from Eden,
yetser hatov,   *the good inclination*
yetser harach,   *the evil inclination*
coursing the
human race.

God's lips
spell 'yes':
promising lips
to watch,
together
making one,
never zero.

13 Beating on the door

'How long, O Lord? Will you forget me forever?' *v. 1*

I'm beating, God, upon your door.
I screw my eyes to read your lips
but I am shaken to the core

by covid, climate, and what's more
you've morphed into a God who sleeps
when I would worship and adore.

On glib response I set no store
nor on those charismatic cantrips   *charms*
which have left me raw and sore.

How long before I rant and roar,
or worse, when my whole being slips
to shadow life upon the floor

I will ooze death through every pore
while casually the Devil rips
my fading faith to shreds. Therefore

I'm beating, God, upon your door;
with these mantraps I'll get to grips;
I'm pounding, Lord, upon your door
and I *will* worship and adore.

14 Tuim-heidit

'Fools say in their hearts, "There is no God".' *v. 1*

They're a wee thing tuim-heidit,   *empty-headed*
them as beats the drum fir science
an cannae fin God ony place.

Whit dae they expeck? Angels
stottin oot o test tubes, cherubs   *bouncing*
ridin quarks, a derk god bleck-holed?

We niver really thocht o angels
dancin on the heids o peens,
yon wis jist philosophers flytin.   *wrangling*

32

Heivin is whaur God is, aw aroon;
wioot, the universe is tuim indeed,   *empty*
sae tuim it faas tae less thin stoor.   *dust*

Can ye hae guid wioot a faith? Aye,   *goodness*
whiles. It taks a wheen o generations   *a good few*
tae pit a ceevilisation back in clogs.

See 'Darkest Hour' – thon Churchill film?
He gat is ken an wit fae chiels   *know-how insight people*
wha traivelled wi im unnergroon.

An see yon King wha cam tae back im,
Geordie ca'd a realm tae cruik its hochs;   *bend its knees*
nae wird o thon on the big screen.

Tuim-heidit? Tuim-hairtit? Tuim-saulit?
Fin yir ain metaphor, but listen up,
Israel: God will hae the hinnermaist wird.   *last*

15 Postmarked

'O Lord, who may abide in your tent?' *v. 1*

Innocently she smiles, placing
two envelopes in my hand.
She will walk down the road,
busy with bills and brochures,

her daily postal business.
I am just opening metaphors
for holy man and hypocrite,
worried that they use one typeface.

Two letters in the same post,
one for me, one for my shadow,
speaking of money, promises,
gossip, neighbours, friends.

Soon I shall walk down the road,
hoping my holy smile reaches
two corners of my mouth,
and holds my face together.

16 Bless my Kidneys

'I bless the Lord who counsels me,
at night my heart [*Heb.: kidneys*] instructs me.' *v. 7*

Bless my kidneys, one might say,
reading Hebrew body language
with a knowing smile: away

with careful, icy comprehension,
make for the warm choppy wake
of David, his sweet and salty passion

for a God who wants to ravish,
sandblast, sort and wrap the soul
secure within its deepest wish.

When the sea's a trampoline,
bouncing plans, churning guts,
settle your skis, laugh, lean

back into the breeze behind,
hold God's line, let God balance
body fluids, brace your mind.

Whereas in English the heart is the seat of the emotions,
in Hebrew that is for the mind and will, with emotions
(and conscience) seated in the kidneys or belly.

17 Eye to Eye

'I have avoided the ways of the violent.' v. 4

What a sweet and salty psalm,
titbits, tough bits trauma trawled
from fearful years: blogging bald
as a bullet head, yet strangely calm
as David facing Saul, half certain
of the peaceful power of prayer,
but left with anger in his hair,
close-cropped, a violent disdain.

His hope? God's look. It seeks out fruit,
the apple of a human eye,
God's sweet endgame. A butterfly
flaps wings, slow tempest follows suit
and evolution blossoms, fades out
primal instinct, fades in choice,
the hearing of a crucial voice,
the entry of debate about

genetic fate. Adam unlearns
the violent lust to cut and tear,
stab, butt, rape, swear
at Eve. By grace, Macadam spurns
those vicious habits never formed
in Eden, but maybe concealed
in code upon the playing fields
of Eton. Can he live unarmed?

The battle rages fierce within
the cave, the dark night of the soul.
At dawn, when he awakes, he will
be thrilled to feel God close, begin
to wax his grown pupils, meet
the gaze of God, far-seeing light
which surely must put all things right
and nail the cosmic balance sheet.

18 The Nature of God

'He made darkness his covering.' *v. 11*

God is not – not this, not that: so say
the sages of the all-negating way.
You rode the dark
and bent the sky
when I was tumbling
into hopeless night.

God is not some stuff to be defined.
Faith rests upon the things God does, they're kind.
You flashed a spark
and lit my lamp
when I was fumbling
with a broken light.

God is not as dim as humans are;
God is not vague – God is particular.
You made a mark
upon my map
when I was stumbling
and a sorry sight.

19 Art and Science

Experimental Inca scientist,
Pachacutec, emperor, was left
alone for three days to his curious self
upon an island in Lake Titicaca,
studying the sun, its daily progress.
A god, he thought, would roam the sky,
unchained in orbit as the sun.
'There must be Someone other.'

Vincent, artist, troubled saint of sorts,
gazing at the sunflowers and the sun,
dreaming on the star rhymes of the sky,
bears witness in the court of art.
Though passers by at night might glimpse
only a little smoke from the chimney,
that great fire in Van Gogh's soul
burned light onto a canvas.

C.P. Snow, scientist and writer,
sketching two divided cultures: bright
fixers with the future in their bones,
poets locked in a sunlit past.
Art and science maybe need each other,
but in burnt up, bitter years, who comes
with sunny words and sweeter tweets,
like hexagons of honeycomb?

20 Royal Rule

'Give victory to the king, O Lord.' *v. 9*

When Adam delved and Eve span,
who was then the gentleman?

'God save the king – or maybe queen.'
Have we no republican psalms,
no hint that what's aye been
might be a changing scene?

Who is this chosen royal king?
Anointed, haloed – but by whom?
This psalm has lines which fling
a spanner into everything
that might accommodate a fan
of democratic government.

If Eve dug deep, and Adam span
would we have then a gentle man?

With every age, its royal crimes.
Is there another Adam
that might flype the rhymes   *turn inside out*
and rhythm of the times?

21 That's it, then

'Blessings forever.' *v. 6*

No least hint of sorrow
  no flaw in the gold
    no prayer unanswered
      not one word of weakness
    no sin undiscovered
  no chance for the wicked
Not a paradox in sight

22 Worm Weary

'Many bulls encircle me.' *v. 12*

No cuddly pets in sight: there lurk
just savage beasts – and me, a berk

God-forsaken, hurling out
a prayer, a groan, a rasping shout

from broken lips, from East Damascus,
every hell scene that would ask us

how much bloody longer, why
set monsters on humanity?

A talking, swearing, crying worm
one minute, and the next a sperm

of hope, yearning for a womb
to offer God some living room,

a womb to tend my worst afflictions,
tomb to end my contradictions.

23 Shepherd Sonnet

Contradictions, with a sudden dark
to overtake our cosiness, our rosy
hopes. The unexpected snakes devour
the flimsy ladders that we pick and park
for easy climbs to happiness. Who knows,
we might today be falling, calling out
for God to hear us, hold us, help us, fold us
in those arms that felt the hammer blows
to nails through ankles, wrists – such love to meet
the cost of shepherding the likes of us;
or finding courage in the cold of night,
the daytime heat, the struggles of the street.
You fill my cup with hope again: indeed
I find, with you, I've everything I need.

24 Behind the Door

'Be lifted up, O ancient doors.' *v. 7*

Every thing,
every blessed thing
that God has made
was placed upon the piers
love built out of the years
of evolution's readiness
to tiptoe at the pace of God.

Every one,
every blessed one
or ninety one
who climbs a temple stair
and leaves behind their share
of human dirt and emptiness
will seek and see the face of God.

Every king,
every blessed queen
who fronts the queue
at mystic doors, and waits
outside the glory gates
– such royal lowliness
will find the living space of God.

For every thing
and every blessed one
who knocks in hope,
with heart and soul sick
of our inauthentic
puff and stuff, in holiness
will revel in the crazy grace of God.

25 A New Lexicon

'Do not remember the sins of my youth.' *v. 7*

Back in my youth, wrapped up and gone,
I was no angel: but it's age
that opens a new lexicon,
puts loss and pain centre stage.

CARPET

I was no angel: but it's age
and wrinkles make a tender soul,
put loss and pain centre stage
and start to make the person whole.

Yes, wrinkles make a tender soul,
reflect the crooked paths of life,
start to make the body whole
for break and make are man and wife.

Reflect the crooked paths of life,
reveal success, translate defeat,
for break and make are man and wife,
they share a house in every street.

Reveal success, translate defeat,
play on my heartstrings and my gut
which share a house in every street
I drive through mindfully; so please,

play on my heartstrings and my gut,
sound blues and rhythm in the glen
I drive through mindfully; but please
deal with me kindly, even then.

Sound blues and rhythm in the glen
where trip wires cross, and boulders roll;
deal with me kindly, even then
make music in my empty soul.

Where trip wires cross, and boulders roll,
I'll wear the hurt, I'll bear the wrong.
Make music in my empty soul
and I will answer with a song;

I'll wear the hurt, I'll bear the wrong.
Back in my youth, now it is gone,
I longed to answer with a song
that opens a new lexicon.

26 Aye Right

'I have walked in my integrity.' *v. 1*

If Davie gat tae screivin they lang wirds,	*writing*
strang wirds lyk integritie, an nae jist yince,	
he maun hae thocht himsel agen a laddie.	*must*

Nae a gang leader, wi bluid on is hauns.
Nae a guerilla fechter, teuch an gleg,   *tough and smart*
playin aff yin agin the ither aa the time.

Nae a king wi a gled ee, wha spuliet   *roving eye plundered*
anither's wife, and kilt hir guidman   *husband*
tho he wis his ain aefauld sodger.   *loyal*

Nae a stickit faither, yin wha coudna
dale the richt wey wi the bairns e hid.   *children*
Lads and lassies arenae aa that guid,

ken, sae whit wey did yon son o his,
the yin they cry the Christ, hoo cam
he telt us tae become like smaa bairns?

Aiblins it wis curiositie?   *perhaps*
The wey they gie ye aa they hae tae gie?
Wis it they cud tak the hauns o Jesus

wioot bein pit aboot lyk aulder fowk?   *upset, embarrassed*
Davie langit tae be born agen,
A kin jalouse – wioot yon lexicon.   *guess, work out*

27 From Caskie to Cosmos

'He will hide me in his shelter.' *v. 5*

What was Donald Caskie's mind on,
when Gestapo failed to climb the stairs
and find them hidden in the gallery?
Inquiring in God's temple, scheming,
dreaming of a life beyond the walls?

Tent or temple, build it radical,
porous, see through, pop-up church,
open sided, roofless. Roller skate
along a corridor, find a door
which opens to a vault of stars.

Abseil to the crypt, dig out
a tunnel under faulty towers
of privilege and vice. Leave limpet
bombs of word and witness, learn
to gaze on God deep underground.

This maze of God is where I lurk,
passionate about a charged cosmos,
its cool mystery. This is the faith
I share with Paul, affirm the universe
is all Messiah's, yet still ours.

Like Solomon I lift my holy hands
to heaven, and proclaim God vaster
than the space God seems to fill.
What sort of God is this, who wears
our skin, and keeps such human hours?

I seek your face, I search your cosmic fields
to find you stellar occupant
of every kitchen, cellar, gallery:
I search your cosmic files, I seek your folk
to find you present in a feast of smiles.

28 Pinnacle or Pit?

'If you are silent to me, I shall be like those who go down to the Pit.' *v. 1*

The universe has six dimensions,
seven double letters father Abraham
could see, a cubic universe,
the temple at its heart –
so said Creation Book *Sefer Yesira*,
moving meaning from a public knowledge
base to private words and lego thought.

My hands feel their way to the centre:
sanctuary, the holy hexagon,
the space with six edges, where
the heart beats something
old and fierce. It is my journey
to the sun, my Parker Project
over seventy-seven years, not seven.

Is this your holy place, my God?
Might cabbalism turn the cry of David
into echolalia? From Pinnacle
to Pit, where God is silent?
Will the temple change to clever text,
or could the holy word become again
our flesh, our fate, our faith?

29 Mind Map

'May the Lord bless his people with peace.' *v. 11*

Five steps to meeting fire with fire
of love, five lasting steps to bury Baal,
that chancy god, for good and all.

    First up, reconnaissance, go over
    ground, with Caleb's can do attitude;
    live in their skin, think as they would

        up to a point, step number two,
        for human thought is never watertight,
        not Israelite, nor Canaanite.

        The third is battle for the mind:
        because *the pen is mightier than the sword*
        they sang the great voice of the Lord

    who (fourth) stormed through the Middle East
    and mocking, cut foes down to size
    with shafts of truth instead of lies

which leaves a fifth much later step –
non-violence – take it, later Joshua's way,
and leave to God the power play.

30 Playing and Praying with David

'You have healed me . . . you brought up my soul from Sheol.' *vv. 2-3*

Playing away with Bathsheba instead of his mates,
called out, sent off by Prophet Nathan,
David swopped God's face for Sheol's gates.

Yet David never sought to take a tour
with Dante in the nether parts of Hell.
It was enough for God to make him sure

of mercy, smile upon his mourning soul,
control the damage, re-engage the covenant,
returf the pitch, remark the goal

for me and all who want forgiveness fervid,
reeled and jigged right down the field,
yes, everyone who plays and prays with David.

31 Holocaust Denial

'I have passed out of mind.' *v. 12*

The gas chambers have exited
the screen, so what else brews
behind a face which wants to frame
the Holocaust fake news,
its documents all doctored,
witness just a shred?
  I've passed right out of mind
  like someone who is dead.

The death certificates died,
their owners disappeared,
ghosted into mist and myth,
a sleight of hand that's geared
to turn the not so distant past
a little less blood red.
  I've passed right out of mind
  like someone who is dead.

A custom of nay-saying,
a library of lies,
the truth dropped out of Dropbox,
no store cloud in the skies.
My first prayer was too easy,
my second is unsaid,
  I've passed right out of mind
  like someone who is dead.

32 Silence

'While I kept silence, my body wasted away.' *v. 3*

My gutted silence
groans to God,
for keeping quiet
is not a mark
of Jewish faith
or modern doubt.

The noise of silence
fills my head,
loud memories
keep battling trolls,
rattling facts
I can't refute.

A wall of silence
breaks my heart;
things unsaid
are dissonant,
a cloud of sound
that shuts me out.

Locked in silence,
fearful, gagged
by those who keep
harsh tabs on you?
Let this psalm be
a parachute.

To break that silence,
choking speech
and life itself,
takes all of God
and all of us:
one saving shout.

33 Judgment

'He spoke and it came to be . . . the Lord brings
the counsel of the nations to nothing.' *vv. 9-10*

One shout
to cheer the players,
call attention
to the score,
brace the music,
fire the psalm,
a singing arrow
winging skilled
parabolas of praise
across the pitch.

One melody
to seed the storm,
astound the dawn,
feed grass and ground,
reveal a world class
wicket keeper
on a field
where what
we pick or pass
may not be cricket.

One quote unquote
for Holyrood,
for Belfast,
Dublin, Cardiff,
from Westminster:
while fools queue up
to riff that note,
beware! The Umpire
may not play
by English rules.

34 Fears – a List Poem

'I sought the Lord and he answered me, and delivered me
from all my fears.' *v. 4*

'The fear of the Lord is the beginning of wisdom.'   Proverbs 9:10

Ahmed's anger
Bella's blackmail
Colin's court case
Dai's divorce
Erzsébet's ego
Fran's fake film
Gregor's guilt
Helen's hate

Isobel's insomnia
Jean's jealousy
Kati's kidneys
Lisander's leukemia
Mary's madness
Navin's nightmare
Owen's obsession
Peter's poison

Quentin's question
Rachael's rape
Stephen's sexual abuse
Tasmin's terror
Umberto's ugliness
Viktor's violence
Winston's whip
Zach's ugsome zeal   *repulsive*

What are you afraid of?
Never mind the unknown X,
there is Yourself and holy fear,
where Wisdom tackles fools,
and God plus U is W.

35 Enemies

'Fight against those who fight against me!' *v. 1*

When it is too easy to say
'Love your enemies'
When it is repugnant to say
'Love your enemies'
When it is impossible to say
'Love your enemies'

I shall seize this great aggressive psalm
I shall load it with these righteous bullets
I shall smile and slip the safety catch
    and – oh horror –
God has stepped into the line of fire
nodding his head at my complaint
opening his heart to all my anger
holding his hands up in surrender.

36 Change of Subject

Enough of enemies
rattling words,
dropping turds
to grease your way to the pit.

Change gear,
dress for a place where skies expand,
where goodness has no prey to fight,
no animal goes out of sight,
and stealing land is banned.

Raise barriers,
find space for refugees,
grit some just political teeth,
new brief the army and police,
release the feast, in peace.

All those friends,
sharing passes,
raising glasses
to the star of a lit up heaven.

37 Don't Fret

'Do not fret because of the wicked.' *v. 1*

To the short-term victor the spoil:
Nazi loot or Assad's boot.
How can you say, 'Don't roil

yourself', when they conspire
to make land contraband
for Sunnis fleeing fire

to live as refugees
while lesser folk possess
their homes – no 'if you please'.

CARPET

Weep *After the Last Sky*:
Said's lament for bent
Jew-Arab history;

duck as Ngũgĩ's sinews
flex at Kenyan men
who slip into White shoes

and steal land from *The Poor*,
who *Have no Lawyers*. Raw
research, tracking spoor

laid down in memory
for Wightman's legal fight
for land and liberty.

What about Ostriker's quote,
here set: try not to fret
'at the meanness of men' she wrote,

but she knew how to add,
this psalm has bitter balm,
it's counterfactually clad.

A *Volcano Sequence* indeed,
although, for the lava to run
and bite our memory, read

Dead Men's Praise, and thrust
your tender nose in Osherow's
damning take on trust,

as Auschwitz Jews rehash
'don't fret or feel regret'
to *a shovelful of ash*.

Takes faith to understand,
long-term, and to affirm
the meek shall farm the land.

Books referred to in
this poem are listed in
the Notes at the end.

53

38 Dialogue with Pain

'Your arrows have sunk into me.' *v. 2*

You squeeze me in your holy grip
I shrivel up – it's all my fault
although you sent me on this trip
you squeeze me in your holy grip
and let your questions run full rip
to bring me to a grinding halt.

You ease me from your holy grip
I answer back – it's not my fault.

39 Tanka for the Passing Guest

'I am your passing guest.' *v. 12*

Each day a dice cup
shaking sunshine or shadow;
each prayer a hiccup
bouncing questions off the wall
that hides us from the future.

40 Mine Shaft Music

'I waited patiently for the Lord.' *v. 1*

A song from the mine shaft, a cry to God's ear
in a psalm Bono felt was more Gospel than Blues:
I'll sing in the darkness, and wait without fear.

Lost deep in a maze without freedom to choose
my way out, reshuffled, discounted, debarred:
I'll praise from the pit, gloom and panic refuse.

Attacked with a blog knife, half pen and half sword,
lambasted by critics who mock a false me,
I'll ignore their fake idols, I'll stick with the Lord.

Walked over by cynics who trash my integrity,
squeezed like a grapefruit, impaled by their taunts,
I'll talk from my heart, and I'll sing my lips free.

To hell with false comforters, agony aunts,
spin doctors, celebrities, all just the same,
I'm here and I'm willing, I'll do what God wants.

Farewell to the pinball and thin wall of fame,
a good reputation, a solid career,
I'm poor and I'm needy, but God knows my name.

41 The Cosmic Synagogue

'They think a deadly thing has fastened on me . . .
even my bosom friend, in whom I trusted,
has lifted the heel against me.' vv.8-9

You would expect to hear the word amen
within the mosque or church or synagogue;
the cosmic record shows, for rich and poor,
throughout our history the road is hard,
the way is narrow, dogged by human snakes
who trip and trap the amens of the blest.

While godly psalms preoccupy the blest
who long to see a cosmic great amen
transforming every sloth and slug and snake
into the dolphins of the synagogue,
the savvy sigh: they know how very hard
it is to change the ways of asset rich, time poor.

Cosmic is as cosmic does; the poor
survive on scattered crumbs among the blest
and wish for more than words; it's hard
for broken refugees to say 'Amen'
and 'Praise the Lord' when synagogues
of any faith play racist cards with snakes.

With just a touch of irony, the snake's
acknowledged as a sign of healing, poor
joke for the sick within the synagogue
who think that healing's in the deal, a blest
inclusive gospel for our glad amen:
a package with no comfort – just too hard.

CARPET

To hold together different worlds is hard,
to keep believing humming birds and snakes
both share a cosmic plan, to say amen
to theft of time and assets, seems a poor
and dour response, when dozens of the ablest
minds have banned snakes from the synagogue.

So who is welcome in the synagogue
to sing these psalms? Should I include those hard
unholy enemies of mine, say 'Blest
are you' regardless if you're saint or snake,
a sloth or slug, labelled rich or poor?
And while I pray, I hear them hiss, 'Amen'.

This cosmic synagogue has snakes
who make it hard for all, even the poor,
to say 'Blest be the Lord: Amen, Amen!'

Notes on Book 1 Poems

1   Chiasm means 'crossing', from the Greek letter X; Psalm 1 may not be the best example, but in v. 6 'the Lord watches over the way of the righteous' is followed by 'the way of the wicked shall perish [when judged by the Lord, v. 5]', which reverses the sentence order as happens in a chiasm. The term is expained more fully on page 75.

3   Using two Finnish sayings cited in Horatio Claire, *The Icebreaker*, Chatto and Windus, London 2017, 44, 111.

7   The 'shiggaion' (Hebrew word) is a lament of some kind.

10 The quotation is from Thomas Halik, *I Want you to Be*, Notre Dame University Press, Illinois 2016, 2.

17 The rhyme pattern A B B A mirrors the chiastic psalm pattern. I owe the concept of 'Macadam' to Andrew Philip.

19 The Van Gogh quote is from his 'Letter 155', June 1880, http://www.vangoghletters.org/vg/letters/let155/letter.html   accessed 4/3/20. The book referred to is C.P. Snow, *The Two Cultures and the Scientific Revolution*, Cambridge University Press, Cambridge 1961. Snow was a fan of George Davie's 'Democratic Intellect' (Paul Scott, *Towards Independence*, Polygon, Edinburgh 1991, 97).

27 The story is in Donald Caskie, *The Tartan Pimpernel*, Oldbourne Book Co., London 1957, 148-9, republished Birlinn, Edinburgh 1999.

28 See Peter Hayman, 'Some Observations on Sefer Yesira (2) "The Temple at the Centre of the Universe"', *Journal of Jewish Studies* 51 (2) 1986 176-182. The Parker Project is a NASA probe to the sun launched on 12/8/18.

29 The poetic conceit of 'five steps' reflects the step parallelism of this psalm, which is found also in Canaanite poetry. The title 'Mind Map' is a concept developed by Tony and Barny Buzan.

37 Books referred to in this poem:
Edward Said, *After the Last Sky*, Faber & Faber, London 1986.
Ngũgĩ wa Thiong'o, *Petals of Blood*, Penguin, London 1977.
Andy Wightman, *The Poor Had No Lawyers*, Birlinn, Edinburgh 2013.
Alicia Ostriker, *The Volcano Sequence*, Univ. of Pittsburgh, Pittsburg 2002.
Jacqueline Osherow, *Dead Men's Praise*, Grove Press, New York 1999.

40 The italicised line in stanza 1 is cited with permission from a song by Maggi Dawn (Kingsway Thankyou Music/EMI/David Cook). The reference to Bono is based on *Revelations*, Canongate, Edinburgh 2005, 136.

Chapter Two
Ballads and Bridges

Like a bridge over troubled water, I will lay me down
(Simon and Garfunkel)

Part 1

1 Sense

2 Connection

3 Inspiration and Freedom

Part 2

4 Agendas (hidden or not)

5 Seeds of Democracy

6 The Psalms as Poetry

7 How Poets have Treated the Psalms

8 Poetry and Preaching

Part 1

1 Sense

Ballads are directed to intellect as well as soul, mind as well as heart, sometimes to 'ease your mind' as in Paul Simon's song, sometimes to stretch it. This is an intensely personal task. The singer does have to lay himself down, if his song is to affect us, as Hugh MacDiarmid wrote,

> A Scottish poet maun assume
> The burden o' his people's doom.
> And dee to brak' their livin' tomb.[1]

The song may bring us questions and even more trouble, as well as what Paul Simon describes as 'ease'. But ease is a rich word, it speaks of more than just comfort, it speaks of the relief which comes when we begin to make sense, or new sense, out of what has happened in the past, and what is happening now.

We are long past the time when, according to the story, a man was discussing with his companion the preacher they had been listening to. 'Man, was the sermon no grand the day!' 'Aye, but did ye understaund him?' 'Understaund him? I wadna presume!'

I have heard people say they love listening to a poem read in a foreign language simply because of the beauty of the sound, but most of the time we want to understand what we hear. When poetry swung into the modern era with Ezra Pound's cry to 'make it new', one of the common criticisms was that poetry was no longer easy to understand, and for that and other reasons we find serious poetry today a minority pursuit – even if there has been an explosion of self-publishing, with more poetry ISBNs each year than ever before.[2]

One form of poetry which has remained accessible is the ballad, whether the famous epics from Homer and Virgil, the medieval poetry of Chaucer in England and the poems about Scottish heroes like Wallace and Bruce, or modern Country and Western ballads, Scottish folk songs and the like. I use the term loosely to cover poems which are essentially telling a story, albeit with a slant, like all stories. Many song lyrics are ballads of sorts, usually they retain a rhyming scheme, and it is significant that Bob Dylan was awarded a Nobel Prize for Literature.

I chose a ballad form for the long poem on Book 2 of the Psalms because I was comparing two stories with one another, and because one story was from ancient times, and the other from medieval Scotland. Tony Conran wrote that epics deliver us from the scatter of lyric moments, the divorce of the lyric moment from what is public and social.[3] Even if a long ballad is something short of an epic, it still has something in common with a symphony, which the composer Gustav Mahler said should contain the world.

'*Journey*', which comes next, has its three movements – 'Blood Lines' (the prelude), 'Border Warfare' (the body), 'Broader Places' (the finale). Its form is like two different instruments (Robert the Bruce, and David) who develop the theme but keep handing it back to the other. Bruce had to escape from English kings much as David had to flee from Saul. Both display the pattern of threat, survival and ultimate triumph. While you will always find common features in leadership from one civilisation to another, the similarities between David and Robert the Bruce are remarkable, whether or not I am the first to notice them.

Like these two characters, the psalms 'dodge about'. Many of their verses reflect the twists and turns of David and Bruce, not because the writer planned such an outcome, but because these psalms reflect human life. *'Journey'* borrows ideas and experience from the psalms of Book 2, with direct quotations in italics. To let the poem grow like two trees with interweaving branches, I wrote shorter poems alternatively dealing with the OT and with Scotland; 'David' has the traditional iambic pentameters, in four line stanzas, to establish the genre, and 'Bruce' has tetrameters, in three line stanzas. I also wished to model the work of a bard in making connections which would encourage people to think in new ways.

Someone said, 'The past is another country'. We do well to be modest about our claims to understand it. Gordon Donaldson wrote in 1990,

> With all the information that ultimately becomes avail-
> able, it may still be impossible to form a complete and
> coherent picture of what Scots believed and what effect
> their faith had on their actions.[4]

Even when a protagonist quotes the Bible as a reason for his or her actions, what motivates individuals is always complex, and history more so. The Psalms were certainly influential – preached and sung on Sundays, studied in private and in universities, seminaries and schools, in both Jewish and Christian contexts, in Europe and America as well as Scotland:

> The Psalms have rung through Scottish religious life
> for centuries, sung in the monasteries in Latin, sung in
> translation in kirks and on hillsides in the post-Refor-
> mation and covenanting years.[5]

So we should not ignore the Psalms, even if they no longer have the currency in public life that they once had. We know that the past has shaped us, and so we try to make connections with it, using images that historians and poets alike suggest to us.

2 Connection

Connections are the bridges that we cross daily, with our feet, with our heads, with our mouths and fingers on a phone or laptop. Familiar ones keep the world safe and sensible, new ones challenge us, disturb us, delight us and give us fresh understanding, and may even give us opportunities to become better people.

The Psalms are full of connections with other parts of the Old Testament, and with the history of Israel. One thing I tried to explore, writing the poetry about David and Bruce, was how particular psalms in Book 2 connected with the two men and their life situations, and I have put some phrases in the poems into italics to suggest this. This is of course my reading, and it raises the question of how you interpret a text. Is there a single meaning, which was in the mind of the writer, as you might expect with a Civil Service document? Is there a hidden meaning which you might expect from an oracle? Is there no particular meaning at all, as we might say of ordinary dreams which are merely the brain sorting itself out overnight? Or does the reader require to impose her own meaning on a text?

The connections, or bridges, between David and Bruce I made as follows:

• Nationalism has always had to defend itself against racism, so *Poem G* on Psalms 46-48 begins, 'A bit of foreign blood improves the gene pool'. David was from a different tribe than Saul; Bruce had Norman blood.

• In both situations, religious leaders decide that a new king is required, and make their choice. In each case, priests suffer for supporting the king of their choice.[6]

• Both spend time on the run or in exile, and barely survive. Both live in caves, with legends attached. Both have to learn to wait, and not take wrong advantage:[7] 'The bishop bad im / bide is time, fur aiblins God / wad *brak the bow, ding doon the axe . . .*' (*Poem H* on Psalms 46-48).

• David is saved when Saul calls off pursuit to fight in Philistine country,[8] Bruce takes advantage of Edward being away in France.

- Bruce kills Comyn, David arranges the death of Uriah.[9] Both are conscience stricken afterwards, though David is condemned by the prophet Nathan (then forgiven), and Bruce is exonerated within a month by Bishop Wishart.[10]

- Both spent time at the court of the king they would later replace, and were even offered their wives (for political reasons) by that same king.[11] In each case the death of that king, in circumstances they had no control over, would start their comeback, which was a gradual increase of power until a decisive event in each case led to full power.[12]

- Both men enjoyed a celebrated reign and died peacefully.

Of course there are differences – David was a commoner, Bruce a noble. David was less restrained in love than Bruce (though Bruce did father six children out of wedlock). Bruce lost several family members, David seems to have saved his.[13] Bruce fought against Edward I's son, David was best friends with Saul's son Jonathan. Bruce had problems with his impetuous brother Edward, David faced a civil war because he would not manage his own extended family; David's family conflict lasted into his dotage,[14] with Bruce the De Soules conspiracy was nipped in the bud.[15]

Clearly David and Bruce shared a role as leader through a time of dramatic political change, to unify their country and to establish or re-establish what today we would call state religion. Of course there is an ambiguity about David in the Old Testament,[16] whereas Robert remains generally one of the great kings of Scots. Did Bruce and his contemporaries make the connection? Certainly not out loud:

- The Declaration of Arbroath modelled King Robert on Joshua and the Maccabees, not David;

- There was another David (born about 500 CE) associated with Wales;

- Early poets did not connect Bruce with David – Walter Bower (1383-1437) in his *Scotichronicon* compares Bruce to Socrates, Cato, Julius Caesar, Achilles, Ulysses, then to Samson, Solomon and one of the Maccabees – but not to David.[17]

But then, to connect a murderer like David with a king wanting free of the accusation that he murdered the Comyn would not be what you did in the days before a free press, or at least a plane waiting on the tarmac! And his enemies would not want to connect him with any kind of king. Still, David must have been a figure for Scottish monarchs at least to be aware of. David was generally a popular name.[18] David was the name Bruce gave to his son, and more important in this context, it was the name of King David I (1124 – 1153). We know that legal scholars of Bruce's reign were keen to portray that David as the author of Scots law, and to associate Bruce with him.[19] He was the eighth son of Malcolm III (the sixth son of his second wife Margaret), and John Davies says:

> We should at least notice the prophetic significance of the name David, as bestowed upon an eighth son who was to rule over a united kingdom, as the biblical David ruled over a united kingdom of Judah and Israel. Like the biblical David, as prince of the Cumbrians, he was the ruler of a southern territory who then inherited the rule of a united realm, taking in the greater kingdom to the north.[20]

So I suggest that I am not simply 'reading in' this connection between David and Bruce. But thinking of the role of curator or poet, it is useful to consider this in the context of the wide-ranging 20th century study of interpretation associated with names like Paul Ricoeur, Jacques Derrida and Northrop Frye. People still take different positions, whether sitting harder on text, on the reader's freedom, on the community that interprets. Some are happy to trust the text, others 'deconstruct' it on the assumption that the writer has a hidden agenda. This is a big issue, considered in more detail in section 4 of the chapter, with the Battle of Bannockburn as one example.

Just as in science (and politics!) there are 'fashions' which only change with a 'paradigm shift', so with the interpretation of texts – whether medieval ballads, or the Psalms themselves. And events – a pandemic, or a war – accelerate these shifts, which we see within the Psalms themselves, as their content has to shift from living with David and his successors as king, to living with

God alone as king. The experience of exile in Babylon, and return to living as a minority under a foreign power, are major fault lines running through Psalms and Old Testament.

As far as I know this is first comparison of David and Robert the Bruce, though section 6 of this chapter looks at other connections made between Old Testament and Scottish history. It is more common to see in the passion of Christ a model for later struggle and suffering – as in the as yet unpublished ballad 'The Fourteen Stations of Johnny Armstrong', written by a descendant of that Border family, Peter Armstrong, or in *The Sair Road*, by William Hershaw.[21]

3 Inspiration and Freedom

Someone speaking or writing about a sacred text will want to interpret it, and bring ideas and context – ancient and modern – into play. A poet writing about the same text will also do this, but with much greater freedom: for example, in *Poem 16 'Bless my Kidneys'* I talk about someone water-skiing in the 'warm, choppy wake of David'; the Psalm is headed l*e*dawid, but the Hebrew could mean 'written by David', 'in honour of David' or 'following David', and my expression not only signals the ambiguity, but picks up David's character (warm *and* choppy).

Psalm 8 talks about tiny children being special. Malcolm Guite in his poem on that psalm has decided that he will include the elderly along with the children, even though they are not mentioned.[22] Such is the freedom of the poet as interpreter – poetic licence. The poet is not a preacher responsible for communicating what a psalm means, whether within or beyond the mind of the writer. The poet is a free spirit, working at a different level from a preacher – and yet I have tried to accept the discipline of writing *on* the Psalms, and not simply *off* them. This raises questions far beyond the scope of this book, but I simply give my testimony that writing as a believer dealing with 'an inspired text' has allowed me to travel to places on that magic carpet that would be inaccessible otherwise. However, you as reader must also be the judge of that.

Yet what is an inspired text? One that just inspires the mind and heart of the reader or listener, or one that is inspired by something or someone beyond the human spirit, however we choose to name it? The Latin poet Ovid began his *Metamorphoses* by asking the gods to inspire his work. During the Scottish Cambuslang revival, psalm verses would come into the mind of those affected, often interpreted in a very personal way as direct communications from God.[23] Going even further, can the poet be like God, as Paul Valéry hinted? 'The poet is recognised ... by the simple fact that he causes his reader to become "inspired"'.[24]

Malcolm Guite expresses a common idea in a sonnet called 'Bible Study':

> Open the text again, for it is true,
> the Book you open always opens you.[25]

When we turn round the phrase 'read the Psalms' to 'the Psalms read me' that brings together mind and heart. Athanasius said that the psalms become like a mirror to the person singing them. Yet that mirror, and that process, remain mysterious, even hidden like God in Psalm 97:2, who is surrounded by 'clouds and thick darkness'.

A modern approach locates inspiration not in God but in human experience. Adam Kirsch said that Rosenberg's *Poet's Bible* (which has many psalm versions) is 'replacing the doubtful miracle of divine inspiration with the genuine miracle of poetic inspiration'.[26] Others will prefer to hold a higher view of sacred texts, as A.N. Wilson argues:

> The experience of reading the Bible becomes a way of reading off our own experience and backslidings and emotional life against the template of the Myth . . . in no other book of Scripture is this more the case than in Psalms.[27]

By 'the Myth' (a rather loose term), Wilson means the life and faith and history of Israel, and the headings attached to many psalms tell us that those who compiled the Psalms would have agreed with him. In typically paradoxical fashion, the atheist Hugh MacDiarmid (the pen-name of Christopher Grieve) expressed a high view of the inspiration of the Psalms:[28]

Interviewer: You still believe in inspiration then, Dr Grieve?

MacDiarmid: Oh no, no, not inspiration. Inspiration means something coming from above, although in Scotland it comes from below as a rule! We have a shepherd poet here who writes doggerel. Well, he says to me, that's where shepherds have the advantage, they get away up in the mountain-top and there is nothing between them and God and it simply flows in upon them. And I said, yes, any examples of this process? He couldn't give me one. I gave him one. I said, the Psalms of David, but that was the only one in history.

Inspiration is seldom used of contemporary poetry. John Betjeman once was handed a manuscript by a young aspiring poet, who said that God had given him those words. The English poet laureate looked at it, then tossed in into the waste bin, with the comment, 'The Lord gave, and the Lord has taken away!'

What about the poet who writes on the Psalms? For example, when I link 'bow down toward your holy temple' in Psalm 138:2 with 'Samson bowed with all his might' in the temple of the Philistines, in *138 'Hair'*, is that inspiration, lateral thinking, or both? The question must be answered by the reader. A sculptor may start with a plan, but find that the material he works with has its own ideas – that happens with poems also. Imagination? Inspiration? The Spirit? Or a mixture?

Inspiration and interpretation are like the pillars of the bridge which a reader must cross in order to profit from what is in front of her, in a book or on a screen. And now **the reader may decide to skip Part 2**, and move on immediately to read **'Journey'**, the long ballad about King David of Israel, and King Robert the Bruce of Scotland. Or read on to discover more about agendas, about the Psalms themselves, how poets have interacted with them, and some further thoughts about poetry and preaching.

Part 2

4 Agendas (hidden or not)

The poet today, like the curator of a museum, no matter how fairly she wishes to preserve the past, will have to make her own choices and accept that she has an agenda.

In my Book 2 poetry, I am suggesting that the life of David and Bruce follow similar trajectories. But overall, I am seeing David and the Psalms and the history of Israel as a lens through which Scottish leaders in Church and State understood their own identity, from early Scotland through medieval Scotland up to and beyond the Reformation. Others have written about this,[29] but what I want to underline at this point is how poets, like historians, use an agenda to curate the past. To say this involves imagination is not to say it is untrue, but simply that it presents one angle on 'what actually happened'.

According to Abbot Bernard of Arbroath, on the first day of Bannockburn Bruce himself addressed his men, and included these words:

> For us, the name of the Lord must be our hope of victory in battle. This day is a day of rejoicing, the birthday of John the Baptist. With our Lord Jesus as commander, Saint Andrew and the martyr Saint Thomas shall fight today with the saints of Scotland for the honour of their country and their nation . . .[30]

Like the English martyr Thomas Becket (and the Old Testament David), Bruce had endured hardship and exile, with the death of Edward I on 7th July 1307 a potential game changer, a 'sign from the Almighty: for "Longshanks" had been gathered to God on the Translation feast of St Thomas'.[31] His devotion to the saints is better shown than his devotion to the Psalms; but it is unlikely that Bruce was unaware of the kingship models in the Bible, given the character of King David I, and the importance of David as a devout king in the Old Testament.

This kind of connection was common enough in Europe. Not many Scots appear in Dante's *Divine Comedy* – but Michael Scott appears as a sorcerer in the eighth circle of hell.[32] Scott was tutor to the Pope, born in Fife (or the Borders) in 1175 and celebrated in folklore as a magician.[33] Having a Scot as tutor to the Pope was a sign of the connections between Scotland and Italy, as were the journeys made by Scottish churchmen to solicit the Pope's backing. Robert the Bruce had a brilliant brother – Alexander, educated at Cambridge and afterwards Dean of Glasgow, and he would have been aware of Dante's writings. Considering he spent much of his life in exile from his native town of Florence, it is not surprising that the three epic poems which make up Dante Alighieri's *Divine Comedy* have many political references, and that the first poem is forthright about the kind of people who occupy the infernal region.

Today we think it odd, and probably dangerous, when a country's rulers and religious leaders are close (as in Iran, or again in Russia today) – but this was normal in ancient times. The Psalms have this double thread, binding religion and rule. As do epic poems like Blind Harry's *The Wallace*, or John Barbour's *The Bruce*.

Through the period of the Wars of Independence Scotland emerges as one country with one king. The hints of how some Scottish kings modelled themselves on the David of the OT,[34] seeing in 'the sweet psalmist of Israel'[35] a necessary link of church and state, become clearer, at least with hindsight, in the life of Robert the Bruce.

It has been said that poetry helps us put into words things we have nearly forgotten; poetry as curating also has the task of reminding us of things we might otherwise forget, preserving memories that the historian might miss, becoming 'an antenna capturing the voices of the world'.[36] But inevitably, voices captured take on the inflection of the choirmaster. Sometimes this is dramatic, distorting the truth. The bard knew only too well that his employment depended on being able to punt his leader's prowess over against his rivals. Historians are accustomed to reading between the lines. One example where contemporary historians are only now beginning to sort out what probably happened is the Battle of Bannockburn. The poet John Barbour wrote his famous epic *The Bruce* for Bruce's grandson, Robert II, in the 1370s, long after the 1314 battle itself. From *Barbour's* poem,[37] it would appear that

(a) the key battle was fought on the Dryfield (where the current National Trust Centre is located);

(b) Scots cavalry had significant involvement on that second day of battle – so today there is even a statue of Bruce on horseback (true enough on the first day of battle, which was small scale);

(c) the appearance of a crowd of 'small folk' sealed the rout of the English.

There are at least five earlier sources which between them make clear that the battle was fought on the Carse of Balquhidderock, that the Scots fought on foot, and that if a crowd of 'small folk' were present at all, it did not affect the battle.[38] Does that mean Barbour wrote a bad poem? No, because he was writing a romance, not a history – that's what bards get paid for (if they are lucky). Of course, it doesn't mean that everything he wrote is historically untrue, just that it needs to be checked out. And it's not only Barbour's account which was likely to be biased: a poignant example is the English Carmelite and court poet Robert Baston, who was attached to the English forces so that he could write up their victory, but captured by the Scots and forced to write up their victory – talk about conflicting loyalties!

> The poetry of the Psalms presents the history of Israel as the story of God's work in that history, whether it is the mistakes of Israel that are on display, as in Psalm 78, or the survival and blessing of the nation, as in Psalm 105. Sometimes that survival is in question, as in Psalm 74, or acutely by the genocide feared in Psalm 83:4. *Poem 83* features anti-Semitism and the Holocaust, but *74* goes further in considering 'Identity Theft', and *31* 'Holocaust Denial' is based on Psalm 31:12, 'I have passed out of mind like one who is dead'. For John Knox, 'the vision of a Christian nation . . . would be realised in Scotland through the preaching of the Word of God and through national examples drawn from Israel's history . . .'[39]
>
> Particular events, with their religious claims, can be airbrushed from history. A modern example is noted in *14 'Tuim-heidit'*. It uses Psalm 14:1, where 'Fools say in their hearts, "There is no God"'. The poem asks why in the recent film *The Darkest Hour* there was no mention of King George

VI calling the nation to prayer, when churches were filled with people in a way inconceivable to millennials today. Exactly the same point could be made about the film *Dunkirk*.

Donald Davie quotes André Malraux: 'In his library of art books or of long-playing gramophone records, the modern artist has an imaginary museum . . . more comprehensive and convenient' than any museum or gallery. Davie goes on to say that since the invention of printing, 'poetry has had [500] years of such an inhabitation'.[40] But nowadays the poet has too many mythologies to choose from, nothing to tell him which of all the galleries in the imaginary museum he should frequent,[41] and the film script-writer likewise may choose a secular mythology even though it subverts beliefs widely held in the time of the film.

Key events like Bannockburn, or the Scottish Reformation, changed the museum of the Scottish mind – mindset if you prefer. Real museums change their displays for big events, and after the biggest events. Two more recent are the Union of Parliaments in 1707 and the (re)opening of the Scottish Parliament in 1999. Iain Crichton Smith was careful to write, 'Let our three-voiced country sing in a new world' for the opening of the Scottish Parliament, whereas a century earlier, Scots and even Gaelic were not taken very seriously as literary tongues.[42] Religion is a strong feature of Gaelic literature, where pre-Christian beliefs are found alongside the religion of the Psalms[43] – less so in contemporary Scots writing.

In his Introduction to *The Faber Book of Twentieth-century Scottish Poetry*, Dunn discusses MacDiarmid's attack on T.S. Eliot, who dismissed Scottish literature as 'provincial'. MacDiarmid wanted more than Stevenson's 'strong Scotch accent of the mind'. He meant that

the poet was obliged to remake Scottish poetry on the basis of a pre-1707 mentality. That is, write as if history had never happened; or write in such a way that history would be rewritten, and unknitted, in the work.[44]

MacDiarmid is recognising that key events in the history of a nation change the mentality of writers. This is certainly evident in Psalms like 137 which reflect the experience of exile, and in poetry written after the Holocaust.[45] *78 'Israel – a*

Melting Shop' presents the fire of suffering as the Old Testament presents it, as part of the mystery of God's providence in judgment – Egypt as a refining blast furnace,[46] the wilderness troubles (a feature of Psalm 78) as discipline,[47] the experience of exile as purification from idolatry.[48] The 'Writings' of the Old Testament still present a choice of how to respond to cataclysmic events like the Holocaust, or lesser but significant changes in the evolving history of Scotland – they offer us the cynicism of Ecclesiastes, the despair and smidgin of hope in Lamentations, the godlessness of Esther, the protest of Job, the anger of the Psalms.

MacDiarmid claimed, 'There lie hidden in language elements that effectively combined / can utterly change the nature of man'.[49] The language of the Psalms is held by many to display this.[50] The book of Psalms has held a unique place in the lives of both Christians and Jews, and out of the history and religion of the Old Testament, the Psalms offer a particular kind of devotion and questioning which has proved transferable to countries like Scotland. Right through early and medieval Scotland, study and regular singing of the Psalms shaped the spirituality of Scots, and the Psalms themselves shed an unexpected light on the people and periods in question. By the time of the 18th century, the Seceding pastor John Brown of Haddington would write a liturgical manual for psalm-singing called *The Psalms of David in Metre with Notes* (1775) which annotates the metrical psalms of the Scottish Psalter (1650). He could say that he wanted them to be sung as 'a spiritually transformative act of Christian worship'. His Kirk Session meetings consisted largely of prayer and the singing of psalms.[51]

5 Seeds of Democracy

This questioning spirit has a long history, and each chapter of this book touches on the way the Psalms, with their spirit of enquiry, have planted seeds of social and political change, even if nowadays such changes are seldom credited to religious faith.

In general, medieval citizens were well served if their monarchs ruled with justice, and were not threatened by other rulers. In William Dunbar's poem 'The Thistle and the Rose', composed for the wedding of James IV and Margaret Tudor in 1503, the lion leans humbly and gracefully on his lady's knee, and she tells him clearly to 'exercise justice with mercy and conscience'.[52] In another poem, 'Surrexis Dominas de Supulchro', the 'lyone' is pointedly Christ (not an Edward or a Richard or any English king), and Dunbar refers indirectly to Psalm 24:7-10.[53]

Ideas of democracy were awakened by the Renaissance: 'A crucial aspect [of the 14th to 16th centuries] was the recovery of classical republican and democratic ideas, and their reapplication in the early modern context.'[54] But there were other sources which challenged the divine right of kings. Scotland's problem at the start of the 14th century, explains Neil Oliver, was that King John Balliol was a lame duck. Bishop Lamberton is likely to have consulted the Scottish theologian Duns Scotus in Paris in 1302, where Duns Scotus would tell him that the real root of royal authority was not inheritance but the consent of the people.[55] In 1309 this bore fruit in 'The Declaration of the Clergy', which declared that 'by knowledge and consent of the same people, [Bruce] was received as king . . .'[56]

> It may be impossible to prove a direct connection, but the use of the Psalms by the clergy over so many years[57] must have led to what might be called a proto-democratic way of thinking. The Psalms show a people coming to terms with the loss of their king, grasping the idea that the Lord was the sole king, and that the people corporately could occupy a high place – whether as 'God's sanctuary' in Psalm 114 or as 'Mount Zion' in Psalm 78. Susan Gillingham points out that even after the final compilation of the Jewish Psalter, Zion referred not only to a place, but to the people as personifying that place: the term was 'democratised and spiritualised' to refer to people of the community of faith rather than the temple in Jerusalem[58] – as indeed by the NT writers.[59]

How far faith should be democratised and *not* spiritualised has been a matter of dispute.[60] *Poem 113, 'Height and Depth'*, celebrates the proto-democracy which the gospel writers saw Jesus inheriting from the Old Testament:[61]

> . . . that loving hand which wraps goodwill
> around the needy, lets them sit at tables
> with the royals, rewrites morbid labels,
> raises wretched, dings to earth high heid yins.

Charles Péguy said, '*Tout commence en mystique, et tout finit en politique*.'[62] How that change takes place, if the Old Testament is any guide, is through a mixture of hard events and spiritual reflection, as Jeremiah and Lamentations reflect on the fate of the king and nobles of Jerusalem. The book of Jeremiah is still ambiguous, as David's throne is to be re-occupied in coming days (33:17-26), a prophecy which soon had to be understood in messianic terms,[63] leaving open the question, what kind of community should Messiah lead, and how should that community be led before Messiah came?[64]

> The early reception history of Psalm 2 is relevant here. In the Septuagint verse 6 is reported speech, so instead of God addressing the king, the king is addressing rebel rulers – more monarchical, less messianic. Another key point of interpretation was how one of the Qumran communities understood verses 1 and 2,[65] to the effect that the whole community inherit the promises to David; 'his anointed one' is in the plural so they together form a messianic community.[66] This way of thinking would be picked up later by groups like the 17th century Levellers, the 20th century Red Clydesiders,[67] or as early as the late 14th century Peasants' Revolt in England.[68]

In Scotland, the issue of the divine right of kings was still to be a matter of fuller debate, but the rights of the people had been asserted.

6 The Psalms as Poetry

There is no Hebrew word for 'poetry', only *šîr*, that which is sung; in Ugarit myth, there is a craftsman God Kothar who could make music; while in English, 'poetry' is derived from 'that which is made'. But the psalm texts themselves show us poetry.

Features like alliteration, onomatopoeia and planned line length are common to poetry in most languages, including Hebrew. Likewise metonymy, as in Psalm 21:8, and metaphor, as in the unique Psalm 22:3, 'Yet you are holy, enthroned on the praises of Israel.' Edward Clarke in his poem on Psalm 14, writes about 'The Word / that's nailed to metaphors.'[69] There is no epic poetry in the Psalms; what we have is a kind of lyric poetry, using a variety of verbal resources – headed in the Hebrew psalter 'Songs of Praise'.

The Psalms do not have fixed metres as in traditional Scottish, English or American poetry, rhyme is rare, but rhythm and word stress are certainly present, typically two or three or four beats to a line. Breaking with the tradition of much modern poetry, I have kept clear stress beats in my poems, with a variety of line lengths. I have at times made a nod to six important features of Hebrew poetry:

(1) **Parallelism** – different ways of repeating a phrase or line, often simply to express the same thought a different way, or to add a little to it – Psalm 31:12 'I have passed out of mind like one who is dead / I have become like a broken vessel.' In *31 'Holocaust Denial'* that particular verse is used as a chorus – a common form of repetition in English.

Something significant may be added ('advancing parallelism') as in Psalm 1 where the Hebrew has three verbs, 'walk', 'stand', 'sit' for growing intimacy of contact with the wicked.[70] Or 'opposite parallelism', as in the last verse of that psalm. Or 'responsive parallelism', as Psalm 118:5.

(2) **Antinomy** or antithesis – a wider case of opposite parallelism. That Psalm 118:5 in Hebrew literally contrasts 'narrow spaces' with 'broad places'. In Psalm 1, verses 1-3 on, the wicked are contrasted with the righteous in verses 4-6; likewise Psalm 112 verses 9 and 10. In Psalm 23, green pastures contrast with the darkest valley – interpreted in *23 'Shepherd Sonnet'* by snakes and ladders.

(3) **Chiasm**, originally 'crossing' (from the Greek X) and therefore putting things back to back – a literary structure typically taking two words or ideas A and B, with variant forms A° and B°, and presenting them as A, B, B°, A°. Some commentators talk about stepped parallelism instead: here is an example from Psalm 29:[71]

Trees (v. 5)
    Animals (v. 6)
        Wilderness (v. 7-8)
    Animals (v. 9a)
Trees (v. 9b)

29 'Canaanite Conquest' not only reckons with the Canaanite background to this psalm but is laid out with a stepped structure. If Psalms 20 and 21 are taken together, Psalms 15-24 as a group have a chiastic structure, with Psalms 15 and 24, for example, both having an entrance liturgy ('Who shall dwell on / ascend God's holy hill?').[72]

(4) Repetition. Psalm 107 has a chorus repeated four times: 'Let them thank the Lord for his steadfast love, / for his wonderful works to humankind.' Psalm 8 repeats the opening two lines at the close: 'O Lord, our Sovereign, / how majestic is your name in all the earth.' I have used a chorus line in *31 'Holocaust Denial'*, since the sense of vv. 1-8 is repeated in vv. 19-24.

All four above could be described as a form of Hebrew parallelism. There are two other features which are less common, but found in English as well as Hebrew.

(5) The pun, an occasional feature of Hebrew poetry, I have used frequently,[73] but not in exact correspondence to the Hebrew, although in the section of poetry for Psalms 60-65 I have made a pun out of the Vale of Succoth in Psalm 60:6, since *sukkâ* means booth or shelter.

(6) Alphabet poems, where the first letter of each line is in alphabetical sequence.[74] The best known is Psalm 119, where each section of eight lines begins with the same letter, and continues in alphabetical sequence. Rather than repeat the form in *119 'Fair and Square'*, I have acknowledged the sequence with 'letters sailing A to Z' and 'mark each passage with eight riding lights'.

In ancient Middle East poetry and story-telling, the climax often comes in the middle, not the end as typical of Western story-telling.[75] But while Chapter 3 of Lamentations in the OT illustrates this, it seldom features in the Psalms, perhaps because they are not narrative poems.[76]

The Psalms like other Wisdom Books deal with ideas, but they share the general OT habit of holding body and soul together, as in Psalm 127. This is reflected in the way 'hymns and psalms' feature alongside 'favours under the blanket' in a more recent Gaelic poem:

> That life
> was to be everlasting . . .
> It would be sweet
> with butter and fish,

and good company,
hymns and psalms,
favours under the blanket,
and porridge in the morning.[77]

7 How Poets have Treated the Psalms

Up to the 19th century, the Tyndale and King James Versions of the Bible 'gave to English literature a treasury of phrases and language which ensured [they] found a central place within the wider canon of poetry and prose'.[78] This intertextuality would include references to the Psalms, consciously or unconsciously, in Italian poets like Dante, or English poets like Herbert (but less commonly in Scotland apart from Gaelic poetry). Here is one example in Gerard Manley Hopkins' poem 'God's Grandeur':

> The world is charged with the grandeur of God.
> It will flame out, like shining from shook foil;
> it gathers to a greatness . . .[79]

A later less trusting response would be Edward Blunden on Psalm 37:25,

> I have been young, and now am not too old;
> and I have seen the righteous forsaken,
> his health, his honour and his quality taken.
> This is not what we were formerly told.[80]

Today references to the Psalms in American poets are common, from such as Scott Cairns, William O'Malley, Jacqueline Osherow; and Ernesto Cardenal writing last century in Nicaragua. But such references are only occasional in England and Ireland, and almost unknown in Scotland. Responses to me from thirty well-known poets in Scotland, England, Wales and Ireland who have used the Bible in their poems, plus others who teach literature, revealed that it is rare for the Psalms to feature in their writing, even if they do cite other passages in the Bible.

A check of all the poems written in five major poetry journals since the start of the 21st century found only three instances of a poet referring to a psalm in a poem (two of them in Scots), though another 27 were found in a sample of several thousand poems in

contemporary pamphlets and books (excluding Psalm 'versions').
This is a small sample of almost 434,000 new poetry ISBNs
published in the UK between 2000 and 2018, the number of which
multiplied between 2017 and 2018.[81]

It would be logical to expect this kind of change in Scotland,
given four factors:

- The rapid decline of church membership
- The change in religious education, away from learning the
Bible
- The multiplicity of Bible versions in place of the 'literary' King
James Version
- The secularisation of Scottish society

The Psalms are a literature known by Scots well into the middle
of the 20th century. As a boy, I recall Psalms 23, 100 and 121 being
sung on public occasions. Back in 1922, the first Scots Labour MPs
left St Enoch station in Glasgow to the singing of two covenanting
psalms (23 and 124).[82]

> The 18th century Michael Bruce, 'the gentle poet of Lochleven',
> authored the 58th Paraphrase, 'Where high the heavenly
> temple stands'; but apart from this indirect allusion to Psalm
> 78:69 via Hebrews 4:14, nothing from the Psalms graces his
> (often theological) poetry.
>
> Of the 19th century 'Ettrick Shepherd', it is said that the
> Psalms were 'the central literary text which Hogg himself
> paid tribute to',[83] although strangely, James Hogg is typical of
> many Scottish writers when he always refers to people singing
> the Psalms rather than to the Psalms themselves.[84]
>
> Indeed, almost all the classic texts in the *Scottish Religious
> Poetry Anthology*, if they mention the Psalms, cite them
> simply as something sung, and when they mention the Bible,
> always refer to doctrine and story rather than explicitly citing
> the Psalms.[85] Robert Allan (1774-1841) weeps for the 'halie
> covenant aith / We made wi our Gude to keep;' and therefore
> asks, 'O wha will gang to yon hill-side, / To sing the Psalm at
> een?'[86]
>
> It is true that Dallan Forgaill's 'Elegy of St Columba' says,
> 'God fixed the Psalms'. There is the prose version of Psalm
> 100 in that *Anthology*, since it was written by a Scottish poet,

along with the prose version of Psalms 23 and 128. There is the reference to psalm tunes in 'The Cottar's Saturday Night'. But citations from the psalms *in the poems* are absent from this Anthology, while angels, apocalypse, ascension, Christ and his work, creation, grace, Job, judgment, law and Moses, love, Mary, saints and popes, sabbath, Satan, the Song of Songs, the Trinity, are frequent.

Robert Henryson's 'The Preiching of the Swallow', a religious poem, is about the swallow as a bird of nature, without reference to Psalm 84 (though the title suggests familiarity). The brown stag of Donald Macdonald is on the moor, not in Psalm 42. Nan Shepherd's 'Licht amo' the hills' has nothing to do with Psalm 121. Donald Macaulay 'listened to the psalm' – while 'the tune was mysterious', that is all we get.[87] Catriona Montgomery's 'blackness of the pit' might have come from a dozen psalms if she had not included 'black', making it come from none.

In their Introduction to the anthology, the authors suggest that the Scottish poetic tradition is better represented by those like Norman MacCaig and Sorley Maclean who manage to link the sublime and the mundane without positing a contrast between this world and another world, since they stay 'locked in the human cage'.[88] So among Scottish writers it is more common today to find 'psalm' used in a vaguely spiritual sense, as John Burnside writes of 'the people in a psalm . . . arriving here by chance, just passing through',[89] or indeed Scott Cairns' use of 'Idiot Psalms'.[90]

A few contemporary British poets, like Michael Symmons Roberts[91] and Maria Apichella,[92] have hinted at 'psalm' in the title of their books. Roberts wrote 150 poems all with 15 lines, reflecting ideas and emotions from the psalms without a one to one correspondence (he emphasises that *Drysalter* is spelt without a p). Apichella presented her partner as a 'contemporary David' in her long poem.

With the perseverance of psalm singing in the Highlands and Islands it is not uncommon to find a Hebridean context, as when 'the psalms lift and fall in long waves' in a new poem by Kenneth Steven.[93] But 'psalm' has been used for a religious lay in earlier generations, as in 'A Psalm of Ben More' written by John Blackie about Mull in the late 19th century.[94]

The paradoxical Psalm 46 has the words 'Be still and know that I am God' in the mouth of one who 'breaks the bow and shatters the spear'. Harry Smart muses on the idiocy of someone setting Psalm 46 to the tune 'Dambusters', with the terrible collateral effect of the bombs downstream of the dam:

> And my mind had turned to the Möhne Dam:
> how the voice of engines went over the waters,
> the voice of the Lancasters,
> the bombs of glory thundered, the bombs of God.[95]

Maoilios Caimbeul writes in a lighter vein:

> Ministers
> in black clothes,
> buses coming from the communions,
> and we singing psalms. Elders
> praying and laughing . . .[96]

Poems referring to particular psalms are found in minority languages like Gaelic (Maoilios Caimbeul), Scots (Jock Stein), Shetlandic (Christine de Luca).

> This indicates how rare it is for published writers in Britain to feature a verse from the Psalms.[97] One obvious reason for this is that the Psalms are already poetry. That, however, has not stopped poets using epigraphs from the Classical poets; of the poets consulted who do write on the Psalms, some have simply worked psalm themes into their poetry, and some (like Caimbeul) have used psalm epigraphs.[98] It is unusual to find contemporary UK poets (like Edward Clarke, Malcolm Guite, Diana Hendry,[99] Theresa Lola,[100] and Lyn Moir[101]) who have written directly on a psalm without simply making a devotional text.
>
> In ten years of attending poetry readings in Scotland, I have only heard one poem focused on a psalm,[102] though devotional poetry on the Psalms may come to light in websites like *Church of Scotland Weekly Worship*, or *Sanctuary First*.[103]

8 Poetry and Preaching

Poetry and preaching seem very different. Preaching is putting across a message. Norman MacCaig, the poet, said, 'If you want messages, go to Safeways!' Of course, poetry does contain messages, but MacCaig was subtle, and MacDiarmid less so. They certainly wrapped their messages in very different paper.

Poetry does not even have a clear starting point: every poem begins in the dark, the writer does not know where she is going until 'something happens'.[104] This parallels Jacques Derrida's commentary on an exhibition of prints he hosted at the Louvre, where he suggests that drawing proceeds from a structural blindness, begins where it cannot see or know.[105]

At first sight, the difference is one of constraint and freedom: the preacher or commentator is tied to the meaning of the text, using interpretive tools, while the poet is free to run with her own vision. But the constraints have weakened – while traditional exegetes would not hesitate to 'compare scripture with scripture',[106] today feminist preachers (for example) would be asking whether the perspective of Psalm 2 is biased by its assumption of male despots,[107] and these questions may set a poet also off in new directions.

After the positives of Psalm 1 and *Poem 1* come the questions in Psalm 2 and *Poem 2*. So these first two poems present the hermeneutic of trust and the hermeneutic of suspicion, and the two remain in dialogue all through the Psalms, which is just one way that the Psalms are both ancient and modern. The two are not always separate. The King James Version opening of Psalm 121 confused them by mistranslating 'from whence comes my help' as a statement, not a question – the Hebrew context implies a question – and the contemporary poet Toby Martinez de las Rivas picks this up in a poem:

> He would lift his eyes past mine to the hills
> '. . . from whence cometh my help . . .' & I could not
> detect whether that was statement or question.[108]

Here is what poetry and exegesis share:

(1) Both, in different ways, affirm and question, though the preacher will question more carefully, and the poet will affirm more obliquely – as Emily Dickinson wrote, 'Tell all the truth but tell it slant'.[109]

(2) Both reach beyond the text, though the poet will travel much further. But like the preacher, she can be open not only to the text and its meaning in an impersonal sense, but in a personal sense to the God (or for some 'the transcendent') behind it.

The task of the poet is to see, and to sing – and the poet's song 'may reach where the words of the philosopher do not reach,'[110] or as MacDiarmid wrote: 'For I've nae faith in ocht I can explain, / and stert whaur the philosophers leave aff.'[111]

> This starting place, according to Psalm 139, is God's knowledge of us, and Augustine relates this specifically to the memory.[112] Rowan Williams develops Augustine's view as follows:
>
>> Thus, the most spiritual reading [of the Psalms] for Augustine will always lead us most directly to humility. Where literalism is to be rejected, it is because it proposes to us a static object of knowledge capable of possession and thereby fails to stir us to longing for the greater fullness of God. So there is a paradoxical dimension to his hermeneutics: what most locates us in our earthly experience in all its reality is what most opens up the fuller sense because it most prompts desire . . . the Psalms offer a particular way of structuring the time of the believer's life, so that the present is always oriented to Christ's future.[113]
>
> It is a paradox that such humility – if indeed there is 'more' beyond the text – helps us to discover new things. Long before Ezra Pound in *Canto LIII*, Quintilian – the ancient authority on the memory[114] – spoke about 'making things new'.[115] Such new things come both from the memory, which embraces our life experience, and from the transcendent. Just as the Psalms themselves hold together the transcendent and the immanent,[116] so a nuanced understanding of God as in all as well as over all will encourage the imagination of the poet as well as the application of the exegete.[117]

Preachers and poets work at different levels, and produce very different material, but share the challenge of communication in a way which leaves God and the reader free to do their own work in response.

Book 2 Poems: Journey

1 Blood Lines

Psalms 42 – 45

A

Where is your God? A question never marked
on Abraham's mind map, given what we know
of this great ancestor, just told to go
from Haran, up and round that Fertile Crescent

Canaan bound, with basic Bedouin stuff
– a tent, a wife, a nephew, goats and sheep,
maybe a camel, servants, just enough to keep
together soul and body, *build an altar.*

Sheikh and shepherd, wandering warrior,
hearing desert recitative by night
as God kept telling Abraham he might
expect *as many children as the stars.*

One God, one note, such faith and faithless play
with Abraham's women, trial on Mount Moriah
when his trust was taken to the wire
and Isaac brought the song back from the dead.

B

Columba learned that music, flew
(or fled) across the Irish sea
to beach his coracle on I.

Columba, lord of wind and whirlpool,
whales and wells, *the cataracts*
of Scripture, named prophetic facts

that opened hearts and kingdoms,
thundered godly psalms at Brude,
changed a heathen land for good:

a saint of spiritual songs,
thirled to God *by light and truth*,
heaven's music, Spirit's breath.

C

Led, or driven, into wilderness,
wildscape where songs and dreams and men expire,
Moses saw the light, the bush on fire,
found the God of all his nomad fathers

calling him to go to Egypt, face his fears
and Pharaoh, free his people from the grind
of slavery, the helpless, hopeless mind
that takes disgrace as heaven's final word.

Take off your sandals, Moses, keep your distance,
this is holy ground. So Moses hid his face,
but not his failings, tried to dodge his place
in history, argued long with God, and lost.

Loose ends tied up, great ends ahead, the man
went back to win his people living space
as God fought for them, making them a race
unique, a lighthouse to intrigue the world.

D

For all their common Christian light
those Europeans fought for power,
and this meant refugees like her,

the Saxon Princess Margaret,
discipled at the court of Stephen,
wrecked on Tyneside coastline, even

then in Scottish hands, and taken
north to wed that nasty Malcolm,
roughest king in Christendom.

Did he poison his Orcadian
queen? And then exchange that potion
for his passion, for his notion

that he wanted, needed Margaret,
some firm and feisty woman who
would take him, change him, make him new?

Forget your kin, your father's house:
tough words for any royal bride
'mid rumours of uxoricide.

Who else would leave her husband's bed
to tryst with God, and let him be
all eaten up with jealousy?

He crept behind her to that cave –
but when he found her true, he knew
he had some making up to do.

He bowed to God as well as wife,
and so Dunfermline Abbey stands,
his penance, built to her own plans.

Her soul kept thirsty for her God,
saw statecraft joined to piety,
new learning, health, sobriety

and pilgrimage an economic
asset for the realm, Queensferry
hers in name for car or wherry.

E

Romance, command, arrangement, hit or miss,
the chemistry of fate has many forms
and ceremonies, taken as the norms
of ancient or today's society.

Let's find them in the text, those hidden
early brides, from Eve to Zipporah,
with thanks to Shiprah and her colleague Puah,
who both saved the race from genocide,

fulfilling words to Abraham, that he
would have descendants, so that those who share
his faith in God might call him father, bear
his name beneath their own religious label.

F

What a roll call from her womb,
no virgin saint Queen Margaret:
Alexander, David set

to follow Duncan, Edgar, all
her sons, and with a lateral twist
we find King Robert on the list –

the Bruce, whose wife Elizabeth
would suffer exile for the cause
of liberty, its fame, its laws.

Salute the women, pull them out
of hiding, name them every one,
and note the mother of the son,

the countess Marjorie of Carrick,
Bruce's mum, and Agatha,
Saint Margaret's devout mama.

Psalms 46 – 48

G

A bit of foreign blood improves the gene pool,
oils the way to make Adullam's cave
a hospitality tent for any brave
enough to join the loyal opposition,

find the God of Jacob is their refuge,
take the risks of changing faith and truth
to copy David's great-grandmother Ruth.
But none of that is in young David's head.

He watches sheep. He skiffs a stone across
a river carrying his childhood dreams,
still unaware of any brook *whose streams*
will bless the future city of his God.

H

We dinna ken fir shair gin Bruce   *for sure if*
wis born in Ayrshire or in Essex,
wi' his pedigree a mix

o Europe's westies: onyweys,
cried Robert lyk is Norman faither
(no that they were aye thegither),

Bruce wis a sturdie bairn, brocht up   *child*
in Annandale, wi fower brithers
an three sisters, aa wi mither's

Scottish bluid as weel's the French
tae gie the comin King a gene
for joukin back an forrit, tween   *ducking   forward*

the Scots an Edward, eik name Langshanks,   *nickname*
wha cud flether and cud flyte   *flatter   scold*
an if ye thrawed, gang unco gyte.   *objected mad with rage*

Nae mony gaed aboot the land   *went*
tae *coont its tours, conseeder was,*   *towers   walls*
its fierdie heritage an its laws,   *proud*

fir maist wir feart, wi Balliol jist   *afraid*
a tuim tabard. Then, Wallace winnin   *empty*
Stirling Brig, the English rinnin,

Edward laired in Flanders – hooch!
– till Falkirk; efter, aa thing ower,
Wallace lowsed hissel frae pooer.   *released himself*

Bruce wis Earl o Carrick, yokit
wi his sleekit unfrien, Comyn,   *smooth, plausible*
an yin Peebles coorse forgetherin   *rough assembly*

fun the Comyn's twa hauns thrapplin   *choking*
Bruce afor the ithers mad im
gie richt ower. The bishop bad im   *give up, stop*

bide is time, fur aiblins God   *wait   perhaps*
wad *brak the bow, ding doon the axe,*   *cast down*
an mak the English turn thir backs.

Bit nae jist yet. Edward wis back,
the mountains shak, the braid seas raired,
an Bruce wis forced tae cry im 'laird'.   *call*

I

Far from Rhine and Danube, Tyne and Forth
another river waters not a garden
but a city; not the river Jordan
but a river from the heart of God;

not even Gihon in Jerusalem,
but God's own blessing for all humankind.
Meanwhile, the prophet Samuel puts his mind
to changing the succession: no more Saul,

but David, chosen for his sparkling eyes,
his shepherd soul. The last shall end up first,
the youngest best; while Saul might do his worst,
the giant-killer David swerved, survived.

One day they'd crown him in Jerusalem,
a city David took by stealth; ascended
by the water tunnel; God defended
him, and let him star in his own film.

Glorious things of thee are spoken, Zion,
city of our God. A hillock morphs
into a cosmic diamond dwelling, dwarfs
the future monarch's modest place of birth.

J

Who know what stark theology
drives prelate, monk or priest
to put a fast before a feast?

God is the king of all the earth,
the Psalmist says: and therefore, since
an English king is but a prince

a Scottish bishop ponders long,
decides God's temple has no gate
that closes out a Scottish state.

2 Border Warfare

K

David had no qualms that Saul was king;
he was a commoner; he knew his place,
for *low and high, both rich and poor, all face*
one judgment, leave their wealth behind.

Saul was the foolish man, the paranoid,
fearing failure, dreading death; obsessed
with David's popularity, possessed
by jealousy, he tried to kill the one

he saw as rival, offered him his daughter
as a prize, set the bride price high
enough to guarantee that he would die
at enemy hands. But faint heart never won

fair lady – David, smitten, never blinked,
brave enough to outstare dangerous billies
like King Saul: tossed a hundred willies
at his feet, and married Princess Michal.

Still, *no price is high enough for life,*
in spite of fame we die like animals.
No way Saul and David can be equals;
David seeks the truth, and finds the lie,

as Saul is taken over by his hate,
sits there, beilin, *speaks against his kin,*   boiling
calls out his son, flings his spear at him
for loving David more than father's pride.

Michal is wife – but Jonathan is more,
a friend that loves more truly than a brother,
tragic, doomed to perish with his father,
death his shepherd, Philistine his foe.

90

JOURNEY

L

Another Saul perhaps, this Edward,
making Robert *protégé*,
not guessing *lésé majesté*

would prove a double-ended spear,
their friendship just an episode
as border warfare ebbed and flowed.

These English kings *named lands their own*,
but rich and poor, *the wise, the fool*,
must enter death's own boarding school.

Robert made three pacts: he pleased
himself and Edward, as it were,
and wed Elizabeth de Burgh.

The second pact, with Lamberton,
he made to *solve his riddle*, keep
the flame of freedom burning deep

within himself. The third compact
was Comyn brain-child. Robert
trusted him, used all his expert

skill at politics, until
called back to Edward's oversight;
Bruce played for time, fled overnight,

deduced the depth of treachery
on Comyn's part; confronted, slew
him at the holy altar, knew

the die was cast; the time had come
for Scots themselves to call the tune
and crown this Robert king at Scone.

M

Some psalms are written to enthrone the king,
and some are written when the king has fallen
foul of God and humankind, all in,
shit-soiled in sin, and flat upon his face.

King David, older and no more that bright-eyed
boy who charmed all Israel with his art,
his handsome, giant celebrity – his heart
cries out in pain: 'O God, have mercy on me,

I am crushed and broken, filthy in your sight.
I stole Bathsheba, made her pregnant, got
her husband killed, then went and tied the knot
with her in haste to hide the awful crime.

You want the truth bored deep into my soul,
so make me clean, and scrub my dirty heart.
I'm torn in bits, but every single part
is pleading with you, begging your forgiveness.'

N

Maybe King Robert used this psalm,
acknowledged what he'd done before
the altar of a church, his war

with Comyn bringing him to crisis,
daggers drawn, shedding blood
within the holy house of God.

Barbour glossed it in two lines,
a bishop soon absolved the king,
but still it was a dreadful thing

that seared the conscience of the Bruce,
besmirched the virgin Scottish rose
and gave a weapon to his foes.

Psalms 52 – 59

O

Young David took Goliath's sword, and fled
from Saul, left Doeg clyping to his king: *telling on (someone)*
'I saw your son-in-law, worshipping
at Nob, and all the priests supporting him.'

Saul summoned them and had them put to death,
his chief of shepherds, Doeg, *treacherous*
in heart and tongue, his dagger lecherous
with misdirected lust for sacred blood.

All alike perverse, no one does good,
the litany continues through the strife
of Saul and David, running for his life
from town to town, from countryside to cave,

where once he hid, as Saul crept in to crap,
and David's men said, 'Get him, now's your chance!'
But David said, 'No dance of circumstance
will let me murder God's anointed king.

'*I cast my burden on the Lord, for he*
will save me, and throw down my enemies
into the deepest pit. Vengeance is his,
and I shall live *to give him all my praise.*'

P

Bruce almost lost his life at Methven.
With his cause and kingdom doomed,
he fled far west, while Edward fumed.

Barbour never mentioned spiders,
but the legend fills a vacuum;
history needs some wiggle room,

for truth is strange, and providence
embraces fiction as it acts
through circumstance and stubborn facts

– like those two women caged like doves
without their wings, four hideous years
a spectacle, exposed to jeers,

nowhere *to fly and be at rest*;
while Alexander, brilliant brother
(Dean of Glasgow), Thomas, other

sibling, lost their lives for Bruce.
How will he spin the story, win
the hearts of kith as well as kin?

(And how will future thinkers link
the simile of *olive tree*
and difficult theology?)

Q

No kin were Ziphites: '*Rude and ruthless strangers
seek my life,*' said David, as he dodged
King Saul again at Horesh, went and *lodged
in wilder country, rescued from his troubles.*

Would it always be like this? A weary
fugitive? Pretending to be mad
in Gath? Or could he ask the seer, Gad,
for help? '*All day I utter my complaint.*'

R

Guerilla warfare's what you see
when Bruce comes back. In Galloway
he worked his faith, day after day

evaded capture, *kept his feet*
from slipping, proved that God could *shame*
those who would trample on him, came

at last to tipping point, the fight
at Loudoun Hill, and, well rehearsed
off stage, the death of Edward First.

S

This royal lion, *greedy for its prey,*
its teeth an arrow, tongue a sharpened sword,
had lashed its tail at David and the Lord,
but when King Saul and Jonathan met their fate

on Mount Gilboa, David would compose
a song of lamentation, praise the one
who *loosed the dogs*, respect the Saul who'd done
so much to hunt him down and take his life.

Yet David knew the words to slag a foe:
'*Let them be like the snail that turns to slime*
under my foot. Let them slip out of time
like an aborted child. Give me revenge!'

In Carmel David carried thoughts like these
against a man called Nabal, who refused
a payment for protection, then abused
his future king, preferring his own feast.

He had a wife who knew which side her bread
was buttered: waited till her man was sober,
told him how she'd gone and cleared the larder,
taken loaves and wine, dressed sheep and grain,

a hundred raisin cakes, two hundred figs
to save the day, keep David's wrath at bay.
A stroke ensued, her husband died, a doorway
to a better life, as David's wife.

3 Broader Places

Psalms 60 - 65

T

A better life indeed: *repair*
the breaches, fill the cracks
with smeddum that the country lacks.   *courage*

A bolder life – although the Bruce
falls sick, his people pray, '*Prolong*
the monarch's life, let him be strong

again, for he belongs to us,
and we to him. Returning health
became a sign of commonwealth,

a king and people working out
how *low and high estate* will both
commit to treaty at Arbroath.

But first to set a nation free,
keep and castle, raid and ransom,
North Sea trade another transom.

Bruce is found beside his soldiers,
wading through Perth Castle moat,
water reaching to his throat,

in such like ways declaring status,
tightening screw and turning spanner,
raising up a godly banner.

Slowly, slowly, wins this race,
until his brother, who had wedged
his men round Stirling Castle, pledged

that Mowbray could remain
one year without relief. This made
the English force bound to invade

before Midsummer, 1314,
giving Robert just a year
to mount the fight of his career.

U

David makes the *flight* of his career
to Achish, King of Gath, a Philistine
no less, and serves him well, with every sign
of loyalty, by raiding foreign parts,

pretending plunder comes from Israel.
Then a blow: his base at Ziklag falls,
the women, herds, are stolen. Hear the calls
his men make hard against him – *then he prays;*

his heart is faint; God leads him to his foes
through an Egyptian slave he rescues, makes
the raiders raided – finds the flocks; takes
his trophies; *fainting turns to feast and praise.*

V

Now Edward marched his men past Falkirk,
thought he'd quickly sweep the board,
failed to take St Ninians Ford,

had to take the long way round,
pitch his camp down on the carse,
there rest his weary royal arse.

Scots creep through Balquiderock Wood
that second day, before midsummer,
Edward's army due a *bummer*   *blow, knock out*

for their spurning of the peace
that Bruce has offered. Oozing swank
but poorly led, they slumber, drunk

until they spot the Scots advancing
down the carse. King Edward likes
to think that when they place their pikes

and kneel, they offer to surrender;
close advisers grimly cackle:
'Sire, they kneel before God and battle!'

One knight charges at the Scots
– too late, no room to gather speed,
he falls; the Earl of Gloucester *deid*.   *dead*

The English archers have their famous
arrows ready by the gross,
but now the Scots are far too close,

they cannot shoot without their targets
being friend as well as foe;
they are disqualified. And so,

the Scots are winning; pinned between
the Pelstream and the Bannock Burn
the English see the battle turn.

The river of God is full of water,
yes, but now it runs with blood
and buries men in gore and mud.

Two days later, Bruce reflects,
and through the squint at Aberdour
takes bread and wine: 'This is my hour,

for you have heard my promise; also
Scotland's hour; our time has come,
we're no more under England's thumb.'

W

King Saul is off the field, now dead, and with him
Jonathan: *have you not left us, God?*
Must we repeat that awful *Ichabod*?   *glory has departed (Heb.)*
The land is torn, and *human help is vain.*

David, off the pitch by providence
can pray, 'O God *you heard my vows, and gave
me heritage with those who fear you.* Save
me, *let me be enthroned for ever.*'

So it was. He took the throne at Hebron,
fought for seven years to bring the nation
into one. '*My rock and my salvation,
God my castle*, confidence and King.'

X

If riches grow, set not your heart
upon them. Bruce dealt well, and fairly
with the captured English, early

on he ransomed Bishop Wishart,
with his Queen and Marjorie
his daughter, now at last set free.

Needing further fields of glory,
Edward Bruce went into action
overseas, but some distraction

Ireland proved to be; *set no*
vain hopes on robbery, the psalm
makes clear, it only leads to harm.

Ten years after Bannockburn
the Pope acknowledged Bruce as King.
So underneath your wings, I sing

for joy, and all who swear by him
shall glory, for the mouth of liars
will be stopped. Priests, monks and friars

now invoked St Andrew patron
saint, and Edward, always late,
agreed in 1328.

He turned the sea into dry land.
While Pharaoh may have lost his son,
his daughter Scota proved the one

progenitor the Scots might claim
to link them with the Bible story,
according to the ancient foray

into history on which
the Declaration of Arbroath
itself depends. For, nothing loath,

the document rides roughshod through
the facts, to make the case for Bruce
before the Pope, plays fast and loose

with Picts and Scots; but what it says
on people, kings and common weal,
for freedom making such appeal,

is what has stamped its glorious seal
on minds and hearts for centuries.
Without it, Bruce would be the less,

for he has only one more year
to live. The Douglas takes his heart,
after his death, and makes a start

on pilgrimage. Jerusalem
he fails to reach, is killed in Spain,
the heart is saved, comes back again

to find a home in Melrose Abbey.
Blest the man whom God shall choose:
so rest in peace, Robert the Bruce.

Psalms 66 – 71

Y

David gathered thirty mighty warriors,
battle heroes, ambidextrous slingers,
archers, men who understood the King as
well as fought for him; they knew him, loved him,

risked their lives to bring him just a drink
of Bethlehem water when he mentioned thirst.
Such energy and love behind him burst
a leaking dam, installed a new regime.

After all the trials, *a spacious place*
to rest and reign, to build a civil service
(and some houses for his wives). His verve is
there until he comes to middle age,

and teenage sons, each with a different mother.
Once girls thrilled to sing of David's fame,
later *played their tambourines*, and came
to bless God in a massive congregation.

Now these girls have married David's soldiers,
and the King has gleaned a dangerous
hareem, one bound to nurture venomous
ambition, to which David's eyes were blind.

The Bible spills these family secrets, David's
crafty nephew Jonadab abetting
Amnon's incest lust for Tamar, letting
him deceive her, rape her, then reject her.

Absalom, usurping God and father
(*who alone should judge with equity*
the people given him), showed no pity
for his father nor his concubines,

abused them, while his father fled for life
across the Jordan, *waters to his neck*
and weary with his crying. What a wreck
he's made of fatherhood, this famous king.

Meantime Absalom took bad advice,
let David rally, find his friends, fight back,
see Absalom's rebellion falter, crack.
To God alone belongs escape from death.

'*O Absalom, my son, my son! Would I*
had died instead of you, O Absalom!'
Thus David threw away, without a qualm,
the courage of his troops who fought for him.

His flaw? He could not bear to discipline
his sons, or make the kind of firm decision
that his kingdom needed. Lack of vision,
nesting, no more worlds to conquer, lulled him

to a lonely end. We find him senile,
appetite gone cold, while Adonijah
makes a sudden grab for power. Bathsheba
confronts David: why not Solomon?

Do not cast me off when I am old,
do not forsake me when my strength is spent.
Benaiah, Nathan, Zadok, all three went
to crown King Solomon, at David's word.

King David's voice: still present, whispering
lament and praise, thanksgiving, song and prayer;
a commonwealth of psalms, with words to wear
around the forehead, and within the heart.

Psalm 72

Z

The past seems far away,
the future's now upon us,
knocking, scowling, mocking
our attempts to pray
for rulers, be they kings
or queens or ministers
or sheiks, Theresa May

or Sturgeon, Mao or Xi
Jinping, Pol Pot or Trump,
imam or president,
yes, all the powers that be
who hold elected seats
or fill by fouler means
the stage of history.

How does rude rule play out
in war and peace games? Could
the unseen prayers of common
men and women, doubt
and faith, lament and praise
mixed up in cries to God
be what it's all about?

*Grant the king your justice
God*, and *may he give
the poor a break*, the rich
a fright. In fact, is this
the sort of king a God
might be, or is that just
a faint hypothesis?

So, does it really matter
if the psalm is full
of jussives, 'may it be',
or something more than that, a
'he shall be', so dear
to Christians seeing prophecy
in lots of Bible data?

Our stories start with fire,
then flicker to their close,
limp off the stage, and cough,
apologise, retire.
Without some thread of hope,
the tales of David, Bruce
and everyone expire.

Long may he live! He will,
with *gold and grain and glory*,
when the common weal
is all his care, a temple
built of living stones,
such potent prophecies
a leader must fulfil.

Notes on Book 2 Poems

To let the poem grow like two trees with interweaving branches, I wrote shorter poems alternatively dealing with the OT and with Scotland; David has the traditional iambic pentameters, in four line stanzas, to establish the genre, and Bruce has tetrameters, in three line stanzas. The final poem combines the two in seven line stanzas.

D   While Margaret was born in Hungary and brought up in the royal court, it is uncertain whether she had Hungarian blood – I follow the story that her mother Agatha was *'filia regis Hunorum'* (though she may have been his niece, or unrelated) – but she certainly was influenced by the Christian royal court.

V   It is likely King Edward camped on the knoll at the north end of the Carse of Balquhiderock (below Bannockburn High School today) before the second day of battle – the knoll (not a pit bing!) is shown in Thomas Jeffery's map of 1746, and the Carse is now accepted by historians as the battle site.

Historians question the story that Bruce went to Aberdour Kirk, though it is claimed at that church.

Y   As in other sections, this uses material from other parts of the Old Testament.

Z   This frames the whole poem, as Psalm 72 frames Books 1 and 2 of the Psalms.

Chapter Three
Migration and Identity

Ilk vaigin is aye steekit till
the last lanesome path's uncleekit
fae the fankle o gates:
we follae our faithers
ower the hill

> (William Hershaw, '*Solvitur Ambulando* II' in *Saul Vaigers*)

Part 1

1 Identity

2 Roads, Gates and Tribes

3 Land and Spirituality

4 Migrants

Part 2

5 The Psalms and National Identity

6 Israel and Scotland: Comparison and Covenant, the Psalms and Scottish Nationhood, the Use of Typology

7 The Psalms and Today

8 Book 3 Poetry

Part 1

1 Identity

'Journey', the long poem based on Book 2 of the Psalms described how both David and Bruce discovered themselves and their life work, curating their experience from the sources available – but their nations changed at the same time, and the people of Israel and the people of Scotland found their sense of identity developing in new ways. This 'national identity' is distinct from the sense of personal/individual identity which has such prominence in the West today. In the earlier psalms, and not least in Psalm 72 which closes Book Two, national identity is focused on the character of leaders like David or Solomon, on the nature of the God they worship, and on the prospect that the nation of Israel will be righteous and prosperous.

Other psalms, like the more direct attacks of the Old Testament prophets, describe who the people of Israel are supposed to be, their true identity, and contrast this with what is actually going on. People need to *know* who they are, and then *be* who they are. The Psalms not only did that for Israel, with their place in the Old Testament story, they gave a country like Scotland a sense of identity – but more on that later in this chapter. The key thing to note for now is that to assert identity is to make a prophetic statement, and the thread of this chapter and its poetry is prophecy.

In the Old Testament, when things go wrong, it is not just 'bad luck', although a book like Ecclesiastes toys with that idea (for example, in chapter 6). The cause is human sin, and a protest poem describes the outcome for those sinned against, as do many of my poems in 'Migrants', the Book 3 poetry in the next chapter, often set in the form of a lament. One of the poems (on Psalm 74) is called *'Identity Theft'*, an issue which links refugees today with the Jews who saw their sacred symbols destroyed and the cream of their community deported to Babylon:

> Our flags have gone / from mast and heart,
> and no one knows / the past . . .

Sometimes, however, the injustice allows a community to refocus their identity, as did the Jews after exile, as did Scots who emigrated during the Clearances. *Poem 82 'Clearance'* contains a critique of law and landlords, gaeldom and even God himself, but ends by acknowledging that 'Scots and powerful doctrine / cleared the ocean'. This sense of identity has not only been a resource for survival, but often a force for good – except when it morphs into 'civil religion', as it did in 'the troubles' of Northern Ireland or in Apartheid South Africa. When the Boers went on their 'Great Trek', they identified themselves as the chosen Israelites travelling through the wilderness, and the Khosa people as the Amalekite enemy.[1] This then was adjusted to become the doctrine of Apartheid, separate development.

Even today it is an area of dispute, with one church leader describing nationalism as 'a dark whirlpool of error' (thinking of ethnic nationalism) and the SNP careful to promote a different kind of civic nationalism. Prophetic poetry risks this kind of misunderstanding.

2 Roads, Gates and Tribes

'Pilgrimage' is used nowadays solely for a journey taken with the intention of spiritual growth and maturity. But traditionally it was also used to describe life's journey, intentional or not. Philip Doddridge's hymn 'O God of Bethel' has the lines, 'who through this weary pilgrimage / hast all our fathers led', signalling – from a reference to the story of Jacob – both the randomness and discomfort of our journeys, and the providential hand of God in them.

William Hershaw in the poem cited at the start of the chapter wrote of 'gates' in Scots, which translates as 'roads' in English – but of course when we look back over our journeys we can always identify some key 'gates' we passed through. His work[2] is a celebration of pilgrimage and Scottish saints, bookended with two short poems about how the journey itself changes us, and how the pilgrim who sets out is worn away like a pilgrim badge by the journey. 'We follow our fathers over the hill', but travel roads and go through gates that we may not choose for ourselves, as in the forced migration that followed the Scottish Clearances, or the equally forced migration that the world sees today.

Psalm 74 describes how the enemy took axes and smashed the interior of the temple in Jerusalem before destroying the temple and city, as described in more detail in the book of Lamentations. Those who have fled places like Aleppo and Homs and Mariupol know how such wanton destruction is an attack not only on familiar surroundings but on the identity of a people. As in Syria and Ukraine, sometimes they are people within a people, which was true of the Scottish Clearances, or more recently the closure of the Scottish coal mines.[3]

All nations have their tribes, in their origins and as a factor of present life. 'Tribe' has outgrown its Victorian primitive connotations, to resume its place as a neutral word for a human social group, typically sharing a common language and culture.[4] Israel had its twelve tribes, linked to the twelve sons of Jacob; these twelve re-emerged from Egypt in the Exodus, settled in the land of Canaan, later merged into a ten (Israel) and a two (Judah), who went into exile separately and returned to form a single people – although of course by the time of Jesus there are new tribes like the Essenes and the Pharisees and the Sadducees, or those who live in Galilee and those who live in Judaea.

In the Psalms, Judah emerges as the chosen of the twelve tribes of Israel (Psalm 78:67-68), and this chosen tribe has become God's temple dwelling (Psalm 114:2); in Psalms 147 and 149 'Israel' is once again the name for the whole people of God, not just the northern kingdom. By the time the books of Psalms were put together, Israel has learned to worship in a synagogue as well as a temple, and after the Roman destruction of their second temple in 70 CE, worship was only in the synagogue.

In Book 1 Poems, *41 'The Cosmic Synagogue'* is a sestina which keeps on raising the difficulty of a tribe retaining its unity, morality, and common vision, not least when there is a gap between rich and poor. This relates to the differences between political parties in Scotland and England, and to whether a system of social security is for the poor or only 'the deserving poor'; it relates to emigration and immigration, and whether a future Scotland will retain a sense of 'providence' at all.

Faith is faith precisely because, as in the best detective novels, the hidden reasons and the true identities are not revealed till the end of the journey. The *poem on Psalm 134* affirms this:

> When we get there, questions dry
> up, silenced by the sounds of heaven;
> no more need to puzzle why
> the journey felt like being driven
> off road, off stage, just off key.

The Psalms, with all their questions and dark moods, affirm that life with its 'fankle o gates' is a pilgrimage. This is celebrated within the lives of the Scottish saints themselves. Take Munro (or Kentigern), whose mother is supposed to have been hurled down the cliffs of Traprain Law, a few miles from my home in Haddington. In the popular account, she was rescued, Mungo was born at Culross and grew up to become the spiritual leader of West Scotland, but not before being kicked out of Scotland and spending time in Cumbria and Wales. See *86 'Mungo the Migrant'* in Book 3 poetry.

3 Land and Spirituality

In this age of the internet, tribes form, and identities are often shaped virtually. After the pandemic, more people work from home. The great gathering of people into cities is being shaken apart again. While land is still an important part of geopolitics, it is easy for many people in the West to feel detached from land, and attached to family and virtual tribe without setting foot anywhere.

Historically this was never the case. To understand Israel, to understand the identity of any nation today, we have to take the land seriously. When Alastair McIntosh was invited to address the Russian Academy of Sciences on the renewal of cultural identity, he spoke of 'the spirituality of nationhood', and how MacDiarmid (in his 'Farewell to Dostoevski') saw that vested in the land.[5] Said McIntosh from his work in community empowerment,

> Certain principles in biblical theology – whether we believe in God or not – are powerful in offering the constellating vision to achieve necessary integration between land economics, political power and national identity.[6]

Poem 1 'Temple Garden' refers to 'our subway roots' which 'know the truth of good and evil'. It is there, unseen, that the life of a nation is nourished or starved, and the poet as prophet waits (Psalm 130:5), listening to what is deep in the soil (Psalm 1:2-3). The poet is frail, but the word is strong, addressed to the land and the people on it, as with Jeremiah 22:29, 'O land, land, land, hear the word of the Lord!' – a counterpart to Jeremiah 7:4, 'Do not trust in these deceptive words: "This is the temple of the Lord, the temple of the Lord, the temple of the Lord".'

In the time of the Old Testament, there was the 'land of Israel' and the 'land of the nations'. Today with so many international links we have a wider view of land, perhaps – that wider view includes a solar system where travel is starting to be possible. *Poem 28 'Pinnacle or Pit'* uses a space capsule on its way to the sun as metaphor for the journey of life, and the risk that this might end up burnt out in a pit of silent flame, instead of reaching the pinnacle of heaven. But 'native land' still resonates.

While the morality of the Israelite occupation of Canaan, like all occupations, is contested, for the Israelites it was a gift of divine providence, and certainly not due to their own power or virtue or skill.[7] Land for the twelve tribes (and for the whole tribe of Israel in later years) was a matter of providence. and Brueggemann calls it the central theme of biblical faith.[8]

The ordinary context within which providence happens is land. This gives it an importance which is both economic and spiritual.[9]

This is expressed, continued Alastair McIntosh, in Psalm 104:30, 'When you send forth your spirit, they [creatures] are created; / and you renew the face of the ground.' A sense of equal divine providence was the vision which inspired Henry George,[10] whose idea of land value taxation is on the agenda for Scotland.[11] Both George and McIntosh argue that land ownership is provisional, McIntosh from Scripture (Leviticus 25:23) and George from equal rights to what the Creator has provided.[12] Landlords are simply stewards responsible to God. This concept is actually enshrined in Scots law.[13]

In *1 'Temple Garden'*, garden – with its 'subway roots' – is both metaphor and land itself. The underground railway with its roots and fungi makes a metaphor for word and spirit as well as genes, and both land and human skin are 'enlightened by the psalms'. The garden is a temple garden, because it is sacred, and a world garden, because it is universal. The land of Israel was sacred, and so, if the land of Israel is a model for other nations, then land as such is sacred, and land is universal. Hence the need for land reform.[14] The Psalms simply assert the ownership of God (24:1), who entrusts land to a people rather than to individuals (Psalms 66:12, 80:9,

105:44 – the basic allocation in Joshua 14 – 18 was first of all to the twelve tribes).

Poem 37 'Don't Fret' ends with the line 'the meek shall farm the land', not 'the meek shall inherit the land', to show that land use is as important as land ownership. The Scottish Government has been right to try to work with landowners rather than simply against them. And yet such collaboration is often pragmatic rather than principled. Now that we no longer agree on something like being a 'Christian nation' it is hard to find common principles – a common place to stand and take a view, like the 'outlook towers of the famous town planner Patrick Geddes. He grew up in Perth and fell in love with his local high point, Kinnoull Hill. It was, in effect his first 'Outlook Tower', and he would find later Outlook Towers on the Castle Hill of Edinburgh and at the Scots College of Montpellier in the south of France. An Outlook Tower served as an essential visual aid to Geddes' educational work, as from its physical eminence people were enabled to perceive and ponder relationships between diverse phenomena spread out below and before them.[15]

Tom Hubbard wrote a praise-poem to Patrick Geddes in 2000 ('The Hoose o Licht'):

> We biggit a land:
> a mony-layered tenement . . .
> We riggit oor space
> that we could constellate the years
> o the lang mirk and the tentit base
> wi the words o oor ain and the warld's seers;
> this is oor ootleuk touer; a guide
> fir the passin pilgrims ower the tide.

In this book, temple and tartan together represent a kind of outlook tower from which can be seen the connections that have mattered in Scottish history, and which may continue to be a guide for passing pilgrims.

4 Migrants

I open the poetry on Book 3 of the Psalms with *73 'Open Questions'*, a lament for Alan Kurdi, the three year old Syrian boy who drowned, and whose story brought the dangers of forced migration to Western attention. The poem rehearses the trials of people trying to escape by boat across the Mediterranean, but ends with a nod to hope, as does that psalm, seeking to find some 'good work' of the Lord even in these dire experiences. The second poem, 'Identity Theft', looks further at what is happening, and the third poem, 'Selah', uses this mysterious pause word found in Psalm 75 and other psalms to signal the fact that our enquiries often leave us without an answer, so that we have to live intellectually as migrants who are still *en route* to their destination. Hence the significance of Hershaw's poem at the start.

When these psalms were put into a psalter, Israel had begun to experience exile and migration on a scale not seen since the period of their time in Egypt, and the exodus which followed. Historians generally believe that the move out of Egypt is unlikely to have been in a single movement, as portrayed in the book of Exodus; be that as it may, the return from exile in Babylon certainly had many waves, and when the Passover festival was celebrated later on, Jews would come from many parts of the Persian and later the Roman empires. That festival celebrates how, out of protest against cruelty under Pharaoh, came the possibility of escape, then rescue and the forging of a new identity.

In *78 'Israel – a Melting Shop'*, the journey is presented (as the psalm presents it) as migration to a holy mountain, a symbol for the land of promise. As if in a steel furnace, a new identity is forged by that journey, however mysterious, however much 'a place of dark as well as light'. The psalm itself offers a sense of identity if we identify with the people of Israel as a kind of 'first nation' – not in the sense of being superior or protected from the vagaries of human experience, but as a model of what it means to be chosen by God to be something and do something special. That 'specialness' is controversial and has attracted anti-semitism, in the Old Testament it fails and leads to exile, in Isaiah's servant songs it involves suffering. Its 20th century re-emergence in modern Israel has divided Jews themselves let alone the Middle East, but it continues to offer one understanding of identity which has shaped Scotland and other nations in the past, identity as a migrant journey to some kind of 'holy mountain'. While sometimes presented as other-worldly – 'this world is not my home, I'm just a-travelling through' – many whose hearts were in heaven have proved to be of great earthly consequence.

Dante's famous three-part work of literature called *The Divine Comedy* is an epic poem featuring the poet's journey through hell, purgatory and heaven in the company initially of the Roman poet Virgil. It celebrates the 'new exodus' of people leaving purgatory just as the children of Israel left Egypt. His work was inspired by Psalm 114:1-2 and 'all the psalm that's written after this'.[16] Souls are being shipped out of purgatory like the children of Israel coming out of Egypt. These biblical analogies are not uncommon in literature – in Blake's 'Annotation to Laocoon' we have 'Israel deliverd from Egypt is Art deliverd from Nature & Imitation'.

Poem 114, 'Exodus' therefore features Dante:

Dante finds his feet, plays hopscotch

with his Classic friend, blurring the line
between the polysemous squares
of old interpretation, adding rhyme

to link the Exodus to all of us. He bares
his chest: it's gospel truth, he swears.

That journey out of Egypt, which Jews celebrate annually at the Passover festival, is a migration. The Israelites were migrants – the theme of Book 3 poetry, the reality of life for so many refugees today, and an increasing reality for many more if climate change continues.

No one sets out on this kind of journey unless they hope that it will bring them to a different place, and a better life. Even in the worst circumstances – flight from bombing, use of people smugglers who may be exploiting or even trafficking their clients – the journey would not begin without the desire to find something better, a new home if not 'heaven'. This is a theme of nearly every epic poem, whether *The Odyssey*, *The Rime of the Ancient Mariner*, Edwin Morgan's *The Cape of Good Hope*,[17] or *The Birlinn of Clanranald*.[18]

The author of the last named poem, Alasdair Mac Mhaigstir Alasdair (Alexander MacDonald), was known as 'the bard of the Gaelic Enlightenment', and familiar with the literature of Scotland, England and continental Europe. He was also an army captain, a Jacobite, and after Culloden a fugitive – all that was the context of his epic poem, which describes the journey of a birlinn, or galley, from the Hebrides to Carrickfergus in Ireland, through a terrible storm. He offers us this hope of something better at the end of the journey, as do Homer, Coleridge and Morgan.

Many of the poems in 'Migrants' are laments, corresponding to the psalms in question. One in particular is different, *78 'Israel – a Melting Shop'*, because that psalm celebrates the Exodus, and the journey to a promised land with all its storms on the way which tested and formed the people. It is another pantoum, since the journey often seems to take steps backward as well as forwards. So:

> Keep on wrestling with the true,
> a sacred fire, a melting shop;
> digest it, live it, make it new
> in earthly tent and mountain top.
>
> A sacred fire, a melting shop,
> God draws us into sanctuary,
> an earthly tent, a mountain top
> to match the mystery of the journey.

Migration is a feature of the 21st century, significantly from the Middle East. So **'Migrants'** is the title of Book 3 poems, which consist of individual stories of migrants, in dialogue with the third book of Psalms and the story of Israel which these psalms rehearse. They include two stories of Scottish migrants, and one migrant missionary to Japan.

Now is the time to move on to the poetry, if you wish. The rest of this chapter will explore how the Psalms and the Old Testament gave Scotland a sense of identity, will look at tribalism and Scottish politics today, and set Book 3 poetry more firmly in the context of life today.

Part 2

5 The Psalms and National Identity

What Adrian Hastings said in his Belfast Wiles Lectures, focused generally on *English* nationhood, is also true of Scotland. He said that the Bible provided for the Christian world the original model of the nation, and that 'the world is a society of nations originally "imagined" through the mirror of the Bible, Europe's primary textbook.'[19]

Hastings added that in Scotland, religion played 'no more than a subsidiary role' in forming identity. He was writing in 1996, just as the modern Scottish Nationalist movement was on the upsurge, and religion was by then not the motivation of most protagonists.[20] The Psalms are seldom quoted by opinion formers today, unless at the funeral of a national figure like John Smith: on 20th May 1994 there was a reading of part of Psalm 121 as a preface to that service, and the singing of Psalm 23 in Gaelic. Doug Gay's book *Honey from the Lion* has only one mention of the Psalms,[21] and Gay has to show the relevance of other texts in a contemporary world where 'civic discourse in Scotland and the UK is becoming less hospitable to books that address public policy questions from an explicitly theological angle'.[22]

The Old Testament in popular understanding has now merged with ancient heritage in a way inconceivable to those living before 1900. It is now possible in the Church of Scotland (though not in the Scottish Episcopal or Roman Catholic Churches) to attend public worship without hearing or singing the Old Testament or the Psalms. This 'dilution' of public worship reflects a tension in the Third Declaratory Article of the Church of Scotland, where the Church calls itself 'a national Church representative of the Christian faith of the Scottish people'.[23] Since the proportion of Scots professing the Christian religion has declined,[24] there is a tension between representing 'Christian faith' and representing 'the beliefs of the Scottish people',[25] which are now plural.[26]

Is this a contemporary version of the old Caledonian antisyzygy, being pulled between two opposite poles which contradict one another? Neal Ascherson argued in 1988 that only one contradiction in Scottish society remains fundamental – the old contradiction between self-assertion and self-distrust. To introduce his theme he quoted Covenanter James Renwick, on the scaffold in 1668: 'There is a storm coming that shall try your foundation. Scotland must be rid of Scotland before the delivery come.'[27]

A way of understanding this is suggested by Martin Buber. Every nation has a guiding spiritual characteristic, its 'prince',[28] which can become a god rather than a serving angel. Walter Wink distinguishes this 'higher calling' of nationhood from its 'fallen personality', and Alastair McIntosh uses these ideas to speak of the spirituality of nations, with a lower form relying on law, hard sanctions and force, and a higher form relying on spiritual authority, empowerment and non-violence.[29]

Another way is to acknowledge multiple identities. As there are two identities in the Church of Scotland – one purist, one more pluralist – so there are at least two Scotlands, one independent, the other more comfortable with a dual identity (British and Scottish), and we live today with the tension between them.[30] Ascherson went on to cite Walter Scott, for whom 'Scottish history was only safe when it was certain that the beast's limbs, the Cameronian tradition for example, had finally lost the power of movement . . . Live Scottish history was to be feared.'[31]

> Scott was conservative and wanted to resolve peacefully the antinomies he recognised in his novels about the past. He was in fact mirroring the editors of the Psalms, who celebrated David when his kingdom was dead, and supported second temple religion under foreign rule. Books 1-2 of the Psalms deliberately terminate 'the prayers of David son of Jesse'. The Asaph Psalms of Book 3 reflect the destruction of Jerusalem and its temple, and hark back to Moses and Aaron with a modest acknowledgment of David at the close of Psalm 78. In Books 4 and 5, religion is more about God, Mount Zion and the temple – it is spiritualised, closer to the wisdom tradition than to the prophetic challenge.

1 Maccabees 7:16-17 might be cited against this; it links
Psalm 79:2-3 from the Septuagint, concerning the suffering
of the Exile, with the murder of martyrs in the 2nd century
BCE; more assertively, Psalms of Solomon 17 'recalls psalms
about the protection of the Davidic king in Psalms 2, 89 and
132 and applies them to the impending punishment on the
Roman nation after the capture of Jerusalem by Pompey
in 64 BCE'.[32] But generally the Psalms themselves simply
complain (as 73 and 74). In the time of Jesus the authorities,
unlike the Zealots, were quietist, and found the crowd's use
of Psalm 118:26, as recorded in Matthew 21:9, threatening.

How is it that in the words of Hastings earlier, the Bible provided
'the original model of the nation'? It is partly, of course, in the way
Israel finds its identity in the Exodus from Egypt, in the sufferings
in the wilderness, in its later struggle and political failure, and
in its remarkable return from Exile. But the New Testament
perceives a more basic pattern: the existence of nations is derived
in Acts 17:26 from the creation of the first man. Paul has in mind
Isaiah 42:5, which says that God 'gives breath to the people' upon
the earth, but 'giving breath' is associated with creation in Genesis
2:7 and in Psalm 33:6: 'By the word of the Lord the heavens were
made / and all their host by the breath of his mouth'. By this time
'the nations' were familiar enough to feature strongly in Psalm
33:8-12, the nations at which God laughs in Psalm 2. So Acts is
not saying anything unfamiliar to the Old Testament or the Book
of Psalms.

National identity, then, is recognised in the Book of Psalms,
even though its focus is almost entirely on the particular nation of
Israel. It is really only in the prophets, e.g. in Isaiah 42:6, that Israel
is given a continued calling to bless other nations. In the Torah,
after the early stories of creation and early peoples, the promise to
all nations through Abraham (Genesis 12:3), and the promise to
Ishmael (Genesis 21:18), Israel's calling becomes limited to verses
like Deuteronomy 26:19, where Israel is to be set 'high above all
nations'. Such language, as Adrian Hastings recognised,[33] is a
powerful factor in shaping identity. We now need to see in more
detail how this worked out in Scotland.

6 Israel and Scotland

Comparison and Covenant

Ever since Jesus called twelve apostles to match the twelve tribes,[34] ever since Paul compared the Christian journey to the journey of Israel through the wilderness in 1 Corinthians 10:1-6, people have tried to compare their own pilgrimage with the history of Israel[35] – though it is already happening in psalms like 44, 78, 90 and 105. Jewish communities make a whole series of connections with Torah (with the story as well as the teaching).[36] But the attempt to compare the story of one's nation with the story of Israel goes further than a spiritual exercise for the individual. Herbert Butterfield wrote, just after the 1939-45 War, that the history of the ancient Hebrews

> was fundamentally of the same texture as our own. There is ample evidence that in their own great days . . . they looked back upon their own distant past in the way in which we now look back to *them*; and in manifold ways they express the thought with which the twentieth century itself is so familiar – the longing of Psalm 44: 'We have heard with our ears, O God, and our fathers have told us, what work thou didst in their days, in the times of old.'[37]

The early, weak attempt at such comparison was in the *Declaration of Arbroath*, which put more emphasis on the mythical journey of Scots from Greater Scythia than on the OT. It did compare King Robert to 'another Maccabaeus or Joshua', but its ethical foundation was freedom from the English rather than covenant. A stronger example of is the belief that Scotland, like Israel, was a 'covenanted nation'.[38] Whereas James Cameron was content to say that 'a Protestant country, according to the Reformers, is one which agrees to live in conformity with *the Gospel*' (my italics), the chapter of the *First Book of Discipline* which he is considering specifically cites a series of *OT characters* as godly examples (not the Gospel).[39]

Jane Dawson goes further. For Knox, the reintroduction of
Roman Catholic worship in England 'was a breach of the
covenant the kingdom had made with God' during the
reign of Edward VI.[40] Knox's *History of the Reformation
in Scotland* was designed to call the people of Scotland to
embrace God's covenant.[41] Ironically, the 'Covenanters'
a century later were less inclined to model Scotland on
the Old Testament, than to assert the 'crown rights of the
Redeemer', what J.H.S. Burleigh calls 'their preposterous
claim in the name of Christ to domineer over the civil state',[42]
and others call simply standing against crown interference
in church affairs.[43] But the idea of 'covenant' itself was an
important political device which the Presbyterian elites of
Scotland in the 17th century used against Charles I and his
successors.[44] Anthony Smith 'observes how the Hebrew idea
of a community formed through a unique covenant with
God has carried over to numerous "Christian" nations'.[45]

Section six of Chapter Two underlined the often vague way that
Scottish poets referred to the Psalms. But they bear a clear witness
to the fact of psalm-singing and the idea of a covenanted nation.

Sometimes a specific application would be made. In 1638
a preacher called Alexander Henderson used Psalm 110:3,
'Thy people shall be willing in the day of thy power', to
encourage people to sign the National Covenant.[46] In 1719,
Isaac Watts published a translation of the Psalms in which
he rendered 'Israel' as 'Great Britain'. An extreme version
of this is the British Israelite Movement, which holds that
the British peoples are the descendants of the ten lost
tribes of Israel.

In all this I make no claim that Scotland (or Britain, or America)
is specially chosen above other nations,[47] though such a view,
'exceptionalism' is the name for it, can be traced in colonial
attitudes: simply that just as the Psalms shaped the faith of Israel
(and were no doubt shaped by it),[48] so the Psalms, when known and
sung, shape the faith, and therefore influence the history, of other
nations.[49] Jonathan Hearn points out that religions do not simply
provide solace and sources of meaning, they are also 'profound
meditations on the nature of power';[50] the Psalms from 2 onwards

stress the overarching power of God, even more so in the later psalms which acknowledge the demise of the Davidic monarchy, leaving God alone as king.[51]

While there are references to the psalms, and concepts like temple, in Scottish and especially Gaelic literature, English literature is richer.[52] However, Scotland was closely connected in social and academic circles with England[53] (and the Continent), and so reference to English literature is appropriate.[54] For example, William Law (1686-1761) wrote a devotional book which commended not only using a number of psalms in daily devotion, but actually singing or chanting them.[55]

The Psalms and Scottish Nationhood

> Psalm 144 ends with: 'Happy are the people to whom such blessings fall / happy are the people whose God is the Lord'; Psalm 33:12 gives us 'Happy is the nation whose God is the Lord / the people whom he has chosen as his heritage'. In the former and in the second half of the latter, *yām* is translated 'people', in the first half of the latter, the different word *gôi* is translated 'nation'. However, *yām* includes in its meaning something of what we understand by nation.[56]

Although early Scotland was made up of different peoples,[57] the medieval understanding of a nation was of a people who obeyed a king, rather than an ethnic community with a single language[58] – just as the Psalms show Israel gathered first around the king of Israel,[59] then when the Davidic kingdom failed, as a people who acknowledged Yahweh as king.[60] Likewise in Scotland, the nation was gathered around the medieval kings – three of whom were children of the Margaret who was made a saint. But when the kingship was shared with England in 1603, and Scotland subsequently entered a period of conflict over forms of government (initially argued around religion and later around democracy), new ideas of national identity emerged which are still in dispute.

These range from the 'Christian vision' in William Storrar's *Scottish Identity* – which ends with a twist to MacDiarmid's lines, 'She canna Scotland see wha yet / canna see the Christ / and Scotland in true scale to him' (with 'the Christ' substituted for 'the Infinite') – to the McIlvanney joke, 'Having a national identity is a bit like having an old insurance policy, you know you've got one somewhere but you're not sure where it is.'[61] Doug Gay contrasts two ideas of national identity illustrated in 20th century South Africa – the racist National Party, and the African National Congress.[62] Although the books of Ezra and Nehemiah appear outright racist,[63] the book of Psalms is inclusive in the same limited sense as the book of Ruth, in that the rule of Yahweh and the fellowship of Israel may be enjoyed by people of any and every nation, and that all nations will one day acknowledge that rule.[64]

The Use of Typology

In my Book 2 poetry, I am not only putting side by side David and Robert the Bruce, but the land of Israel and the land of Scotland. This has precedent. Adrian Hastings refers to both Bede and Barbour seeing 'an Old Testament style providential role' in how they understood their respective nations of England and Scotland.[65] Here are four other examples of Scotland being identified with Israel:

(a) The ambition of James VI and I was to reunite the offices of king and psalmist.[66] In Scotland James attempted to restore Song Schools on a civic basis in 1579.[67] James Doelman comments more generally:

> In what a contemporary described as 'his almost private and studious days in Scotland', James had shown his avid interest in theology by writing biblical commentaries or meditations. Both Scottish and English poets called attention to James's poetic vocation, claiming that James would be remembered as a poet rather than as a king.[68]

He is best known for the quality of the King James Version of the Bible, translated by the best scholars of the day (with a balance of Puritans and Churchmen) – a Bible whose psalm versions were used in the 1637 Prayer Book which caused a riot in Edinburgh St Giles. James was also notorious for royal attempts to gain control of the Church in Scotland, and influence its worship, which culminated in the time of his son Charles I and his attempt to impose that particular prayer book.[69] But the Stuart interpretation of the Old Testament model of king as worship leader (Psalm 144:1,9,15) failed in its 17th century Scottish context.

(b) Murray Pittock argues that groups like the Jacobites saw the Old Testament as a model for a Scotland with the true king:

> Typological history does not evolve along timescales: it takes a mythic or remote historical era and glorifies it either to lament its passing or lament [*sic*] its return. The prophets of ancient Israel provide one of the clearest examples of typological history in action, with the nation's past covenant with God always being betrayed and always renewed . . .[70]

This is congruent with Book 3 Psalms like 78, and verses like 74:20, 77:8, 79:5 and 80:7.

William Hamilton, a Jacobite, was born in 1704 in Scotland and died in France in 1754. In 1747, when he was a captain in Prince Charles Edward Stuart's 'Lifeguards', he wrote 'an imitation of the 137th Psalm' which is in the National Library of Scotland and cited by Nelson Bushnell,[71]

> On Gallia's shore we sat and wept,
>   when Scotland we thought on,
> Rob'd of her bravest Sons, and all
>   her ancient Spirit gone.

Gallia is France, not Babylon. Later stanzas refer to the French attempt to enlist exiled Jacobites against the English force in the Netherlands, and use Psalm 137 to denounce the French failure to support the 1745 campaign effectively.

Referring to Scottish Jacobite song, Pittock speaks of 'its own underground continuance through biblical typology'. In doing so, the sacred song referred back to the Royalist ideal of a Davidic king and forward to a second Stuart coming: it was 'a millenarian voice for royalty': 'Have Israel's nor Judah's men no thought / that David should be over Jordan brought?'[72] In the 'Taorluath Doubling' of 'The Iolaire', 'kingship energy renewed' hints at Jacobitism.

(c) John Murdoch edited The Highlander, a weekly in Inverness. He pushed for land reform in the 1870s and 1880s, comparing land reform not only to the liberation of the Israelites from Pharaoh but to 'the restoration of the twelve tribes of Israel to Palestine'.[73]

(d) In a late 20th century Gaelic poem, '*An Tuagh*' / 'The Axe', Fearghas MacFhionnlaigh uses 49 lines to set up a battle encounter on a national scale, linking the axe with which Bruce slew de Bohun to the slaying of Goliath, and then suddenly ends his poem:[74]

> but your axe was broken, O King
> and another we have yet to find

thus linking the current confusion over Scotland's identity not only with medieval Scotland, but with the crisis in Israel's life, where Books 4 and 5 of the Psalms reflect the change from trust in a Davidic king to trust in something bigger, yet still to come.

7 The Psalms and Today

A late section in Chapter Two illustrated how poets in Scotland at least have largely ceased to use the Psalms, let alone relate them to current events. Clearly writers, following the secular spirit of the times, prefer to leave them safely in their historical period, rather than seek a relevance to the present day – a prophetic relevance – whether this is claimed to be 'reading out' or simply 'reading in'. And even with religious writers, the relevance of the Psalms is now restricted to personal life, rather than extended to the life of a nation.

Up to the 19th century, the Psalms themselves were always seen as prophetic text in one way or another, with a remarkable consensus that they speak of a coming Messiah, albeit with different understandings of who such a person might be. This is true of the Septuagint, the Psalms Targum, the Peshitta, the Qumran communities, the Pharisees of Jesus' time, the rabbinic commentators, as well as Christian writers.[75]

Typically, as in Psalm 2, the *nations* conspire against God – but their rulers are enjoined to be wise (Psalm 2:10), and Israel is instructed to live in a way that encourages other nations to recognise God (18:43-44, 98:2-3, 115:2). The nations will be judged (Psalm 9), but there is some hope that one day all nations will be blessed by God (22:27, 36:7). Can poetry link this to Scotland?

Book 2 poems suggested that David is a 'type' for Robert the Bruce, teased out in the last chapter. *Poem 142 'In the Cave'* asks 'Who is in the cave with David / and his band of desperadoes?' In stanza

3, the question is turned round, 'Who is in the Scottish cave . . . ?' implying that David (and other 'real and phantom figures') huddle with us, and if David, then at least the psalms linked with him.

> Although Psalm 33 has no superscription, it may well be part of Psalm 32,[76] which is 'a *maskil* of David'.[77] Psalm 33, like many psalms combines praise with judgment; so *33 'Judgment'* also does this, but judgment there has an immediate reference (to relations between the British and Irish nations), and an ultimate reference ('where bowling / is not cricket / as we know it'). Prophecy, like poetry, works with more than one layer of meaning.
>
> *Poem 144 'Stuff'* recognises the multiple images of God in the psalm, and in stanza 1 translates them into modern images, and the idea of a 'shape-shifting God'. Both personal and impersonal images are found within many psalms, and typically bridged with the concept of 'order speaking', as in Psalm 19:1, 'The heavens are telling the glory of God.' The word of God is linked with wisdom in Proverbs 8, and more generally with Torah, and thus is not simply a *fiat* but an ongoing feature of how the universe develops with a word which is contemporary as well as ancient.[78]
>
> Generally those later psalms were seen as in Churches today, sublime poems about God rather than challenging poems about politics and society, and the leaders of Jewish society under the Romans wanted things kept that way. Like much lyric poetry today, psalms would be read and enjoyed for what they had to say to the individual, not as a manifesto for change. But at Qumran, the Psalms were read as prophetic text, both predicting the future and challenging the present.[79] Mika Pajunen argues that 'psalms in the late Second Temple Period could be interpreted as prophecies, and fresh prophecies were written in the form of psalms.'[80]

Some of the Psalms are best seen as prophetic texts, especially Psalms like 2, 72, 89, 110. It is often said that the New Testament is out of step in seeing so many messianic references in the Psalms, but in fact early Jewish interpreters took the Psalms in exactly the same way (without viewing Jesus of Nazareth as the Messiah). The Pharisees accepted that David wrote Psalm 110, which is key to the way the Gospels present that psalm. *Midrashim* regard the writers of the Psalms as prophetic. The Septuagint and the Qumran texts saw them that way, as did the medieval rabbis later on.[81]

Scotland is not of course today like those communities at Qumran in the final centuries BCE, who saw the Psalms being fulfilled in the events of their own time. Yet the Psalms and their poetry in the past became part of the identity of the nation, and just as identity was celebrated at Qumran by remembering, through psalms like 78, 105, 106, 114, 135, 136,[82] so it happened in Scotland – even if the Psalms themselves did not feature widely, being left to be sung in churches and remembered in hearts. *Poems* were certainly seen as prophetic in Scottish literature, whether presented as words from beyond, as with Thomas the Rhymer,[83] or a critique from within society, as with the poetry of William Dunbar cited in Chapter Two.

A major reason why bible and faith are no longer plausible in Scotland in the way they once were, lies in the current secularism. While this is sometimes presented as the result of 'the scientific outlook', other factors make better sense, since (for example) the majority of Christian leaders are admirers of Darwin, and many scientists and philosophers are embarrassed by the excessive claims of the 'new atheists'.[84] Two major, but very different reasons are

• the breakup of the National Church in the Disruption of 1843, which led to the State taking over social work and education from the Church.

• the change in understanding personal identity since the 1960s,[85] when many young people ceased to follow their 'faithers ower the hill'.

8 Book 3 Poetry

Migration is a movement from one place to another, with all that means for a person's, and a people's sense of identity. Normally this is seen as a movement from one land to another, but it can also be a migration of ideas, from atheism to faith and vice versa, from one political ideology to another. Such migration, while it has an intellectual component, is also a migration of the whole person, with implications for the identity of people, communities and nations. In exploring examples of this, Book 3 poetry brings together the Psalms, the history of nations and contemporary life.

The poetry goes well beyond Scotland. Outwith secular Scotland, religion has retained its importance. In different ways, none of the bigger religious tribes of Judaism, Christianity, and Islam are other-worldly, though each would also affirm that hope is not limited to this world. Christianity in particular faces the temptation of either limiting faith to ethics, or lapsing into an extreme other-worldly position, as issues of world poverty, refugees, war and climate crisis seem so hard to solve.

Book 3 poetry does not offer solutions, but like the Psalms behind the poems, it keeps our attention on what is really going on, through the testimony of those facing dire situations, and the witness of the Psalm writers. Sometimes the psalm does not get further than asking a question, so in 73 'Open Questions' I write in stanza 3,

> Yet Israel keeps asking these big questions,
> giving us hard words in psalm and silence,
> fleshing out the tearing of our bodies,
> flashing out a challenge to belief.

At other times, the psalm spins the thread of prophecy and ties it to the ribbon of hope. Maybe it is just casual, whimsical, as in 77 'Through our Eyes', where a fleeing refugee woman remembers how she served tea to the very soldiers who have just beaten in her door. Maybe it is just a vague reaching for the transcendent, as in 83 'Beyond',

> God, is there something else
> beyond the reach of reason
> beyond the frontier of pain . . ,
> beyond the throat of any word?

Maybe it is a message from the birds of Psalm 84. In Poem 84 'The Highways to Zion', the dove is herself a migrant, a bird of passage 'which makes a draught around my soul', and even 'life's ordinary deal' might be 'soft feathered with the plumage of God's love'. And it is birds, like humans, who are

> looking for a righteous wind somewhere in the atmosphere,
> hoping for a faithful current and a friendly pier.

David Smith in a recent book says that the loss of lament is one of the reasons for the irrelevance of Christians in the West.[86]

Certainly many church services show an inability to 'weep with those who weep' where music is concerned. Since 'lament' is a major category description of many of the Old Testament Psalms, the loss of psalmody outside, say, the Catholic and Free Church traditions is serious. The Psalms offer a tradition of lament and hope when justice fails.[87]

Book 3 poems, being about migration, often forced migration, major on lament. *Poem 80 'Malala'* includes this:

> The tears
> of broken walls and shot up nations
> trickle gently down the conduits
> of our holy books, and down
> the face of God, beloved parent
> whose own face shines behind its tears.

It is important, but not controversial, to picture God lamenting with those who suffer. What is more difficult traditionally is to accept that God might, on occasions at least, be powerless, as in *82 'Clearance'*, where God has to accept that when his ministers (in a double sense) fail, that reflects on him also:

> God failed.
> His ministers of state were far away
> in London, centre of the world;
> his ministers of word were far away
> in soul, appointed, bought
> by greedy landlords.

In that stanza there is a reference not only to the Clearances, but to a controversy in the Church of Scotland over who appoints parish ministers, a dispute which led to the Free Church 'coming out' from the established Church in 1843, that break which led to the State taking over poor relief from the Church, and hastened the process of secularisation.

Book Three Poems: Migrants

73 Open Questions

'Show me bodies floating in the water, I don't care'

Katie Hopkins in the Sun

'I was envious of the arrogant; I saw the prosperity of the wicked.
They have no pain; their bodies are sound and sleek.'
They are not in trouble as others are;
They are not plagued like other people . . .' *vv. 3-5,13*

Alan Kurdi, toddler, drowned en route to Kos,
island of healing and some hope of passage;
a photo speeded evolution, changing migrant
cockroaches to human casualties in hours;
it might have seeded revolution, ranging
righteous sympathy against the gates
of fortress Europe, reeling from the hordes
who push the boundaries of Superpowers.

Can God be good as well as great? Abu
Hamada's never troubled by these issues,
handling boats and migrants from a distance.
Like every smuggler, business first – and other
jobs are hard to come by; he has family
to put through school; and if he was to stop,
demand would thrust another in his place.
Philosophy is seldom worth the bother.

Yet Israel keeps asking these big questions,
giving us hard words in psalm and silence
fleshing out the tearing of our bodies,
flashing out a challenge to belief.
And if the psalm does bookend fear with faith,
and seem to close enquiry with a visit
to the holy place, consider this: what doors
can open through a body on a reef.

74 Identity Theft

'No one remembers his own history . . .'
                    Tsegaye Tesfaye

'They set your sanctuary on fire,
they desecrated the dwelling place of your name,
bringing it to the ground . . .
We do not see our emblems;
there is no longer any prophet,
and there is no one among us who knows how long.'
                    vv.7,9

Pharaoh tried,
Nebuchadnezzar,
great Alexander,
grim Antiochus,
then the Caesars.

Russian pogroms,
Nazi policy,
Western eyes shut,
ships turned back,
a holocaust.

*Our flags have gone
from mast and heart,
and no one knows
the past; our art
is crushed, and now
the last dread part
of life has come.*

*Our flags have gone
from mast and heart,
and no one knows
the past; our art
is crushed, and now
the last dread part
of life has come.*

Refugees
are swimming
into Europe,
pressing on
our politics.

Our flags have gone
from mast and heart,
we never heed
the past; our art
is weary, and
the last dread part
is still to come:

when we are all
turned refugee
from history
and who we are,
a hidden steal.

Our flags have gone
from mast and heart,
we never heed
the past; our art
is weary, and
the last dread part
is still to come:

that solemn slippage
out of memory
and into something
larger, little known
but held by God.

Our flags have gone
from mast and heart,
and all we know
is past. The art
of faith in God?
Entrusting every part
of who we were.

75 Selah

'When the earth totters, with all its inhabitants,
it is I who keep its pillars steady. Selah'   *v.3*

Zabiullah sips tea in a tent;
stench of sewage hangs around
him and seven thousand others,
waiting for news of asylum,
watching a rat scuttle past.   *Selah.*

'This is worse than the boat,'
he says, caught in an eternity
hung around his neck:
queueing for toilets, ten minutes,
queueing for bread, ten hours,
queueing for asylum, ten months.   *Selah.*

Lesbos, island of loitering,
loitering in tent and trauma,
loitering in mental breakdown,
loitering under the leaky umbrella
of that deal with Turkey,
put up fast to block
the heavy rain of refugees.   *Selah.*

'We are treated worse than animals,'
Somali teen Saida says,
fighting months of boredom,
fighting for a doctor,
struggling for identity
against the lure of suicide.   *Selah.*

God has set a time, *Selah,*
to judge with equity, *Selah.*
Selah – silent pause
which echoes all our questions,
leaves us none the wiser.   *Selah.*

76 The Wrath of Teens

'Human wrath serves only to praise you,
when you bind the last bit of wrath around you.' *v.10*

A stone thrown,
a rubber bullet
to a cousin's head,
the soldiers slapped
and kicked by Ahed,
age sixteen; her parents
Nariman and Bassem
are so proud of her,
a teenage hero
reunited with her village
after the Israeli jail.

Violence, counter-violence,
escalation eddies
round the Middle East,
a vicious storm
that feeds on hate
and catches everyone.
Surely, says the psalm,
this all too human wrath
will praise the God
of Arab and of Jew.
Some hope. Somehow.

Ahed Tamimi spent time in an Israeli jail in 2018 for slapping and
kicking Israeli policemen following a clash which involved her cousin.

77 Through Our Eyes

'I think of God, and I moan; I meditate, and my spirit
faints . . . I am so troubled that I cannot speak.
I consider the days of old, and remember the years of long ago.'
vv.3-5

The razor wire cuts through me,
separating past, serrating
present, future gutted.

I walk beside the endless fence
with a thousand companions,
locked into our bleeding selves.

Assad and his army were the worst,
firing out of nowhere – even
snipers taking out the children.

We served them tea, after
the army had beaten in our door.
What is happening to respect?

My husband works away
from here; if he's late back
I fear the army took him.

My mum is sick, no blanket.
Even close to the border,
the planes come to bomb us.

The children have only the clothes
in which they fled. They remember
paradise, and cry, and cry.

I never imagined it would come
to war; nor that we'd need
a visa just to stay in Lebanon.

We don't want parcels, nothing
from you – just to return,
go back to our own country.

The world sends weapons, bombs,
then settles down to watch us;
they must want the war to stay.

The planes come. They don't
kill Daesh or the Free Syrian
Army. They kill the likes of us.

Children need a home, not camp.
To those with nothing, Daesh
offers money and a future.

Why join Daesh? No one
wants to say 'I am a loser'.
Daesh offers power.

'When the waters saw you, O God,
. . . the very deep trembled.
Your way was through the sea,
your path through the mighty waters;
yet your footprints were unseen.
You led your people like a flock
by the hand of Moses and Aaron.'   *vv.16,19-20*

Migrants struggle overland,
fling themselves across the seas:
salvation wears a European face.

A Bosnian refugee gets an award
for film. At age thirteen, a Syrian
girl wins Betjeman's poetry prize.

God's way is rough, God's steps
unseen, but still the world is big
enough for every one of us.

78 Israel – a Melting Shop

'I will open my mouth in a parable; I will utter dark sayings from of old, things that we have heard and known, that our ancestors have told us. We will not hide them from our children . . .'   *vv.2-4a*

'Then he led out his people like sheep, and guided them in the wilderness like a flock. And he brought them to his holy hill, to the mountain that his right hand had won. He built his sanctuary like the high heavens, like the earth which he has founded forever.'

vv.52,54,69

God drew them back to sanctuary,
a place of dark as well as light
to match the mystery of the journey,
echo patchiness of sight.

A place of dark as well as light,
profound enough for everyone
to echo patchiness of sight,
admit the race is hard to run,

profound enough for everyone
to learn from Israel's special case:
they found the race was hard to run
and made a tent a worship place

to learn that God, in every case
of trouble warned them, and then said
to make the tent a worship place
and trust him for their daily bread.

When trouble came, God warned and said
'I drop the manna, send the quail,
so trust me for your daily bread,
and don't keep saying God will fail.

'I drop the manna, send the quail,
I spread the table, flush the fountain,
don't keep saying God will fail
to bring you to his holy mountain.'

Spread the table, flush the fountain,
follow God for all you're worth;
keep on travelling to the mountain
temple, sure as heaven and earth.

Follow God! Yes, all you're worth
is what he tells you in that holy
temple, sure as heaven and earth.
You're his image! Chew that slowly

when he tells you in that holy
time of wrestling with the true -
you're God's image. Chew that slowly
but digest it, make it new.

Keep on wrestling with the true,
a sacred fire, a melting shop;
digest it, live it, make it new
in earthly tent and mountain top.

A sacred fire, a melting shop,
God draws us into sanctuary,
an earthly tent, a mountain top
to match the mystery of the journey.

79 Another David

'Let the avenging of the outpoured blood of your servants
be known among the nations before our eyes.'   *vv.10-11*

'Happy shall they be who take your little ones
and dash them against the rock!'   *Psalm 137:9*

'May God do his worst to me if Nabal and every cur in his
misbegotten brood isn't dead meat by morning!'
David in 1 Samuel 25:22 (The Message)

Scrunch of a father's head
crushed with a killing club,
hard as the face above it.
Scream of a sister pierced
with a stabbing spear
sharp as the knife in his mind
that cut his childhood
into slices of lean hate.

Three days lying in the bush,
scared to pee or shit, while
soldiers ravaged, raped,
relaxed. He heard them laughing,
boasting, drinking, snoring,
quarreling till their ethnic
lust agenda moved them on,
left behind them awful silence.

Twenty years to live in trauma,
eat the meat of memory,
drink the heady beer of vengeance,
warm his feet at the raging fire
consuming his humanity,
turning him so slowly, surely
into a soldier brandishing
his stabbing spear and killing club.

The story of this 'other David', caught up in the conflict of South Sudan,
changed for the better when he attended a trauma healing workshop.

80 Malala

'Restore us, O God; let your face shine, that we may be saved.
O Lord God of hosts, how long will you be angry with your people's
prayers? You have fed them with the bread of tears . . . You make us
the scorn of our neighbours; our enemies laugh among themselves.
Restore us, O God of hosts; let your face shine, that we may be
saved.'   *vv.3-7*

Her mum wailed, 'My Malala, my Malala!'
recited verses from 'The Pilgrimage',
thinking of this daughter *planted*
in her womb, and *God who causes*
life and death, and then revives:
the hour is coming, have no doubt.

Another father phoned, whose
nine-year old became a programmer
approved by Microsoft – her heart
gave out before she met Bill Gates.
Malala's dad cried too, 'How does
a father live without his daughter?'

He sobbed and told his brother
that the village should prepare
to hold Malala's funeral – this girl
gunned down by Taliban, whose
life was fading into memory, until
the helicopter flight to Rawalpindi.

The British nurse was occupied,
knowing if Malala did not live
it would be said she killed
the teenage saint of Pakistan,
the National Peace Prizewinner,
symbol of a female future.

She lives – in Birmingham, an exile
with her family, not a friend
to tell her jokes to, no flat roof
on which to play, only the weight
of fame to carry, and the silence
from her home in Pakistan.

I was crying as I read. The tears
of broken walls and shot up nations
trickle gently down the conduits
of our holy books, and down
the face of God, beloved parent
whose face shines behind its tears.

81 Freed from the Basket

In memory of the Chinese cockle pickers
drowned in Morecambe Bay in 2006.

'I hear a voice I had not known:
I relieved your shoulder of the burden;
your hands were freed from the basket.'   *vv.5b-6*

Who knew that Chinese immigrants
were mired in such a slaver's pickle?
The Government, as blind as Pharaoh,
blamed their lack of holding pens.

Some British cocklers, coming back,
passed them, tapped their watches.
No communication. Too much
racist water had been flowing.

Then the fast Spring tide, returning,
noticed them, and freed them
from their baskets: yes, the sea
saw every one of them, all 23.

How many Israelites fell dead
beneath the Egyptian lash before
that unknown voice called 'Moses, Moses'
from a burning bush, and Moses noticed?

How many migrants die in lorries,
in the desert, on the mountains,
in the dangerous sea? How long
before a cockled world takes notice?

82 Clearance

'Give justice to the weak and the orphan;
maintain the right of the lowly and the destitute.
Rescue the weak and the needy;
deliver them from the hand of the wicked . . .
Rise up, O God, judge the earth;
for all the nations belong to you.'   *vv.3-4,8*

'Let every person be subject to the governing authorities;
for there is no authority except from God . . .
the authorities are God's servants.'   *Romans 13:1,6*

The heather failed
when factors burned it off before the sheep
were even come. The highland cattle
and the customs perished, while the lowland
Scots Enlightenment
was all the rage.

Justice failed,
it never caught alight, the wick of truth
doused by the dark, the black, black oil
of underground theology, that pumped
predestined poison into
venal veins.

Gaeldom failed,
clan chiefs bewitched by betterment, they hid
behind the law, let houses burn,
the people shift to barren coasts, to live
or die in penury.
No kindness left.

God failed.
His ministers of state were far away
in London, centre of the world;
his ministers of word were far away
in soul, appointed, bought
by greedy landlords.

Change is hard.
To justify the ways of God and men
is not a easy game. But like
the spores exploding from a punctured puffball,
Scots and powerful doctrine
cleared the ocean.

83 Beyond

'O God, do not keep silence . . .
They say, "Come, let us wipe them out as a nation;
let the name of Israel be remembered no more." *vv.1,4*

The crash at the door,

the inner commotion,

the tortured confession,

the cattle trucks,

the camps,

the gas,

a nation driven

to the edge of that last exile

and beyond:

beyond the reach of reason,
beyond the frontier of pain,
beyond the bounds of human life,
beyond the throat of any word.

What turns stones thrown out of protest
into missiles primed to kill?
What turns a leather waistband
to a belt of high explosive?
What overturns the Middle Eastern
table of warm hospitality,
pours poison down our gullets
to block our arteries,
build our biceps
in a devilish gymnasium,
ready to blood the Jews
(or bleed their foes)

beyond the reach of reason,
beyond the frontier of pain,
beyond the bounds of human life,
beyond the throat of any word?

We have the psalms
to make up hard lines,
work up angry questions,
size up all our enemies,
beat up lust for vengeance,
. . . and give up justifying evil.
God, is there something else,

beyond the reach of reason,
beyond the frontier of pain,
beyond the bounds of human life,
beyond the throat of any word?

84 The Highways to Zion

'How lovely is your dwelling place, O Lord of hosts!
My soul longs, indeed it faints for the courts of the Lord;
my heart and my flesh sing for joy to the living God.
Even the sparrow finds a home,
and the swallow a nest for herself,
where she may lay her young . . .
Happy are those whose strength is in you,
in whose heart are the highways to Zion.'   *vv.1-3,5*

I am a bird, created on day five
to pick the insects off sea-monsters,
fly through space and storylines, steal
into psalms where God delights
to name my kind to keep the tune alive.

I am a migrant, seeking sanctuary,
worn out, longing for a corner
I can call my very own, feel
at home, a wanderer no more, where
I can rest those documents I carry.

I am a bird, so flexible in flight:
I swoop, I coo, I twitter, could be
swallow, pigeon, sparrow, as I wheel
around those temple courts, to see
if I can find a holy nesting site.

I am a pilgrim, struggling on the way
with beasts and burdens, worldly fears;
for just a single day with God I kneel
and pray; that's worth a thousand years,
I know; I want to find this, come what may.

There is a bird of passage, say a dove,
which makes a draught around my soul,
suggests to me life's ordinary deal
is played into a pigeon hole
soft feathered with the plumage of God's love.

85 Birds of Passage

'Faithfulness will spring up from the ground,
and righteousness will look down from the sky.' *v.11*

They flock, they fly,
they float, they die.

Some pass the hunters,
some fall from the air;
some lose their compass,
some manage to get there.

I read about a migrant
passing through Libya to Paris,
who grew wings for a wild
ascent, four flights of faith
to pluck a child from a balcony,
replace him in his family nest.

I heard about another
passing through Greece and Italy,
grounded at Calais, every flight
to England full, or turned back,
cancelled till he lost the lift,
the spring of hope that drove him
from an Asian to a European hell.

They flock, they fly,
they float, they die,

looking for a righteous wind
somewhere in the atmosphere,
hoping for a faithful current
and a friendly pier.

86 Mungo the Migrant

'O God, the insolent rise up against me;
a band of ruffians seeks my life,
and they do not set you before them . . .
Turn to me and be gracious to me;
give your strength to your servant;
save the child of your servant girl.' *vv.14,16*

He left Traprain in embryo,
the child of violent royal rape,
his mother's womb a cushion
as they bounced down cliffs,
were frogmarched to the coast,
dumped into a coracle,
pushed out onto the River Forth,
to drift unannounced on the tide
into the arms of Culross monks.

Tannoc named her child 'big chief',
but holy Serf said 'my beloved',
'Mungo' in his local tongue.
When ruffian boys threw stones
and hit a robin, Mungo took it,
asked the Son of God to heal it,
and it flew right into Glasgow's
coat of arms – the city named
from Mungo's 'happy family'.

Made a bishop, driven south,
Mungo walked through Cumbria,
a journey in the truth and power
of God, converting fear to faith,
as far as Wales, establishing
that monastery of migrant souls
who one day would go back with him
to Scotland, to Strathclyde again
to plan and build a Christian land.

Those miracles – the fire that stopped
restarted by a hazel branch,
the ring flung in the River Clyde
that popped out from a fish's mouth
– and far less magical, those steaming
baths he found on pilgrimage
to Rome and took each day at home:
we owe our legends to these migrant
saints who lived and prayed the Psalms.

87 Sabras

'The Lord records, as he registers the peoples,
"This one was born there."
Singers and dancers alike say,
"All my springs are in you".' *vv.6-7*

Moshe Dyan, born on Israel's first kibbutz,
Yitzak Rabin, born within Jerusalem,
Chaim Topol, born in Tel Aviv, but
playing *Fiddler on the Roof* all over.
Sabras, holding blue Israeli passports
without further reference to God
– yet Tevye always shaved his beard
before his children, when the theatre run
was over, so they recognised their Dad.

88 The Torture of the Pit

'I am counted among those who go down to the Pit,
I am like those who have no help,
like those forsaken among the dead,
like the slain that lie in the grave,
like those whom you remember no more,
for they are cut off from your hand.
You have put me in the depths of the Pit . . .' *vv.4-7*

A little slit
above the ear
kept him alive,
hanging upside down
for three days
in the Pit.

He bore it,
blood oozing
from mouth and nose,
his faith strong
for three days
in the Pit.

To knock the shit
right out, they took
him, left him
overnight, hearing
the moans of others
in the Pit.

'Just quit
your faith,' they said,
'You'll save the three
believers hanging
three days
in the Pit.'

The Jesuit
apostasised,
convinced his Lord
would do the same
to save us
hanging in the Pit.

In the early 17th century, Christovao Ferreira migrated to Japan at the behest of the Society of Jesus, and spent over 30 years in Japan, an inspiration to the faithful as he endured years of persecution, until a report reached Rome that, unaccountably, Ferreira had apostasised.

89 In Conclusion

'I will sing of your steadfast love, O Lord, for ever.
. . . Lord, where is you steadfast love of old . . .?
Blessed be the Lord forever. Amen and Amen.' *vv.1,49,52*

Though dead, I hover: Ethan is my name,
insider commentator, leading advocate
of psalmody, this ancient on-off game
we play for ever, questioning the state
of things, rehearsing how and who to blame
for broken promises. Is it too late
to seek God's help? Can we in exile frame
our mind maps faithfully, turn round, migrate
to some more holy ground, discover where
God is at work to comfort, heal, amend,
construct a meeting place of hope again?
I am the patron of each love affair
between our faith and doubt: I end
with 'Blessed be the Lord. Amen, Amen.'

Notes on Book 3 Poems

73 The words by Katie Hopkins in the Sun (April 2015) are cited in Patrick Kingsley, *The New Odyssey*, Faber & Faber, London 2016, 262.

74 The epigraph by Tsegaye Tesfaye is in a Kenyan refugee camp newsletter (*Stormy Seas We Brave*, World Council of Churches). A conference was held at Évian-les-Bains in July 1938, and apart from a few countries like Canada, the Western Powers refused to take a significant number of Jews, even though Hitler was offering to let them go. An example of ships turned back was the German liner St. Louis, carrying about 900 German Jewish refugees, which was denied entrance to the Havana harbour in 1939. The ship was later denied entrance to the United States and returned to Hamburg, Germany. Other ships were denied entrance to Palestine in the 1930s by the British authorities.

75 Based on a story in the Economist, 3Nov18, 'A Small Piece of Hell', 34.

77 A found poem, from a film by Samir Mehanovic.

79 Based on an article published by Wycliffe Bible Translators in May 2018.

80 Based on *I am Malala*, Weidenfeld & Nicolson, London 2013.

88 Based on Shusaku Endo, *Silence*, Peter Owen, London 1969, 19ff.

Chapter Four
Music and Wonder

Music is ... by its very nature so close to the fundamentals of existence   (Joseph Pieper)[1]

It is normal to speak of 'tone colour' and ... 'texture' implying a shared, even inherent, synaesthesia among musicians, ... parallels between music and textile   (John Purser)[2]

I have not now the shadow of a doubt as to every *piobaireachd* being the music of a poem   (C.S. Thomason)[3]

Part 1

1   The Gift of Being Amazed

2   Transcendence: Church Architecture and 'Greek' Thomson, Poetry and George Herbert, Imagination and Freedom, Across Religions

3   Synaesthesia

4   Book 4 Poetry

Part 2

5   Music in Israel: Gematria

6   Early Christian Music

7   Singing in the Scottish Reformation

8   Music Inside and Outside the Church

9   Church Music in Highlands and Islands

Part 1
1 The Gift of Being Amazed

The poetic thread of this chapter is 'singer', with the poet singing her wonder at life in an amazing universe. One of the things even an atheist like Richard Dawkins acknowledges is his amazement at the extraordinary details of the universe as revealed by modern scientific discovery, a *wonder* that believers and unbelievers happily share.

This was true long before radio telescopes or the cracking of the DNA code. John Muir, introduced in Chapter One, was a Scot from Dunbar who as a boy emigrated to Wisconsin in 1849 with his father, and eventually made his way to the Sierra Nevada in the 1860s. He fell in love with the Yosemite valley, and wrote to his brother in 1870:

> Yet this glorious valley might well be called a church . . . the glory of the Lord is upon all his works . . . written upon all the fields of every clime, and upon every sky.[4]

> I have not been to church since I left here, but God could not be more pleased at my worship in this temple [Yosemite].[5]

Muir sent an article to the *Sacramento Record Union* called 'God's First Temples: How shall we preserve our forests?'[6] He railed against 'the devotees of ravaging commercialism' who 'instead of lifting their eyes to the God of the mountains, lift them to the Almighty Dollar'.[7] Although no biblicist, Muir was in tune with the temple theology of the Old Testament, linking trees and mountains and rivers with God, and saying that no temple made with hands could compare with Yosemite.[8]

The sense of wonder can be lost. Charles Darwin in his autobiography says this:

> Up to the age of thirty, poetry of many kinds, such as the works of Milton, Gray, Byron, Wordsworth, Coleridge and Shelley, gave me great pleasure . . . formerly pictures gave me considerable, and music very great delight. But now for many years I cannot endure to read a line of poetry . . . my mind seems to have become a kind of machine for grinding general laws out of large collections of facts . . . The loss of these tastes is a loss of happiness, and may possibly be injurious to the intellect, and more probably to the moral character . . . by enfeebling the emotional (imaginative) part of our nature.[9]

What a profound comment on the arts, by a great scientist who happily did retain his sense of wonder at what became known as the theory of evolution, even if he lost his taste for the arts themselves.

I have two confessions at this point. First, I may be breaking my promise to make Part 1 simpler than Part 2. If you need to, go straight to section 4 which introduces the poetry. Second, until we get to section 3, which explains how the senses ar linked, I hardly talk about music at all. Perhaps I'm back on that magic carpet, steering my curious way through the clouds. But stay with me if you can.

'Wonder' as a verb can be linked with doubt as well as possibility thinking. *Poem 89 'In Conclusion'*, which completed the poetry of Book 3 of the Psalms, suggested that Ethan (the writer of Psalm 89) might be 'the patron of each love affair / between our faith and doubt'. This does at least two things: first, it places the line between faith and doubt not between atheist and believer, but within the psalm, and by implication within the believer. Of course, it is not expressed as the modern intellectual doubt, but the practical doubt of a man who is beginning to wonder if God can actually do anything to change things for the better.

That indeed is taking 'wonder' in a much less sublime sense. Yet second, the poem describes the relation between faith and doubt, not as a struggle, but as a love affair. True wonder! How I think it works is this: God is at work within the psalmist (and within any or all of us) to help him express both the faith of verses 1-37, and the doubt of 38-51. Helping someone to acknowledge and express doubt is here an act of loving attention. That in turn allows a faith-filled conclusion which mirrors the conclusion of the first three Psalm Books: 'Blessed be the Lord forever. Amen and Amen.'

'Wonder' is a staple of poetry: 'A poem is a temple in which epiphanies happen.'[10] It has two cousins. One is **play**, which is a way of interpreting Proverbs 8:30-31, that Wisdom was at play, like a small child, in creation. The rabbis developed this with their word play, and also with number play. Numbers in Hebrew are marked by particular letters, and Hebrew *gematria* plays with their significance in a serious and sophisticated way (see the later section four).[11]

Wonder's other cousin is **hope**. Wonder acknowledges something beyond our grasp, whether or not you have the courage (as the believer might put it) to tie a God label to it. This was one reason, I think, for the hagiographies of earlier days, so debunked by literary fashion today. The wonders in the life of a saint gave people hope that they, too, might see wonders in their own lives. *Poem 86, 'Mungo the Migrant'*, is a simple rehearsal of the wonderful life of St Kentigern (Mungo's other name).

2 Transcendence

Transcendence is the name for what is beyond ourselves and our experience.

The British Library contains the late 15th century Breviary of Isabella of Castile. One of its illuminators also worked for James IV of Scotland, a reminder of how medieval Europe embraced outlying nations like Scotland. The Breviary depicts the reconstruction of the Jerusalem temple, with references to the Psalms. The new temple was the sign of a new age, an age of things beyond, it was a utopian image of the 'Age of Discovery' – Isabella was patron of Columbus' voyage to the New World.

While today we focus on the evils of colonialism, and hidden motives like greed and domination, a historian is also interested in how Europeans of that age understood what they were about. Today some see space travel as earthlings exporting their junk and their problems, while others see it in terms of wonder and discovery – which is how Isabella saw travel. She had a sense of transcendence, which of course she saw as experiencing something of God in her worship and sense of mission. While we can look back cynically and say that the colonial powers were playing God themselves, that does not do justice to the spirit of the times. Here is the poet Keats:

> Then felt I like some watcher of the skies
> When a new planet swims into his ken;
> Or like stout Cortez when with eagle eyes
> He star'd at the Pacific – and all his men
> Look'd at each other with a wild surmise –
> Silent, upon a peak in Darien.[12]

Church Architecture and 'Greek' Thomson

In Europe, while the first churches were simple wooden buildings, the medieval architects designed churches and cathedrals with spires and towers that signalled transcendence, calling people to look up and feel the beyond. This has continued up to the present day, though there have always been exceptions – believers who wanted meeting houses without adornment, citing the practice of the early Church where worshippers simply met in larger homes. For them, transcendence could be felt through God's Word and Spirit, without the help of architecture.

I said in Chapter One that Scots generally reserved the word 'temple' for temples of the past (whether Druid, Jewish or Classical), or used it metaphorically – whether out of a sense of wonder, like John Muir, or out of a sense of loss, as Lord Cockburn used the word when he described the tearing apart of the Church in Scotland at the Disruption.[13] Temple was of course a word familiar to architects, who with the Renaissance moved beyond the medieval view of the world as a 'vale of tears' to the neoplatonic idea that the visible world was a copy of some pre-existing pattern, and that the design of a church should reveal the truth and perfection of God.[14] While architects generally did not spell out these connections, one member of the United Presbyterian Church, Alexander Thomson, did.

Referring to Edmund Burke, who wrote *Sublime and Beautiful*, which deeply influenced Thomson, Sam McKinstry says of that UP Church: 'A Church which virtually revered the Psalms and Paraphrases must often – in all the sonority of its primitive, unaccompanied praise – have been conscious of the Sublime'.[15] Gavin Stamp reports that 'with Thomson, theology and architecture were inseparable'.[16] When in his Haldane Lectures Thomson says,

> The Creator has not clothed with beauty the world which he has given us for a habitation, or filled the Heavens over our heads with glory, without also imposing on us the duty of pondering over these things and laying them to heart,[17]

he is citing Psalm 111:2, and the sense of Psalms 8 and 104.

Nicknamed 'Greek' Thomson, his views were formed by: (a) the 'eternal laws' of Egyptian and Greek (but not Roman) temple construction;[18] (b) a 'temple theology';[19] (c) The Bible, especially Revelation and the Psalms;[20] and put at the service of the people of Glasgow. William Storrar says,

> In his lectures and in his practice, he preferred the horizontal line suggestive of infinity, and the open space in the sanctuary made possible by modern iron beams, as in the three United Presbyterian churches he designed in Glasgow on

monumental, temple-like platforms, rather than the vertical, perpendicular lines and obscuring forest of internal arches in the Gothic churches that were so much in fashion in his day.[21]

According to Christopher Rowland, the book of Revelation is about the overcoming of contrasts between 'above' and 'below', especially at the climax of chapters 21 and 22.[22] Thomson held that architects should transpose the biblical vision of the New Jerusalem and a Protestant sensibility into visionary modern buildings for both slum dwellers and the rising middle-class of Glasgow, as humble co-creators with God. This is well expressed by Robert Crawford in writing about Thomson's relationship to Glasgow:

> Thomson was an elder of the UP Kirk, and loved the Revelation passage where John saw the new city, Jerusalem, coming down from God out of heaven. Drawing on Greek and Egyptian elements, and planning churches based on the temple of Solomon, Alexander Thomson sought to build such a city.[23]

Just as John's vision of the holy city[24] owed much to the ideal temple of Ezekiel 40 – 44, so Thomson's vision was formed by the eternal laws of Egyptian and Greek construction. It is public architecture, in a public space. Transcendence was offered to the whole community.

Poetry and George Herbert

Poets have sometimes used 'temple' as a symbol of hope. *The Temple* is the name given to the edition of George Herbert's poetry (1593-1633) published after his death by his friend Nicholas Farrer. The titles of the poems describe a sequence from church-porch to altar, then from sacrifice up to Good Friday and Easter; there follows a long sequence of spiritual themes, some titles repeating, as varied as Jordan, church music, the bunch of grapes and judgement. Herbert was a man who found 'temple' a universal theme, with all things related to God, his poetry full of dramatic metaphors for the spiritual life and allusions to the New Testament, yet like many after him, he seldom used the word 'temple', and seldom cited the Psalms directly[25] (though David Jasper[26] says the book is modelled on the Sidney Psalter). For example, when Herbert writes about dust, it has no connection with Psalm 90.

In his poetry he refers to the saying of Christ about his body as the temple, and sets out his 'Altar' poem in the shape of an altar. Beyond that, Herbert has one reference in his poetry to Solomon's temple, and one reference to the church as a temple:

> Yet in thy temple thou dost him afford
> this glorious and transcendent place
> to be a window, through thy grace.[27]

While few contemporary poets are willing to reference God in the direct way that Herbert does, this kind of verse chimes with the way which some poets are happy to use 'the transcendent' in place of God.

> When faith disappears . . . the language of transcendence can have a special power because it evokes something that was once familiar, once possible, and is now lost.[28]

However, by the assumption that this 'something' is lost for ever, this 'power' is inevitably restricted, now directly relevant only to those inspired by the language. A Scottish poet like MacDiarmid, influenced by the religion he rebelled against, and friendly with Keir Hardie and his tradition, expected it to transform the social and thus have political relevance. And believers like Jeremy Begbie of Duke University, will claim, in the spirit of Psalm 99:1, that 'divine transcendence is not simply a metaphysical arrangement':[29]

> The Lord is king: let the peoples tremble!
> He sits enthroned upon the cherubim; let the earth quake!

Imagination and Freedom

Transcendence is one place where poetry meets theology. Transcendence is 'this lost-for-words I feel with you that I would call the Lord's work if I were a man of faith . . .'[30] A theologian like Thomas Torrance is happy to affirm the importance of transcendence, but links it both to enquiry (which demands imagination) and freedom: 'Science, faith in transcendent reality, and the free society are inseparably interlocked together.'[31]

This continues a discussion begun in Chapter Two. While imagination has always been a fundamental element of poetry, it has its anchors, recognised or not – rooted in religion, or society, or the conscience of the poet. Even today, while free association rules many poems, there seem to be no-go areas fenced by social media or a fear of giving offence. Indeed, without some anchors of language, intelligibility and acceptance, communication would be impossible. As it is, writings may be only discovered or rediscovered in a different age.

While some believers may have used Scripture and conscience to anchor them to places which have restricted their poetry, I concur with two verses in Psalm 119 which suggest that an anchor in what God says may actually free us to experience wonder and the transcendent, and to write about these things.

> Open my eyes, so that I may behold wondrous things out of your law. (Psalm 119:18)

> I shall walk at liberty, for I have sought your precepts. (Psalm 119:45)

The Psalms invite us to exercise a *moral* imagination,[32] as they were written in dialogue with the Law and the Prophets of Israel. This keeps imagination from becoming a tyrant, like Job's vindictive counsellor Zophar in Job 20 who cited transcendence and claimed wisdom from 'a spirit beyond my understanding'. His companion Eliphaz was playing the same game earlier on in Job 4 when he said 'a spirit glided past my face' and heard it saying things which he then used as a faux moral weapon against Job.

John Paul Lederach examines the use of the phrase 'the moral imagination', and concludes that all the authors he examined [in 2001] agreed, 'the moral imagination has a quality of transcendence'.[33] As expressed by Susan Babbit, the role of the moral imagination is to set in motion 'the bringing about of possibilities that are not imaginable in current terms'.[34] So my *Poem 35 'Enemies'* lets the apparent metaphysical impossibility of God 'stepping into the line of fire' subvert the moral difficulty of loving enemies. Kevin Hart speaks of 'transcendence in immanence ... any poem of value is a record of someone having allowed the impossible to engage the possible'.[35]

Poem 18 'Space Temple' uses the 'broad place' of verse 5 of the psalm to let me 'take this psalm and travel time', with our later knowledge of how space and time are related. It brings in Alfred Edersheim, not simply because his name conveniently rhymes with 'time', but because Edersheim wrote a classic book called *The Temple*.

For the Psalms, transcendence is expressed in images like 'God's holy temple', but, as with the awe-struck prophet in Isaiah 6), the experience of God is expected to make a person cleaner, and act better (Psalm 139:24). The Psalms expect practical outcomes, but the words of the Psalms do their work not so much by arguing for obedience, as through their transcendent impact (cf. Psalm 119:11, or Psalm 139). MacDiarmid had his own way of making a similar point:

> Yet whiles through words can brak'
> A music that can gliff
> Body and brain as if
> Their benmaist secrets spak'[36]

Transcendence is balanced by immanence. Outcomes which are the work and gift of God do not require us to privilege either.[37] *Poem 144 'Stuff'* includes a prayer for deliverance from ricin and cyber warfare as well as knives and family feuds. The poem imagines a temple which takes shape around our praise, and asks for 'a weighted prayer' pitched into a loch, where the ripples consequently 'bless barn and beast, / upend the wicked, / keep a kingdom young.' The hope for such an answered prayer depends upon the transcendent, yet demands that the prayer be voiced. The beyond with the here and now. Transcendence and immanence.

Is such a temple a matter of imagination? Yes. Is such a temple just a matter of the imagination? No, if transcendence is more than simply a useful figment of that same imagination. A choice expressed so simply by George Herbert,

A man that looks on glass,
on it may stay his eye;
or if he pleaseth, through it pass,
and then the heaven espy.[38]

In the Psalms, such a choice is thrown back on God: 'If you are silent to me . . .' (Psalm 28:1), and *28 'Pinnacle or Pit'* puts the question, is the cry of David simply echolalia?

Will the temple change to clever text,
or could the holy word become again
our flesh, our fate, our faith?

Every nation faces choices. At the time of writing, independence is a question for Scotland. Without lapsing into the 'God is on our side' mentality of some belligerents, a sense of the transcendent is what allows a nation and its people to drive through and/or bear with change, and to find hope in such challenging times. It is the task of the poet to open a window onto the transcendent and its wonder.

Across Religions

Psalm 41 completed the poems of Book 1. Its poem, *41 'The Cosmic Synagogue'*, ended with the same final words, 'Blest be the Lord: Amen, Amen!' It recognised the challenge of embracing bad as well as good people faced by any monotheist religion which gathers people together, and took the word 'synagogue' as a gathering point for any religion – indeed the word is used for both the gathering place and the people gathered.

While the synagogue was consciously a meeting-house rather than a place of sacrifice like the temple, Judaism and Islam both have had their mystical sides – Cabbalism and Sufism. The Cabbalists in their imagination put the temple at the heart of a universe shaped like a cube. Just as the Jews had to 'move the temple into the home', so in *28 'Pinnacle or Pit?'* I wrote about them 'moving meaning from a public knowledge base to private words and lego thought'.

Eastern Religions are up front about temples. Sheena Blackhall has written four poems on a Buddhist temple theme in Scotland,[39] two on the Samye-Ling temple at Eskdalemuir, one written at Dhanakosa at Balquidder, and one at the Cave Temple at Dambulla (which is called 'Monkey King', and features a begging monkey and a seller of beads). Themes of cosmos and creation appear, though in a subtly different way from how they feature in the monotheist religions.

'**Samye-Ling**' is about the temple and its life for monks and laity, with the trinitarian chorus 'Samye-Ling, Samye-Ling, Samye-Ling' echoing the hand bells and prayer wheels. It is 'MacDiarmid land', and MacDiarmid is a 'David, who matched the South's Goliath tongue' – 'these pebbles filled his sling . . . / where prayer-flags cling.'

'**Shrine in the Woods**' is also about Samye-Ling. Nearby is a wishing-tree, which is supposed to have been an early Celtic shrine, though this poem is about the lilypool with the Buddha, the 'white marble meditator . . . / the peaceful guardian of this nook'.

'**Diving for Poems**' features the 'little lights set out along the shore' at Dhanakosa. 'Diving for poems / I entered the moon's reflections.' The poem might have been written anywhere, but subtly indicates her oneness with the created world which is more often found in Eastern than Western religion.

A particular and poetic use of temple is found in the writing of Mpu Tantular, a 14th century Javanese poet, who wrote in the foreword to his best known work, the *Arjunawijaya*,

> The purpose of my praise is to implore Him to pay heed to the homage of one who devotes himself to poetry . . . This is what I ask as I build my temple of language on my writing board.[40]

Here 'temple' is used in yet another sense, a cathedral of language. The literary critic Walter Benjamin described his library as a sanctuary, 'with books as the building stones'.[41] This book began with a high view of temple, as a metaphor for cosmos and heart as well as a structure. There could not be such a high view if building were not endemic to culture and nature, whether the library built by a writer, or nests built by the sparrows of Psalm

84:3, as well as the sacred temples of religion. The higher the view, the greater the wonder.

3 Synaesthesia

This is another jargon or summary word, used specifically for someone 'feeling in colour', seeing different images as a melody is played, or neurologically for a person who has different sounds, say, triggered by different experiences of touch – but more generally for the crossover of different art forms when they seem to be doing the same thing but with different media. Speaking of the poet as a 'singer' is another example.

> Seamus Heaney in his essay 'The Government of the Tongue' comments that the poet Dante's tongue is like a conductor's baton, containing 'all the elements of the orchestra',[42] an image combining the inspiration and authority of crafted words. Such synaesthesia, where one art form can be spoken of in terms of another, is particularly true of poetry and music. John Leavitt links music and 'poetic prophecy', seeing the stress and pitch of speech as dynamics and melody,.[43]
>
> There is a ninth CE Frankish volume of music theory compiled by Aurelian, *Musica Disciplina*, which among other things instructs the cantor on how to relate the text and its meaning to the move from verse to antiphon in singing a psalm.[44] This may be the first hint of how a text might relate to the texture of a tune, something John Purser develops in an article on musical structures.[45] In the Highlands, John MacLeod of Inverness analysed a pibroch in terms of 'lines of poetry'.[46] That is synaesthesia. There was a famous blind piper called Iain Dall MacKay, and Maoilios Caimbeul wrote this about him:
>
> *Chitheadh tu le do sprùdan*
> *ged a bha do shùilean gun sholas*
> *bu mhòr na dealbhan bhiodh a' dannsa*
> *nuair dhòrtadh meall den cheòl bhod chorraig.*
>
> You had digital vision although your eyes were dark: many's the picture would dance when a shower of music would pour from your fingers.[47]

Many Highland pipers believed their instrument could actually speak and that pibroch is an extension of the tales told by bards to remember the clan's history.[48] Seumus MacNeill held that the sound of the bagpipes expertly played is like a human voice singing with great emotional and psychological content.[49] Martin Schröder links the pibroch tradition with the Psalms in an unpublished thesis, and illustrates this from 'Gaelic Psalm Tune'[50] by the band Capercaillie and 'The Highest Apple' by Runrig.[51]

Pibroch on a solo instrument makes connections in sequence. A choir or orchestra can make connections as a chord or as interwoven sequences. In 1501 the Scottish poet Gavin Douglas described the techniques of the composer Robert Carver:

> In modulation heard I play and sing
> Fauxbourdon, pricksang, descant, countering,
> Cant Organe, figuratioun and gemmel,
> On croud, lute, harp, with mony gudlie spring . . .[52]

How interesting that in the Scots of that day, 'gudlie' could mean 'goodly' and 'godly'. The words came together again in the Gude and Godly Ballads, the 'Protestant Protest Songs' of the Reformation.

Another approach to synaesthesia comes in Bible texts. Psalm 146:8 says the eyes of the blind will be opened, and Psalm 142:1 says 'with my voice I cry to the Lord', which is what the blind man of Luke 18:38-39 does in hope that Jesus will give him back his sight. Psalms 146 and 147 both echo the words of Isaiah, that the Lord gathers the outcasts and sets prisoners free, words picked up in the 'messianic manifesto' of Luke 4:18 which includes 'recovery of sight to the blind'.

84 'The Highways to Zion' picks up the ambiguity of the Hebrew *tsippôr*[53] and what sounds might feature in its third stanza:

> I am a bird, so flexible in flight:
> I swoop, I coo, I twitter, could be
> swallow, pigeon, sparrow, as I wheel
> around those temple courts, to see
> if I can find a holy nesting site.

That is another example of synaesthesia, the interweaving of sight and sound that a poet often pursues.[54] It can be regarded as a correlate of

Psalm 139:13, which refers to the human person as woven or knitted together. Proverbs 19:17 is more specific: 'The hearing ear, the seeing eye, the Lord has made them both.' Purser illustrates the concept with a poem by Norman MacCaig, who 'crossed the boundaries of music and geology' to link the 'mellifluous din of *canntaireachd*'[55] with

> One sandstone chord that holds up time in space
> Sforzando Suilven reared on his ground bass.[56]

The pibroch song poem '*Moladh Beinn Dorain*' is yet another example. And Hugh MacDiarmid himself wrote 'Lament for the Great Music', which 'attempts to emulate in verse the open-ended, yet formally disciplined, improvisatory quality of the pibroch'.[57]

4 Book 4 Poetry

My own attempt to link pibroch and psalms in a modern poem comes with Book 4 poetry, '*The Iolaire*'. (Pibroch is the English form of the Gaelic *piobaireachd*.) Although many of my poems relate to the crossing over of different arts, this is an open feature of *The Iolaire* – this long poem in the shape of a pibroch. It references the disaster of the troopship *Iolaire*, which foundered in a storm just outside Stornoway harbour in the early hours of January 1st 1919, with the loss of 205 men. The issue of how we come to terms with these sort of tragedies today, has a parallel in how Israel learned to come to terms with their history of exile and return, which is why it could be written in dialogue with the psalms of Book 4.

In '*Taorluath* Doubling: Downhill', I occupy Suilven to contemplate Psalms 98 – 100, psalms placed and possibly written after the disaster of Jewish exile:

> 'If I were on skis,' she said, astride
> of Suilven, 'I'd be away, downhill,
> skimming scree and stretching time
> for you to see things differently. I would
> awaken Moses, shake him, get right through
> to God: howl, groan, gasp, spit
> your prayers, real and raw as juniper.
> I'd breathe on Samuel, make him once again
> a child, living in the Scottish temple
> garden for you, hearing something new.'

Purser gives further examples of linking music with poetry, such as 'Tuis Pater' from the *Inchcolm Antiphoner* (c.1300) where 'the musical structure makes cross-currents with the poetic structure'. Then he introduces weaving, with a 1749 poem (English translation below) possibly by Lachlann MacMhuirich:

> I'm a weaver already
> who weaves very splendid poems;
>   since my careful tutor left
>   I should weave every poem he warped.[58]

Before the music was written with Western stave and bar notation, it was written and memorised with the *canntaireachd* vocables,[59] which are themselves a woven structure, like the *Inchcolm Antiphoner*. This is why General Thomason, cited at the start of the chapter, described a pibroch as 'the music of a poem'.

In that article citing Thomason, Purser relates texture of music to text, and through the metaphor of weaving, to textiles like tartan. Andean traditional flute music, also transmitted orally, makes a direct parallel between music and textile.[60] He also refers to the proposal that interlace patterns in early mediaeval manuscripts and stone-carving may represent a kind of musical notation, as another possible example of linking, for example having a melody associated with the opening letter of a manuscript Latin psalm.

Weaving is of course a basic idea in the title *Temple and Tartan*, and comes into Book 4 Poetry (on Psalm 104) as 'change over templates to weaving and wondering' as well as in a reference to 'God's secret looms'.

119 'Fair and Square' also refers to this kind of link as a paradox of spiritual presence:

> No life complete without God's art and music
> hidden in our sober prose, artless, silent.

In Psalm 119, the art and music of a numerical pattern is woven into the sequence of stanzas as they work through the Hebrew alphabet, painting the prosaic subject of *Torah* in a palette of different colours, inviting us to sing the praise of God's teaching in a sequence of different tunes.

Coming back to *The Iolaire*, like the Book 4 Psalms themselves the poem moves back and forward between weakness, failure and tragedy, and strength, wonder and hope. Every pibroch has a theme and variations, but this form is used explicitly to discuss various interpretations of the disaster, from the supposed drunkenness of the ship's officers to the incoherent rage which often strikes us some time after bereavement. Then as the variations develop further, a bigger theme emerges – the possibility that Calvinism and its downsides might be redeemed into something far greater (perhaps as a tribute to Calvin himself).

Now is the time to skip forward to the next chapter, or continue and look at some snapshots of how music developed over time, with a focus on Scotland.

Part 2

5 Music in Israel

If music can evoke a sense of wonder and transcendence, these things are severely challenged by suffering and exile – 'How could we sing the Lord's song in a foreign land?' (Psalm 137:4). And if the exiled Jews in Babylon were no longer able to offer God their sacrifices, what then could they do? Their solution to this dilemma was revolutionary: they would offer their words and music, their prayers and hymns.[61] Often these took the form of lament, as in that psalm verse – but if they did hang their lyres on the willow trees, they did not abandon them.

We are told that various instruments were used to accompany the psalms,[62] but we know little about the singing, though 'chanting' may be more accurate.[63] Of more than this some say we are ignorant: 'We know as little of the martial tunes to which the Maccabees marched and set their psalms as we do of the songs the Sirens sang. When the Temple fell, instrumental music was banished from the Jewish ritual.'[64] The *Oxford Handbook of the Psalms* has no chapter on 'The Music of the Psalms'. The *Oxford Companion to Music* thinks there may be continuity between plainsong and Jewish 'cantillation': plainsong 'was influenced possibly by the music of the Jewish synagogue'.[65] At the other extreme, David Mitchell has actually worked out a possible score for all fifteen Psalms of Ascent.[66]

John Goldingay lists these words in the Psalms themselves:[67]

> *hālal* = make a lalalala noise (22:22,23)
> *zāmar* = make music (21:13)
> *rānan* = make a n-n-n-n noise (33:1)
> *rûa^c* = shout (95:1)

This suggests that the common translation 'sing' used in the NRSV should not be understood as Western classical singing. It may be closer to chanting, provided that word is used to cover everything from plainsong to singing in tongues.

We know also that music was not confined to temple (or later synagogue) worship. The Israelites sang when they were rescued from Pharaoh's army (Exodus 15), the Song of Solomon is love poetry, and traditional Israeli song and dance is well known.

Gematria

There are subtle links between music and poetry and mathematics, and this is played out in Hebrew *gematria*. Numbers in Hebrew are marked by particular letters, and *gematria* plays with their significance.[68] I have used this idea in a simple way with the *'Song of the Fifteen Steps'*, making each of my Psalms of Ascent poems fifteen lines in length (Michael Symmons Roberts chose to do this for *all* his *Drysalter* poems). In the Hebrew number alphabet, the first letter is 1, and the last 400. A sum totalling 888 is significant as coming just before 999.[69] An example with Psalm 23:3 would be that the three Hebrew words for 'he will restore my soul' are (without the pointing) *npšî yšôbb ynchôt* which have a numerical value of 440 + 320 + 128 which is 888. The Hebrew words in Genesis 2:4 for 'the Lord God made' are *^cśôt yhwh ^clhîm*, which have a numerical value of 776 + 26 + 86 which is also 888.[70] This links the devotion of the Psalms to the creation story, and the creation story to Jewish mysticism.

If you find this compelling, read *The Songs of Ascents*, by David Mitchell. I first met David when he was a rock musician, but he is currently Precentor of Brussels Cathedral, and has always been a Hebrew scholar. His book details the intricate and quite extraordinary way that the Psalms of Ascent (Psalms 120 – 134) were composed in order to celebrate the dedication of Solomon's temple. While these songs may well have been sung later by pilgrims going up to the temple, they were traditionally sung on the fifteen steps descending from the Court of Israel to the Court of the Women. [71] While part of the 'magic' of gematria depends on the way numbers work, it remains a thing of wonder.

The mathematics of the Psalms would be picked up much later in Scotland. John Clerk of Penicuik (1676-1755) used part of Psalm 51 for his cantata *Miserere Mei Deus*. In the Hebrew '400' alphabet, Elohim adds to 86. Three sections of the cantata are 86 bars long. The five sections add to 400 bars, representing completion. At the centre point (bar 200), the text ceases to focus on sin and asks God for a pure heart, the word 'heart' being at the centre of the work.[72]

The link between the devotion of the Psalms and the creation story is also paralleled in the Creation Symphony of William Wallace (1860-1940) which also embeds the numerical values (in English of course) of his name and his wife's name into the structure of the work.[73] Just as 'the heavens are telling', and their voice goes 'to the end of the world' (Psalm 19:1-3), so the words of *Torah* give out the decrees of the Lord, and 'revive the soul' (19:7-9). The praise of Psalm 8:5-6 directly echoes Genesis 1:26-27.

6 Early Christian Music

While Christians between the first century and the fourth were rethinking their categories of social and political life in the eastern Mediterranean, they did not wander so far from the heritage of Jewish psalmody in home or temple, as to suppose that their gatherings should be without song.[74]

Psalmologos and *Psalmōdos* are the Greek terms both found in ancient Jewish inscriptions for 'worship music leader'. Jewish and Christian worship took centuries to diverge, not least in its music – even in the 380s CE, Chrysostom is denouncing Christians who attend Jewish Passover Festivals.[75] They both sang psalms, and both had song leaders. In Latin, Jerome chose *cantor* in his Bible as the term for Jewish worship song leaders, even though Ambrose in the same period preferred lector to *cantor* or *psalmista*. They were speaking about the same function.[76]

For the first thousand years of the Church's life the music used in worship was the unaccompanied melody of plainsong, or Gregorian chant,[77] which one scholar thought to derive from the Jerusalem Temple.[78] The primary intention of the Quire Offices (with the Breviary, for monasteries) was to provide for reading or singing of all psalms in a week.[79] Eight 'tones' (a way of chanting) were used for singing psalms, with a ninth – the *tonus peregrinus*, or 'stranger tone' – associated with Psalm 114 ('When Israel went out of Egypt').[80]

In Scotland worship included psalms sung by a choir, with Psalm 141:2 ('Let my prayer be counted as incense before you') sung three times while the chalice was unveiled.[81] Later, organum, counter-melody and polyphony developed, culminating with the 19 part motet for choral singing composed by Robert Carver.[82]

With the Reformation, music reverted to psalm-singing in unison, but by congregations rather than choirs. Dietrich Bonhoeffer was still rehearsing the same arguments for unison singing in 1939![83] The session clerk or reader often acted as cantor or precentor,[84] and after the acceptance of the Westminster *Directory for the Public Worship of God* (1645) the precentor sang (or read) each line of the psalm before the congregation repeated it.

7 Singing in the Scottish Reformation

At the Reformation all Protestant bodies used versified text for the Psalms. The first metrical psalms in Scotland were translations of Luther, in the Dundee or 'Wedderburn Psalms' (1540s, published 1565), with popular tunes, while other words and tunes came from Geneva. Knox probably followed Calvin's view that music could be a distraction from the preaching – Calvin lost the best organist in Geneva over this – but Knox did not mind music being popular.

Knox in his *History of the Reformation* recounts that the night before George Wishart was apprehended at Ormiston in 1546, he said, 'Will ye sing a Psalme?' and so 'we appointed the 51st Psalme which was put in Scotishe meter', and they sang a version found only in the Wedderburn Psalm Book.[85] In the cities there was a plural tradition, so that when the Geneva versions of the Psalms found their way to Scotland they were given music arrangements by Jhone Angus[86] in the older tradition, while Reformed Scots generally sang in unison (*a capella* in church, but with instruments in secular settings).[87]

The *First Book of Discipline* (1560) was drawn up by 'the six Johns' (Douglas, Knox, Row, Spottiswoode, Willock and Winram), and it exhorted men, women and children to 'exercise themselves in the psalmes'.[88] The complete Scottish Psalter of 1564 does not have the Wedderburn Psalms – the six Johns preferred the Genevan versions.[89] The first version of this Scottish Metrical Psalter appeared as part of the 'Forme of Prayers' in 1564, containing only the 150 Psalms, 104 with their own 'proper' tunes.[90] Older practices continued in some places. The offices continued to be said and sung, involving the psalms,[91] and the Wode Psalter of 1566[92] is an example of polyphony within the Reformed Church.[93]

These 'older practices' were embedded in the liturgies which the Stewart kings tried to make uniform in the joined kingdom; the books contained a lectionary of psalms, and Scottish Episcopal practice of using the Psalms, in public or private,[94] continued alongside use by the Reformed Kirk. At the start of the Scottish Reformation, the English prayer book was used in some places,[95] but in the Reformed Kirk it was superseded by the *Scottish Book of Common Order*, from 1560 on. However the prayer book only 'fell out of favour' during the period of Presbyterian dominance in the 1590s. For Episcopalians, the Book of Common Prayer of 1637 provided that the Psalms be read through every month, as did the later edition of 1657.[96]

Originally, Erasmus and Coverdale had simply wanted ordinary folk to sing the Psalms instead of secular songs. But after Coverdale completed *Goostly Psalms*, Scottish Protestants began collecting a similar set of musical settings, with words put into a Scottish dialect,[97] and the Scottish and English traditions began to diverge.[98] For the Reformed Kirk, while the Westminster Assembly of 1643-53 might have resulted in a uniform Psalter for both kingdoms, in practice the General Assembly of the Church of Scotland undertook a series of revisions which led to the Psalter of 1650;[99] that borrowed from at least twelve other versions – and the text remained unchanged until recent versions of the *Church Hymnary*[100] began to include some modern versions of the Psalms.

8 Music Inside and Outside the Church

As in Israel, so in Scotland: there was music 'in the temple' and 'outside the temple'. How they related changed from time to time. Before the Reformation, church music was chanted, then gradually adorned with the best of contemporary 'high' music. At the Reformation, such music was largely banished from worship. Even though the psalms were set initially to popular tunes, over the years the music declined until with the revival of 'classical' music in the 18th century there was a revival of choral settings of the psalms. Psalm-singing in the Highlands and Lowland developed, and perhaps also declined, in different ways. In the Lowlands the Reformation era was followed by a century of stagnation, and then the growth of a choir movement with four-part psalm singing in the late 18th century, stimulated by the new appreciation of classical music from the European continent.[101]

Generally, however, Yuri Bashmet's view has been followed. Age 12, Yuri formed a rock band and became a teenage idol; then he discovered classical music, and said, 'Classical music puts questions to your soul; jazz music only to your brain and body; and pop music only to your body.'[102] Accordingly composers provided many 'classical' settings of the Psalms, and looked down on other styles until in the last century there has been a transformation[103] – although many cathedral choirs, for example, will stick to 'classical' settings.

Composers have done more than simply provide settings for choirs to sing. Stravinsky said of his *Symphony of Psalms*, 'It is not a symphony in which I have included Psalms to be sung. On the contrary, it is the singing of the Psalms that I am symphonising.'[104] This is an example of synaesthesia.

> While many examples of 'modern styles' are footnoted, one deserves a special mention. At the start of Mackay's Memoirs – a composition based on the pibroch 'Lament for Mary MacLeod' – there is a reading from Psalm 121. The piece was written by Martyn Bennett, who had left Broughton Music School in Edinburgh, and graduated from the RAMD in Glasgow. He was the first traditional musician to be taken at the school. Dr Kenneth Mackay was a medical missionary in Peru who had retired to Kingussie, where Martyn was brought up, and who taught Martyn pibroch. They both liked that pibroch 'Lament for Mary MacLeod'. It was performed first at the school (now the City of Edinburgh Music School), as it was written specially for the instruments being learned at the time, and then later in Princes St Gardens at the time of the opening of the Scottish Parliament in 2004. A recording was made in January 2005 on the very day that Martyn died of cancer age 33.

Psalms like 19 hold creation and *Torah*, the big world of nature and the smaller world of the sacred, in harmony. This harmony was not so evident in Scotland. There were two approaches to what goes on in a church service. One said that only what is found in the Bible may take place (Calvin and Knox), the other that only what is specifically banned in the Bible is forbidden. The first, which ignored biblical evidence of accompanied psalm singing, led to singing psalms (and psalms only) with the voice in church, and this, till recently, has been the position of the Free Church of Scotland. The second led to hymns, organs, instruments, but – paradoxically – it is in the Free Church that the tradition of psalm singing has been best preserved.

The first approach is compatible with a love of different forms of music, but only if they are practised outside worship.[105] Alexander Carmichael's *Carmina Gadelica* bears witness to this, but a narrow understanding of calvinism led to a holy scowl at fiddle and bagpipes. In England, there is an Archbishops' Report which simply recognises difference of opinion on what music is appropriate for worship.[106]

Jeremy Begbie outlines two beliefs which he wishes us to navigate between: a theological imperialism where music becomes simply a gloss for conceptual truths, and a cultural imperialism (he calls it a 'theological aestheticism') in which music itself (typically classical) becomes the way to God.[107] The latter might seem to be a temptation for the cathedral, but is also seen in some independent churches where band-led songs are (pretentiously) described as the 'worship' part of a church service.

9 Church Music in Highlands and Islands

The Gaelic word for music, *ceol*, might be connected with 'birdsong',[108] and Purser also says that the Picts imitated birdsong with their voice and whistling.[109] Unaccompanied Gaelic psalm singing shows an aspect of this in the grace notes 'warbled' by the precentor, and possibly also the grace notes of a pibroch. Allan MacColl notes, 'Congregational singing of the Psalms was also heavily influenced by traditional styles of Gaelic folk song'.[110] Such singing, which is not unlike singing in tongues, has also been compared to the waves of the sea. In the BBC Radio 4 programme 'The Sound Odyssey' of 2/10/19, local precentor Calum Martin spoke of the music 'toing and froing' because we are surrounded by the sea, and a participant said, 'You can feel the waves'. Psalm 42:7 has 'all your waves and your billows have gone over me', in the context of lamenting a state of exile. The Old Testament sees everything coming from the hand of God, and as God is also creator it is natural to use these images, not least for island communities familiar with storms.

> According to Joseph Mainzer, a musicologist who came over from Germany 1842-47, psalms were basically sung to ornamented versions of six original tunes given in the metrical Psalter, 'the melody twining around the notes of its Psalter original like a Celtic knot-pattern'.[111] Gaelic psalm singing preserves this unique style in part because it was not overtaken by the 'proper' tunes set for psalms sung in the Lowlands – instead, these tunes were so transformed as to be unrecognisable.

A major reason is this. The Bible was not translated into Gaelic till the later 18th century, so the Psalms were received as items to be sung. They were first printed in English *with their tunes* in Edinburgh in 1564, but not in metre in Gaelic till 1659 (with all 150 in 1694), so there was oral transmission – however, the metre used for the Gaelic translation was Scottish ballad metre, which is alien to Gaelic, so the tunes had to be sung in a different way, and this gave free reign to a way of singing with a particular spirituality which has been compared to singing in tongues.[112]

In free charismatic worship, this singing may be initiated by any person, and then others take over or join in. In Gaelic psalmody the tunes are still 'lined out' by a precentor (the successor to the early 'cantor' in church music), but again the congregation seems to take over, whereas in conventional psalm singing a fixed structure is held by organ or piano accompaniment. On the mainland, the 'lining' of psalms ceased after the 18th century.

I have no hesitation in saying that this kind of singing witnesses to the transcendent, to something beyond, which we name as God. It is possible to see pibroch in the same way, with its ground increasingly ornamented by clusters of grace notes. I compare its impact to that of the partitas of J.S. Bach for unaccompanied violin.

A modern pibroch starts and ends with a ground or base melody. My Book 4 poem, however, repeats the ground in the middle, to return to the mood of Psalm 102, but also to reflect a much earlier practice in Scottish pibroch playing. The song poem '*Moladh Beinn Dorain*' also repeats the ground in the middle of the poem – something done by older pibroch players, but no longer in contemporary playing.[113]

Let me end this section on a more homely note. If Gaelic singing bears witness to the transcendent, it touches the heart as well as the mind. The poet Harry Smart describes his Free Church father-in-law at Culloden:

> I mind his face was wet with tears
> whose heart had grown generous
> on Gaelic psalms.[114]

Book 4 Poems: Pibroch
The Iolaire

Urlar (Ground 1): Our Dust

Psalm 90

You turn us back to dust, dust blown
off course, unable to make landfall,
ravaged by rocks, the desert sea, and worse,
grounded by our past, our wilderness,
our memory of Moses silent,
our memory of David gone so sour.

Our dust The Iolaire Inquiry gathered
in official vaults for fifty years,
while we had lost the wounded words,
pulled our fingers from the chanter,
placed our fiddles in the closet
where a silent tide washed over them.

A hundred years have nursed this silence,
grown the roots of trauma underground,
with our fury burned up in the psalms,
our sadness shivering on the sands
of Stornoway and every sermon
hinting at some sin still stowed away.

Siubhal (Variation) 1, singling: Easy Thinking

Psalm 91

It was the drink. Always
a reason for the wreck,
the death, divorce, the day's
disaster, not a mystery to check
our dotted i's and j's
that neatly stack the deck
in favour of God's ways.

Siubhal (Variation) 1, doubling: Easy Praise

Psalm 92

The righteous grow like palms,
secure within the church
and flourish without qualms
or queries: 'God won't leave us in the lurch
or fail to do his sums;
let every pagan search
and scowl; we'll sing our psalms.'

We'll sing them to the lute
and call it a guitar;
the praise band has a flute,
a fiddle, mikes, a drum kit, things that are
these days beyond dispute;
we'll build a repertoire
of unforbidden fruit.

Siubhal (Variation) 2: Sovereign God

Psalm 93

The Lord is high above all contradiction,
roaring floods majestic in his ears,
which hear all discords sweet polyphony,
the transposition secret in his will
which rolls a carpet all around the cosmos,
brushes stretti, minor keys, fermatas
into some black hole of providence.

Siubhal (Variation) 3: Rage

Psalm 94

Cum oan, ma Goad ableeze wi wrath,
wha kens the hairt's ill-cleckit airts,   *misbegotten*
jist gie the prood yins thair awmous,   *come-uppance*
ding thaim doon tae chow the stour.   *throw   chew the dust*

They scance yir fowk, they kink thir gams,   *scorn   sneer*
they thraw, jalousin Goad is blin;   *quibble   reckoning*
thiv goat it cumin tae thaim, an
A'll souch them oan thir wey tae hell.   *drive with a song*

O Lord, A'm gratefu fir this saum
at gies me wurds tae lowse ma birse,   *anger*
ma grue at aa thit pizzens yirth,   *horror poisons earth*
an bung it ower tae Goad in heiven.   *hurl*

Taorluath Singling: Over the Hump

Psalms 95 – 97

The century has climbed her mountain,
taken off her jacket, wiped her brow;
upon her face a smile is breaking open
years of stale skin, thirsty for the pinks
and wrinkles of some deep clean freedom.

She makes a curtsey, steps aside
to watch a shadow stay upon the hags
of wet fuel never dry enough to burn
the dark clothes, or the darker habits.
'We do not need these now,' she thinks.

'We can no longer sing a warrior king,
we cannot even serve a shepherd king;
our David died; I will not resurrect him.
Seek a different voice, a new belief
for softened hearts and softer skin.'

But sing we will, somehow befriending
these strange temples, this new world,
riding pillion with a God far bigger
than the one we used to know, and
glimpsing snatches of God's beauty.

Taorluath Doubling: Downhill

Psalms 98 – 100

The century has spoken, pointed out
the coils of wave power waiting, poised
to drive the turbines of a new theology,
or maybe very old belief transformed,
a dynamo to power new-born religion.

Give us kingship energy renewed,
a monarch running rife within our veins,
who blooded, wears our joys and tragedies,
a lord who sings our songs, and woos us
into writing verses lighting up our nation.

She does a chassis, moves into a quickstep,
catches snatches of the heather song
awakening to summer and its colours.
'Take it away, Satchmo,' she cries, gung-ho,
a raid on memory, to comb the silt

for bits and bobs of melody, deciding
that the soil and seas, the air and trees
are sanctified and safe, their whisper
telling us the peat can stay and hold
its share of carbon without guilt.

'If I were on skis,' she said, astride
of Suilven, 'I'd be away, downhill,
skimming scree and stretching time
for you to see things differently. I would
awaken Moses, shake him, get right through

to God: howl, groan, gasp, spit
your prayers, real and raw as juniper.
I'd breathe on Samuel, make him once again
a child, living in the Scottish temple
garden for you, hearing something new.'

We won't see the likes of her again;
she leaves us no repeats, no playback mode,
only the fragment of a tune we heard before
and lost in jags that pricked us into tears.
We'll take each note and nurse it into song;

we'll take the jigsaw of her faith, and let
the Spirit add a third and fourth dimension
so our praise turns gold instead of grey,
and every day we finger all the grace notes,
playing world things right instead of wrong.

Taorluath Breabach: Free Kick

Psalm 101

Play the ball and not the man,
no first team pride of face or foot,
kick out sin and not the sinner,
take care which is which:
but if and when you can't detach them
keep the weak on side, and boot
the worthless out of leadership
and into God's firm touch.

Urlar (Ground 2): Back in the Dust

Psalm 102

Aye, stour yet clags ma thochts, ma doots,	*dust*
A cannae lilt, ma thrapple's smoored	*sing throat's choked*
wi aa the aise o mony years,	*remnants, refuse*
a lang, lang shedda maks ma days	*shadow*
an nichts sae dowf an tuim an wae.	*sad empty wretched*
The Lord is sett me oot o sicht.	

A mane an grane, A fin ma banes	*moan groan*
ir steikit wi a stoun, ma hairt	*pierced ache, blow*
is gowpin, A kin hear the soun	*palpitating*
o fients. 'Dear Goad, be mercifu	*fiends*
tae me, preen back yir lugs an tent	*take notice of*
yir stickit, seik, disjaskit frien.'	*shut out sick downcast*

Crunluath Singling: Zip up your Jacket

Psalm 103

Cool down the cauldron of sin-stewed indictment,
throw in some ice from the poles of God's patience;
pull down the shutters on drunken paralysis,
habits and havers of all such abusiveness;
fall down and worship the Lord who is summoning
islanders, mainlanders, all.

Zip up your jacket that flaps in the slipstream
of blame from the engines of fateful theology;
rip up the packet of sugary half truths that
foul up the bloodstream of Proddy and Pape;
wrap up your ticket for high celebration,
and lodge it in God's banquet hall.

Crunluath Doubling: Stir up the Breeze

Psalm 104

Fly down the alleys of blazars, go deep into
space, with its galaxies, days when the quasars will
lay down a challenge to poets and physicists,
hinting, cajoling our science and art for a
hoedown, a ceilidh, a throwdown, a showdown
to highlight the tartan of God, warp and weft.

Range over centuries, study the plant patterns,
think culture harvest, pick every ripe fruit, don't
whinge over credits to Druid or Christian; there's
room in God's temple, there's heart-food and brain-food, so
change over templates to weaving and wondering,
gather and grow with the Spirit's windfall.

Stir up the breeze in the branches of birches which
dance to the music of warbler and chaffinch, and
cheer up the glens, shelter cowberry, blaeberry,
perch by the burns as they sing liquid notes, run to
tear up the script that rolls solemn from sceptics
who notice life's magic – yet who can they thank?

Tip inhibitions that limit your grasp
of life's options, its chances, its challenges overboard.
Stop overworking your left brain, and roll
to the rock of your right, its superior clock; don't let
sleep overtake your desire to sing praise, to bring
psalms to the Lord, all the days that you live.

Crunluath a Mach: Exegete your Story

Psalm 105

Dig up all your history with stainless steel and expertise:
Graft it onto patriarchs, get a feel for exodus,
know your plagues are not the first ones, nor the last to set you back;
you may have Pharaoh's DNA, but Amram's children count for more
than meets the closing Western eye, so tired of bad religion.
Exegete the memories concealed in those laments.

Deconstruct your doublings, let the notes out of your throat;
like bodies on that awful shore, dress them with respect,
and kneel before your Maker as you bury in the ground
all the pain that stung your parents, all the hurt they left to you.
Think of Jacob, think of Joseph, think of Judah and his tribe,
and claim your resurrection from the endless spinning wheel.

Trust that things in hiding will reveal themselves, so build on
all your past with quiet confidence, like Moses in the wilderness
experience the cloud by day, the fire by night; the spark-filled
darker mystery tugs at our hearts and feet, a guardian angel
opens temple doors in earthy places, conjures up new threads
for the sett of holy tartan God still reels off secret looms.

Urlar (Ground 3): A Dusty Hallelujah

Psalm 106

Our kilts are musty now, we live
somewhere between lament and praise;
we read the riots that our fathers made
like Moses' gang en route to Canaan,
nodding God-squad for a languid minute,
hell-bent on themselves the next.

We have one sovereign now. No longer
Moses, David, or Saint Augustine;
not Fingal, Colum or the Bruce,
not Luther, Calvin and his crowd,
though all had leadership to give.
The Lord, the holy one, is king.

It's all transition now. The road
is different from a hundred years ago,
but pipers, poets, preachers even
share their stories, make their music,
learn to play their human nature,
sing a dusty hallelujah.

Notes on Book 4 Poems

Pibroch is the English spelling of the Gaelic *piobaireachd*. Whereas *urlar* and *siubhal* are translated as 'ground' and 'variation', *breabach* is associated with 'kicking', the derivation of *taorluath* is less clear, and of *crunluath* disputed, though often linked with 'crown'.

This long poem has no connection with the 'Lament for the Iolaire', a modern pibroch written by Donald MacLeod.

Chapter Five

Protest and Praise

For we ha'e faith in Scotland's hidden poo'ers,
The present's theirs, but a' the past and future's oors
(MacDiarmid)[1]

Part 1 WHAT POETS DO

1 The Book So Far

2 The Poet as Prophet: Frailty and Risk

3 From Protest to Possibility

Part 2 TARTAN AND TARTANRY

4 Complexity and Cliché

5 Dressing a Nation: Robert Burns, George MacDonald, Hugh MacDiarmid, Three 21st Century Makars

6 Scotland's Underwear: The Caledonian Antisyzygy

7 The Poet as Rebel: Four Psalms

Part 3 WEAVING IT ALL TOGETHER

8 A Tapestry of Synthesis: Tartan, Temple

9 A Tapestry of Psalms: The Name, Fresh Start, Learning to Live, Coping with the Unexpected, The Gist

10 A Tapestry of Scotland: Lines, Tribes, Capital, Leaders

11 A Tapestry of Praise

Part 1 WHAT POETS DO

1 The Book So Far

Chapter One flew the idea of a magic carpet, using woven fabric to travel time and space, anywhere in the temple of the universe. It introduced the Psalms as the poetry of one unusual people, whose religion gave the nations of Europe and America an identity which has only been departed from in recent times, and paradoxically has become part of the culture of many Africans and South Americans today.[2] While recovery of the Black heritage is a strong and justified theme today, some commentators seem unaware of the strength of the Black churches (found in Edinburgh as well as London) and their reliance on Old Testament tropes. With the 'Carpet' poems, the poet was an **enquirer**.

Chapter Two mentioned poets who remembered the history of Scotland, and became **curators**, inevitably with an axe to grind, whether sharpened for battle or polished for a ceilidh. MacDiarmid did so in his own way, and usually in broad terms, as in the quotation above. Ballads are more specific. They tell a story, typically celebrating a way of life, past and present. What they have in common with protest songs is a sense of identity – this is who we are, affirming *that* over against things that contradict it. The protest song (or poem) then identifies the contradiction in present circumstances, and attacks it, perhaps directly, or obliquely – 'in a parable', as Psalm 78 puts it:

> I will open my mouth in a parable;
> I will utter dark sayings from of old,
> things that we have heard and known,
> that our ancestors have told us. (Psalm 78:2-3)

After the 'Journey' poem sequence, Chapter Three continued to focus on identity, and how this is both threatened and re-formed by migration. It illustrated how the Old Testament story, and the Psalms which arose out of it, influenced the political journey of Scotland as well as the faith of individuals; it contained some reflections on tribes and tribalism. The poems which followed, based on Book 3 of the Psalms, celebrate the suffering and courage of migrants yesterday and today. Here the poet gets closer to being a **prophet**, albeit also a curator of the current events which become history.

Chapter Four, mainly about music and how it relates to poetry, explored the meaning of 'transcendence' and the importance of the arts in general, and for those who didn't skip to the next chapter, outlined how music functions in worship, with some sketches from the time of Israel onwards. This led on to the particular long poem about the tragedy of the *Iolaire*, a poem which also explores how the calvinist heritage of the Highlands and Islands might be reshaped for the present day. Here the poet is a prophetic ***singer***.

Now comes a fifth chapter, which looks at the poet as prophet of protest and as leader of celebration, in a Scotland whose life is compared to tartan, which is a kind of tapestry, with its lines and stitches, a Scotland which Alan Riach describes as a 'performance culture' in his recent book.[3] This part of the chapter looks at the 'dressing' of Scotland, and how poets address the clashes and contradictions of tartan. The third part then changes to see tartan as a whole, and celebrates the weave, before the final Book 5 poetry, which is called 'Tapestry'.

It's hard to choose one word for the work of the poet in Chapter Five – it could be dresser, it could again be prophet, but ***celebrant*** might be the best. There are of course other words, like craftsman, or magician, but those five words, those five threads – enquirer, curator, prophet, singer and celebrant – engage the contemporary writer with poets down through the ages.

Long poems, or sets of poems, like many rituals often have a centrepiece with an introduction and a conclusion. One formal piece of tapestry, the sampler, has a centre with signatures and other work surrounding it. The centrepiece to Book 5 of the Psalms is the long Psalm 119, plus the fifteen Psalms of Ascent which follow, and the structure of Book 5 poetry acknowledges this, with *119 Fair and Square* focused on tapestry, followed by the 'Song of the Fifteen Steps'.

You could skip now and read Book 5 poetry, but to get to the nub of the book you should read on (or come back to it later).

2 More on the Poet as Prophet

Protest is a reaction to injustice. What sharpens it into prophecy is setting it in that wider context of proper identity, with a move from 'I say that is wrong' to 'God says that is wrong'. The secular prophet simply says 'that is wrong', but the derivation of modern Western humanism from Christian belief (rather than as some argue from Greek thought)[4] means that there is usually a commonality – so that figures like Keir Hardie and Hugh MacDiarmid, different as they were in belief, had prophetic stature.

Some words, according to Leavitt, are so powerful 'they are attributed to superhuman agency and called prophecy', some are so beautiful and moving 'they are attributed to a special gift of the speaker and called poetry'.[5] Henri Brémond put it this way: 'The poetic gift corresponds in the natural order to what the prophetic gift stand for in the supernatural.'[6]

Frailty and Risk

The task of the poet as prophet is to bring to the table an alternative perception of reality. But this is very demanding. Poets are frail, as Fearghas MacFhionnlaigh admits:

> I would like to be like Moses,
> inscribing the words of God;
> but a stone tablet would break my plastic pen.[7]
> Not only that, but prophecy deals with risk:
> There is only the choice between fire and ice.
> Our own planet is delicately poised between fire and ice.
> Scotland, there is nothing for you but fire or ice.
> Freedom is fire. Bondage is ice.

Leaders behind their public image are frail, and try to avoid risk. When Michael Symmons Roberts portrays the psalmist king, David, as 'an old man with lungs like empty glasses', with 'the detritus of another Christmas' around him,[8] there is a prophetic edge to that portrait of a leader which the Psalms themselves acknowledge as they bid farewell to the line of David. As Hayim Bialik wrote, referencing Psalm 137:

> And from then till now there's no king in Yeshurun,
> no king – no harp and no music.
> My lyre is the sound of weeping, my harp like a dove
> sighs on the riverbeds of Babylon.[9]

In Babylon, 'Our flags have gone / from mast and heart / and no one knows / the past . . .' (*Poem 74 'Identity Theft'*). A flag is one particular marker of identity, as when the Union Jack and the Saltire compete for the political narrative of Scotland today. Tartan is another, which in the 18th century held a similar resonance to the Saltire today, and was in fact proscribed for a period after the failure of the 1745 Jacobite rebellion. Today tartan is a more subtle statement of identity – sometimes no more than a dress fashion – but in this book, the crossing stripes of woven tartan have been used as a metaphor for the different aspects of our identity, and even the interplay of human and divine.

3 From Protest to Possibility

In *The Prophetic Imagination* Walter Brueggemann says two things about the prophet which relate poetry to national identity, and relate imagination to the practical task. The prophet has to[10]

(a) 'Bring to public expression those very hopes and yearnings that have been denied so long and suppressed so deeply that we no longer know they are there.'

(b) 'Offer an alternative perception of reality, and let people see their own history in the light of God's freedom and his will for justice.'

These tasks mean remembering what is in danger of being lost, helping people see the present in a different way, bringing together the new (the alternative) and the old (the forgotten), both of which are celebrated in the poetry of the Psalms, and challenge the art of the contemporary poet.

In *Phaedrus*, Socrates distinguishes 'telestic madness' (about the past), 'mantic madness' (about the future) and 'poetic madness' (about past and future). This past and future is not only the future of nations and the planet, though prophets are concerned with that, it is also the future of persons and local communities. The great poets, as they remember apparently ordinary things, present their work in a way which brings hope to people. Take Seamus Heaney's poem 'Digging'. All except two lines appears simply to be a loving and lovely memory of his father in the garden, and of course that might vaguely encourage a gardener today. It is the opening two lines, where his pen rests like a gun on his trigger finger, that jerk other writers into the present and the future, and jump start their motivation.

Sometimes a poet like MacDiarmid seems all about protest, or even lament. But take one of his most famous (and short!) poems, 'The Bonnie Broukit Bairn', which starts by comparing the modesty and sorrow of planet earth to the romance of Mars and Venus: it ends, '– But greet, an' in your tears ye'll droun / The haill clanjamfrie!'[11] This shocks us into thinking how sad and down at heel folk today might prove at least the equals of the 'high heid yins' of our age.

There are wider tribal issues which challenge Islam, Judaism and Christianity, as signalled in the *Poem on Psalm 122*, which suggests that their thrones 'now lie buried with the bones / of ancient history.' The thrones, whether the Caliphate, Jerusalem, Rome or Geneva – let alone Holyrood and Westminster – can become an idol. So 'pray for the peace of Jerusalem', and 'every step to build shalom / that lives the meaning of this psalm.'

Psalms and contemporary poetry speak to individuals, tribes and nations, indeed to the planet. In this, the use of the term 'prophetic' can be claimed by believers and non-believers. Modern poetry has generally agreed with Hugh MacDiarmid: 'The transcendental is inherent in us without reference to any religious belief – it comes out of the seed of things . . . it's part of the materialism.'[12] The response of one who reads the Psalms is equally forthright: the heavens ('material' in MacDiarmid's sense) are telling the glory of God,[13] and the psalmist expresses that in poetry. The transcendent may be a secular term for God, but the Psalms earth the transcendent in the wisdom of Israel,[14] which as we saw in Chapter Two, MacDiarmid himself did not hesitate to refer to when it suited him.

Part 2 TARTAN AND TARTANRY

4 Complexity and Cliché

In the weaving of tartan, pre-dyed yarn threads parallel to the long edge are warps, the other wefts. The number and pattern of yarns of each colour is known as the sett, which is repeated as often as required (across the loom) until the warp is complete, then that same sequence is woven at right angles to form the weft and the finished tartan.

Tartan is wool woven as a twill with a check design, but in multiple colours. The word 'tartan' comes from the French *tiretaine* (used for cider made from apples and pears), and the word was in use in Scotland at least as early as 1500.[15] Associated Gaelic words are *breacan*, a plaid wrapped round the body, and *tarsainn* meaning something criss-crossed. An early example was the 'Falkirk Tartan', discovered in 1934 with a hoard of excavated silver coins, dated to the third CE; the scrap of cloth was used as a stopper for the jar containing the coins.

> The intersections and spaces between warp and weft provide a textile template for the collisions, coincidences and ruptures that punctuate the development of any society, so that the merest fragment of cloth contains within its fibres 'the crystal of the total event'.[16] If that is more literary imagination than history, a more modest metaphor comes from the Edinburgh Royal Mile Tartan Weaving Mill, which describes weaving as 'one warp yarn up, the next down – the weft goes through the shed, the space between'.
>
> In the loom, that space is controlled, adjusted and occupied in a mechanical way. In Scottish history, that space between Highlands and Lowlands, between romance and reality, between past and present, is shared by historians, poets, musicians and all who see culture as more than the pixels of a photograph taken at random. It is the job of the poet, said MacDiarmid, to communicate the complexity of the world.[17]

Hugh MacDiarmid's autobiography *Lucky Poet* (1943), says that as boys he and his brother wore the Graham tartan (his mother's). His mother's folk were farm workers, his father's mill workers, and he was always on the side of the industrial workers. But in general MacDiarmid brings together multiple identities into a rightful claim to tartan, linking Lowlands and Highlands[18] – for 'tartan is now a bridge to a mythic identity'.[19]

In the film *Braveheart*, Wallace cuts a strip of tartan from his kilt to give to his wife, and it both represents and betrays their relationship. The strip of tartan cloth is polysemic, a token of love and an index of who Wallace is – and it ties his personal narrative of love and revenge to the national narrative of change and resistance. The film did not 'dig up all [our] history with stainless steel and expertise'; star and director Mel Gibson himself notes that the film is a 'historical fantasy' and should not be taken as the accurate portrayal of Wallace's life. But the film did 'graft it onto patriarchs', 'open temple doors in earthy places', and conjure up 'new threads / for the sett of holy tartan God still reels off secret looms.'[20] Book 4 Poetry is geared to psalms like 105, which gives its own select version of Israel's history, but refines the iron of the past into the steel of a stainless exodus, so that worshippers are encouraged to collect these new threads and weave them into a song of hope for the future.

In 1981 Tom Nairn attacked the kitsch 'tartan monster' of tartanry.[21] Craig Beveridge and Ronald Turnbull then pointed out in 1989 that most critiques of tartanry were assuming an 'inferiorist myth', and that tartan was a much more complex image.[22] Twenty years later, Jonathan Faiers still accepted the view of the English historian Hugh Trevor-Roper that tartan had become a kind of cliché, 'Brigadoon, the fantasy of a fully tartanised society and magical landscape.'[23] But Ian Brown disagrees. For all that making tartan is mechanical, he claims

the essence of tartan – and tartanry – is an absence of certainty. The very design of tartan embodies constant dynamic tension between the clarity, even rigidity, of its grid and the literally endless potential for colour and variety contained within, and visually threatening to break, the lock of that grid. Its impact visually has been compared to that of a flower garden.[24]

The Psalms oscillate between the certainty of wisdom psalms like 1, and the uncertainty of lament psalms like 38, often within the same psalm – as Psalm 22, which begins with a groan and ends with a cheer. Wearing a particular tartan has been a sign of identity,[25] and with loss of identity comes uncertainty. But in the modern period there has been a dissolution of boundaries between different types of dress, as with Japanese and African checks.[26] Humsa Yousef was sworn in as a Holyrood MSP wearing a blend of tartan and Asian styles. And when a new tartan was created in 2019 to commemorate the 15 men who died constructing the

Cruachan power station, that grave connection cemented the seriousness of tartan as an image.[27]

Brown spoke of the importance of the 'grid' in tartan, and that framework is found in Psalm 22.[28] The repeated *rāḥaq* (distant) in vv. 1, 11, 19 signals the absence of God along two axes – the vertical axis of transcendence and the horizontal axis of lived experience. This is how Book 3 poetry has described the experience of migrants, and specifically of both Jews and Highlanders, as 'beyond the bounds of human life, / beyond the throat of any word' (from *83 'Beyond'*).

Like tartan, the Psalms have survived translation into different cultures and different times. They have kept the 'contradictions' analogous to the different directions of yarn in a tartan, but offered some kind of identity, expressed in *22 'Worm Weary'*:

A talking, swearing, crying worm
one minute, and the next a sperm
of hope, yearning for a womb
to offer God some living room,
a womb to tend my worst afflictions,
tomb to end my contradictions.

5 Dressing a Nation

Tartan is a form of dress, and a traditional task of the bard was *dressing* the occasion. Yet tartan has been also a symbol of protest, and poets – whether as outright or closet rebels – have famously been the spiritual engineers of rebellion, when dialogue had failed. Before tartan could be associated with protest, it had to be part of a culture – as poets are part of a culture, whether their poems celebrate it or critique it. Sometimes they have an official role, like the ancient bards or the modern Poet Laureate, sometimes they may be underground, as with the *samidzat* literature of Eastern Europe.

In 1746, following the Battle of Culloden, the wearing of tartan was proscribed by law, with severe penalties, in an attempt to follow the military conquest of rebellion with an act of cultural repression. The Act was repealed in 1782, but it was a time of dearth in the Highlands, and it was not until Walter Scott's stage management of the royal visit of George IV in 1822[29] that tartan became fashionable in all parts of Scotland (although until the second half of the 20th century it was still largely limited to the military and to better off families).[30] Now even the Kirk has a tartan.

How do poets dress a nation, and how in particular have writers dressed Scotland? National costume is often worn only by a minority, and Scotland today is even more of a hybrid nation, so any clear and concise answer from contemporary writers will likely be a contested view. Here is a very brief survey of some key figures representing the four centuries since Scotland lost her independence in 1707, related to the interests of this book. It is selective – no one represents Gaelic culture, for example.

Robert Burns, 1759 – 1797

John MacQuarrie described Burns as a 'Poet, Prophet and Philosopher' and said that he fulfilled the task of any such, which is 'to see and to sing'.[31] His mastery of Ayrshire Scots, his accessible poetic forms, and his human sympathies have made him still regarded by many as Scotland's national bard. If we only had poems like 'Caledonia' we might label him simply a romantic poet and patriot who could also write a 'Lament of Mary Queen of Scots, on the Approach of Spring', but the skill and steel of 'A Man's a Man' and 'Bruce to his Men at Bannockburn' show him to be more than that.

Although Burns had both Jacobite and Covenanter blood, politically he supported the Union – Burns worked as an exciseman at one point; but at the same time he was sympathetic to the French revolutionary cause and criticised the 'parcel of rogues in a nation' who led to Scots being 'bought and sold for English gold' in 1707.[32] He illustrates the way a 'lad o' pairts' from a humble background could find opportunities to mix with all classes, and how 18th century Scotland was a central part of Europe.[33]

Burns was no great churchman, but shared the common faith of Scots at that time, was friendly with the liberal Principal Robertson, and wrote several poems criticising the hard line theology and hypocrisy of some high calvinists. He also wrote a 'Paraphrase of the First Psalm', and 'The Cotter's Saturday Night' which endorsed mainstream Christian belief. At the same time he could write some 'Stanzas of Psalmody' as a parody of the day of public thanksgivings for the recovery of the king on 23rd April 1789. Like other good writers, he used verse for a number of different ends.

George MacDonald, 1824 – 1905

MacDonald is principally remembered for his stories for children and adults, but in *The Princess and the Goblin*, the hero Curdie says 'there was nothing to do but forge new rhymes, now his only weapons'.[34] While his father advised him to 'give over the fruitless game of poetry', and C.S. Lewis regarded him as a creative thinker rather than a great writer,[35] his poems and his stories are deliberately apolitical, crafted to present what he thinks is true through a mixture of fantasy, good theology and common sense. Prose and poetry alike he saw as peaceful weapons for righteousness.

So why choose such a writer as 'dresser' for a nation? Two reasons. First, by the 19th century, the political union of Scotland and England was generally unquestioned; 'issues' concerned health, education, church, poverty, foreign policy, and the welfare of the soul. William Wallace was a hero, but as a patriot, not as a nationalist.[36] There were plenty of attacks on the social and personal evils of the time from writers other than the 'Kailyard School', for example in the Gaelic poetry of William Livingstone on the Clearances, but nationalism as such did not become a serious concern till the 20th century.

Second, the fame of 19th century Scottish culture was found more in the philosophy of J.F. Ferrier, the science of James Clerk Maxwell, the art of Henry Raeburn and George Henry, the town planning of Patrick Geddes, and the writing of Walter Scott (whose Waverley novels were all focused on the past, and whose protests were limited to the saving of Scottish bank notes, or to saying that 'we could aye peeble them wi stanes'[37] back in the time when Scotland had its own Parliament). The English romantic poets, and continental musicians like Frederic Chopin, were prominent. While Scotland had its own education, law and religion, in many other respects 19th century Scotland was coterminous with the British state.

What George MacDonald *does* show us, therefore, is not the earlier tartan of Jacobite nationalism, nor the later tartans of Kailyard patriotism or MacDiarmid's socialist realism, but the common dress of a Christian outlook, which C.S. Lewis would claim led him towards what he called 'Basic Christianity'. That common dress might be eirenic, but it carried its own sharp weapons, pointed (often in the guise of fantasy) at the individual rather than at society. In his long poem 'A Hidden Life', a youth reads old tales of Scotland's warriors, but the poem is not about Scotland; a good death, with the last psalm lingering in the heart, is the climax. His father loved to hear 'the new streams pouring from his son's clear well', but these are for the believer, not for the nation. The wider world ('London' in the poem) will be influenced by each of us doing the best we can in our own little world. The Scots tongue only features in a farewell song found among his papers after the writer had died.

Hugh MacDiarmid, 1892-1978

Christopher Murray Grieve said that he adopted a pen-name to symbolise two very different things:[38] Celtic connections (although at the time he was writing in English), and 'getting rid of Christopher' (which means 'Christ-bearer') – although Christian and biblical imagery continued to pervade his writing. A reviewer of his first book, *Sangschaw*, said that MacDiarmid reflected the authentic Scotland, and his fellow-poet Edwin Muir told American readers that MacDiarmid was starting a 'Scottish Renaissance'.[39]

In Chapter Three we saw that MacDiarmid was trying to remake history, to go back before 1707 in order to remake Scotland in his own day. To this end he put the Scots language at the service of his contemporary nationalism, even though in 1970 he would write in a letter that the process of anglicisation had gone so far that there might be 'only a hundred of us left'.[40]

MacDiarmid's best known work is 'A Drunk Man Looks at the Thistle', and in it he puts together two layers of a critique which were often separated, the thistle being a symbol both of Scotland and of human misery (and more of course). But he achieves the same end in other poems with his use of Scots, so that, for example, in 'The Bonnie Broukit Bairn' Mars and Venus and even the auld mune may be well dressed, but planet Earth is the beautiful but tear-stained place, with a humanism that has a Scottish dimension – and of course MacDiarmid knew well where humanism came from: 'We're ootward boond frae Scotland . . . But the first mate is a Jew'.[41] This made MacDiarmid for me a natural partner in thinking about the Psalms and Scotland.

'Dress' has a second meaning, 'to get yourself in right order' on the parade ground. Grieve served in Greece as a sergeant in the First War, after getting himself into some kind of socialist order through contacts with Keir Hardie and Jimmy Maxton, but he still lacked a suitable form in his writing, according to Alan Bold. His period abroad did, however, allow him to order his political and poetic ideas in a way that would bear fruit later, and allow him to dress Scotland not in the patriotic tartan dear to Walter Scott and the Scottish regiments of his day, but in a national garb which embraced the rocks of 'On a Raised Beach' as well as '. . . the little white rose of Scotland / That smells sharp and sweet – and breaks the heart'.

Three 21ˢᵗ Century Makars

1 EDWIN MORGAN, 1920 – 2010. Morgan was named the first Scots Makar in 2004. While a champion of avant-garde forms, and science fiction, Morgan was influenced by Hopkins as a teenager and retained an interest in 'the last things' – but he also wrote, 'Great Lucretian deep . . . cradle my revolt' and owned six copies of Lucretius' works (Lucretius was broadly an atheist). His *Trilogy of Plays on the Life of Jesus* was looking at the mysteries of space and time as much as the character of Jesus. One of his characters said, 'My job is to rattle the bars', and his response to Ezra Pound's old cry, 'Make it new!' was 'Push the boat out, campañeros!'

Morgan is more interested in the epic stories of humankind than in any narrow nationalism, and his own epic journey poem, 'The Cape of Good Hope' references our common human chains, and the music and literature of Europe, not Scotland's story. While 'On John MacLean' begins with MacLean saying, 'I am not prepared to let Moscow dictate to Glasgow', and later 'letting them know that Scotland was not Britain', it is MacLean's desire for life that brings the poem to its climax. His poem 'Post-Referendum' (the earlier one) is ambiguous – he has a voice say this:

I tell you you must leave your land alone.
... Come on, / you're pegged out on your heathery futon,
take the matches from your lids, it's ended.[42]

Does he simply mean, be realistic about the result? Or that a Scottish Parliament, let alone independence, is just a pipe-dream? Or is the voice itself a seduction from the on-going project?

2   LIZ LOCHHEAD, born 1947, followed Morgan as national Makar. She was a female poet of the people, very unlike MacDiarmid who thought of himself as a poet of the intellectuals. Her sense of, and sympathy with Scottish popular culture is well shown in 'the night I / almost became Miss Scotland'.[43] She wrote a tribute to her predecessor, in a 1990 poem about Berlin and its broken wall, asking who could make sense of it? Eddie Morgan could, which made her want to try.

In 'The Unknown Citizen' she describes the ambiguity of national symbols. In poems like 'Warpaint and Womanflesh' she unpacks the suffering and strength of women. In 'After the War', Scotland is still part of Britain. Her respect for Carol Ann Duffy would evoke 'The Beekeeper', and for Jackie Kay 'Black and White Allsorts'. She reminds us of our common humanity.

Late 20th and 21st century poets generally dress their poems with common issues like sexuality, justice, feminism and poverty. MacDiarmid's outright nationalism is more likely today to be found among Gaelic poets like Fearghas McFhionnlaigh, whose poem in English and Gaelic, *The Midge* was based openly on the image of a fly struggling for its freedom in a spider's web.

3 JACKIE KAY, born 1961, was Makar 2016-21. Adopted child, woman of colour, now resident in England, she represented the international side of Scotland in the post-Brexit world. Her poem 'Threshold', written for the opening of the 2016 Scottish Parliament, referenced past poetry of Russia as well as Scotland, paid respect to Donald Dewar and the wide variety of people and places in Scotland, gave a polite nod to the Queen, but climaxed with a welcome to the world in over 30 languages and dialects.

Like not a few Scots, she had a grandfather who carried shrapnel from the Somme, and represents the body of Scottish people who are ready to move on, whether to independence or some other new constitutional arrangement, without trashing their neighbours or their past shared history. Her latest book, *Bantam*, cites Nan Shepherd, 'It's a grand thing to get leave to live.'[44]

6 Scotland's Underwear

Beneath the bright colours of political clothing, Scotland since the Reformation has on the whole been conservative, and many would credit or blame the national Church for that.

Karl Barth pointed out that people within the church 'who make political comments or declarations' always speak as individuals, since the corporate voice of the church will likely be conservative.[45] The latter follows the ethos of the book of Psalms, which is pastoral, the former the ethos of the OT prophets – while they may hold the same doctrine, the context and application are different.

That corporate voice has in fact been conservative ever since the radical changes of the Reformation era, up to the decision to have a Scottish Assembly (now called a Parliament). Protest at the 1707 Union of Parliaments was unsuccessful. The Jacobites never achieved power. The Highland and Lowland Clearances caused pain but not rebellion.[46] Protest – as in 'the Radical War' of 1820 – was punished severely.[47] The Clydeside Reds had no chance of successful revolution.[48] The modern commitment to democracy, and the traditional Scottish respect for authority, has kept change peaceful – and the official voice of the Church of Scotland has stayed within conservative parameters – for example, the General Assembly has never been pacifist, and when it called for a Scottish Parliament it was always 'within the UK'.

> Reform movements typically address the corruption or failure of authority.[49] *Poem 20, 'Royal Rule'*, cites a couplet from a 14th century English priest, and throws a number of ideas at Psalm 20, which is attributed to David and ends more or less with the words which start the British national anthem.[50] But, 'this psalm has lines which fling / a spanner into everything', even if it does not support 'pure democracy'; the closet rebellion is in vv. 7-8; and since the Psalms as 'word-tools' span the generations, while the original editors may have been quietist,

a Qumran community could interpret them a different way,[51] as could Scots from Medieval through to Covenanting times.

In fact the Psalms (like the Bible generally) have built in spanners waiting to be picked up by theological and political engineers.

This certainly happened at the Reformation. Calvin, who influenced Scotland, wrote, 'For although I follow David at a great distance, and come far short of equalling him . . . I have no hesitation in comparing myself with him.'[52] Not only was psalm singing 'one of the incontestably distinguishing marks of Calvinist culture in Europe and America in the sixteenth and seventeenth centuries,'[53] but 'Calvinists were convinced they could legitimately appropriate the psalms to themselves . . . the psalms were *their* songs which they sang as the elect people of God in a covenant relationship with Him'.[54]

By comparing himself with David, Calvin subverted the institution of monarchy in much the same way as the New Testament,[55] though the Old Testament had its own way of doing the same thing.[56] So Psalm 110, in which 'the Lord will shatter kings on the day of his wrath', could be sung at the coronation of James VI;[57] so James Renwick on the scaffold in 1688 could accuse the current king of being a usurper, as 'Scotland should be ruled by its Kirk' – Renwick quoted from Psalm 103, 'The Lord has prepared his throne in the heavens; and his kingdom ruleth over all'.[58]

But that is all in the past. Since then, protest indeed, but no more than that. The early reception history of Psalm 2 is relevant: in the Septuagint verse 6 is reported speech, so instead of God addressing the king, the king is addressing rebel rulers – more monarchical, less messianic. However, one of the Qumran communities understood verses 1 and 2 (4QFlor I lines 18-19) to the effect that the whole community inherit the promises to David; 'his anointed one' is in the plural so they together form a messianic community.[59] This way of thinking would be picked up later by groups mentioned like the 17th century Levellers, the 20th century Red Clydesiders,[60] or as early as the late 14th century Peasants' Revolt in England.[61] But, Reformation apart, they stayed small minorities. The closest Scotland ever came to rebellion was with the Jacobites in 1715 and 1745.

The Caledonian Antisyzygy

Tartan is both an illustration and a symbol of two opposite directions, which is the main meaning of 'antisyzygy'. Gregory Smith in *Scottish Literature: Character and Influence* (1919) invented the term 'Caledonian Antisyzygy', but Hugh MacDiarmid applied it to current European thinking, and said that it was 'the great characteristic of Scottish literature.'[62] It has been a way of isolating a kind of antinomy thought to be peculiar to Scotland, that yoking of opposites

> delightedly accepted by MacDiarmid as both a true diagnosis of a basic element in Scottish character and literature and a clue to his own work. If we seek for Mac-Diarmid's concern for the divine, it will often be found in his counterpointing of the coorse and the cosmic.[63]

This elaborate phrase has become so much of our landscape of thought that Lesley Duncan could use it to counterpoint demotic Edinburgh with intellectual Glasgow, in a poem contrasting an Edinburgh street piper playing 'Flower of Scotland' with a Glasgow busker from France playing Eric Satie's 'Gymnopedie' on a flute.[64] But it was MacDiarmid who ran with the idea. In 'A Drunk Man look at the Thistle', high national aspirations are yoked to 'a mere weed',[65] as in:

> . . .The thistle rises and forever will,
> Getherin' the generations under't.
> This is the monument o' a' they were,
> And a' they hoped and wondered.   (lines 2231-5)

However, in the poem the thistle is a gravestone as well as a symbol of hope, and the poem like its title careers from one side of the road to the other. The Old Testament speaks of the two ways, picked up in the references to 'the good inclination' and 'the evil inclination' in *Poem 12 'Watch God's Lips'*. Things were less simple for MacDiarmid. He loved both sides of antinomy, even if to others it was plain contradiction – he was expelled from the Communist Party for being a Nationalist, and vice versa!

> Mony ha'e tried, but a' ha'e failed.
> Their sacrifice has nocht availed.
> Upon the thistle they're impaled.   (lines 2641-3)

> You maun choose but gin ye'd see
> Anither category ye
> Maun tine your nationality.   (lines 2644-6)

In other words, there is no escape from the antisyzygy. It belongs to the 'great wheel' of fate, although MacDiarmid is able to add:

> And blessin' on the weary wheel
> Whaurever it may land them! (lines 2653-4)

While MacDiarmid spoke of the 'routh / O' contrairies that jostle in their dumfoondrin' growth' (lines 1111-2), the Psalms are not all as simple as that first psalm; they allow extremes to nestle together even within the same psalm, protecting paradox as a necessary fact of life, as in Psalm 23, and the opening of *23 'Shepherd Sonnet'*:

> Contradictions, with a sudden dark
> to overtake our cosiness, our rosy
> hopes. The unexpected snakes devour
> these flimsy ladders that we pick and park
> for quick ascents to happiness . . .

The extremes may not always clash. Jonathan Faiers describes how in a kilt

> The optical recession and dominance of certain colours results in a visual ambiguity that can produce an oscillation between what the viewer registers as under-check or over-check of a particular tartan.[66]

Like a kilt presenting different tones and patterns, the extremes may give us complementary views of God and of humanity, as when the poet Louis MacNeice wrote: 'We jump from picture to picture, and cannot follow / the living curve that is breathlessly the same', or in Psalm 13 where God both hides his face and deals bountifully within six verses.

MacDiarmid sometimes anticipated this reconciling of things perceived as opposite:

> Said my body to my mind,
> 'I've been startled whiles to find,
> When Jean has been in bed wi' me,
> A kind o' Christianity!' ('A Drunk Man' lines 571-4)

It was less common in his day for sexuality and sanctity to be publicly conjoined, in spite of the presence of 'The Song of Songs' in the Old Testament. And if anyone linked MacDiarmid with the Bible, it would more likely be with Ecclesiastes, or with the Prophets. Indeed, the term 'Caledonian Antisyzygy' was coined to express something of Scottish character which chimes with the Old Testament Prophets, a dour sense of responsibility to keep telling truth to power even when times change:

> For I am like Zamyatin. I must be a Bolshevik
> Before the Revolution, but I'll cease to be one quick
> When Communism comes to rule the roost.[67]

That made MacDiarmid a rebel all his life. Nor was he content to remain simply an observer – according to Alan Riach, MacDiarmid distinguished 'critical realism' (depict present evils and make the best of them) and 'Socialist realism' (concentrate on the germ of transformation): 'Transformation is as central to MacDiarmid's work as contradiction'.[68]

It is not easy to correlate the history of tartanry in Scotland with social transformation. Tartan was proscribed after the failure of the Jacobite rebellion in 1745,[69] and it was only after that time that the Union of 1707 looked secure.[70] The revival of tartanry may have been symbolic of a continuing sense of Scottish identity, but was hardly a determining factor. Even with the Romantic Gothic revival of the 1820s it remained more a Highland (and a Scottish Regimental) interest, and arguably of more significance to Scots overseas than at home.[71]

In the 20th century it was not widely worn. MacDiarmid could wear a kilt when it suited him, but in the 1928 photo of the founders of the National Party of Scotland, no one is wearing tartan.[72] With the decline of home weaving it had become too expensive an item for many families, until it was rediscovered in the 21st century as fashionable dress hired for special occasions. In my own lifetime I have watched tartan move from upper and middle class to mainstream wear.

So tartan remains a popular symbol of identity, though much more today of Scottish than clan identity. For our purpose, it is a metaphor for the weaving of different strands in the Psalms, poetry and Scotland, both as contradiction and as synthesis.

7 The Poet as Rebel

Faiers describes tartan as 'a textile of contradiction, simultaneously . . . traditional and rebellious.'[73] By contrast the Psalms appear at first sight traditional, the prayer book of Jews and Christians. They do not seem to include the subversive irony of other books in the 'Writings', like Ecclesiastes and Job. But if you allow their questioning of God and their own situation to be called a suspicion that faith might be other than just 'simple trust', then you find a series of texts that subverts all false religion.

> Chapter Two noted a historical shift from a hermeneutic of trust, typical of the European approach to the Bible up to the end of the 18th CE, to a hermeneutic of suspicion fed equally by the rise of 'modern' textual criticism and 'postmodern' literary criticism. The current climate is different again, embracing a wide variety of perspectives within the 'methodological pluralism' that William Bellinger noted in his study of Psalm 61.[74] Narrative criticism is trusting, takes the text as it is, and is broadly sympathetic to Ricoeur's dictum, 'Beyond the desert of criticism, we wish to be called again.'[75] It is when we return to trusting the text that we allow it proper effect, when it may turn out to be subversive.

Subversion, secret rebellion, is an important part of the poet's task, As Emily Dickinson put it, the poet tells truth slant. Such truth, and especially God, is never locked up in the poem itself:

> 'God is the poetry caught in any religion,
>   caught, not imprisoned'[76]

Les Murray's aphorism not only gives a view of God and religion, but valorises poetry as a powerful tool for shaping new ideas of God. Many of the Psalms do this under the surface. Here are four examples.

Psalm 139 Language may be subversive

At first sight, Psalm 139 appears to be a psalm of total trust in a God who has formed the poet in the womb and accompanied her everywhere throughout her life. But in her imagination, the poet has visited sea as well as land, darkness as well as light – places that traditional Israelite thought did not associate with God's favour.[77] In Job 10:11-12 (that subversive book), even light is darkness. Here in Psalm 139:12, ironically, darkness is light:

> Even the darkness is not dark to you;
> the night is bright as the day,
> for darkness is as light to you.

But the Psalm does more than this. By stressing the presence of God everywhere, even in the dark, it suggests that temple and tartan, religion and nation, are not ultimate categories. The New Testament does the same thing in Revelation 21:22: 'I saw no temple in the city, for its temple is the Lord God . . .'

Genesis 1, Psalms like 8 and 19, and Psalm 139 in its own way subvert the Ancient Near East view of cosmic powers. They 'demyth the myth'.[78] An example of this in Scottish writing[79] would be where James Hogg subverts the power of religious fanaticism by associating it with psychological mania. The writer spins a tale in order to subvert, to change ideas. And when subversion does its work, and times change, threatening bodies like sun and moon lose their pagan power, and become mere ornaments in a poem:

> The icy haar o Lochnagar,
> Dreid ongauns smored in secrecy.
> Noo, aa is mild as mither's milk
> The meen's bit cosmic jewelry.[80]

Psalm 112 Goodness and generosity may be subversive

This is an alphabetical psalm, which is deceptively straightforward, as if it was a wisdom psalm like Psalm 1. This psalm affirms that goodness and generosity bless giver as well as receiver, but then in contrast to psalms of complaint, it affirms that such behaviour subverts the position of the wicked, who 'melt away' (v. 10).

112 'Wealth and Poverty' is suspicious of a psalm which seems to preach a 'prosperity gospel', like many right-wing regimes. The epigraph hints that great men are greedy and grasping, and that wealth – even with the generosity of Andrew Carnegie – should be scrutinised. But the poem finally acknowledges that revolutions which seek to overturn the wealthy and powerful in the name

of justice often turn sour – and that sometimes, just sometimes, 'some incorrect aristocrat has made this psalm his very own'. We should allow our own suspicion of the generosity of the wealthy to be subverted, along with our ideas of what is politically correct.

Psalm 73 Seeing afresh may be subversive

V. 1 affirms that God is good to Israel,[81] just like Psalm 37. But a look at how the wicked prosper seems to give that the lie, subverting that other psalm – until 'Asaph' goes 'into the temple', perhaps even the ruined temple after the exile (thinking of Psalm 74 which follows) – and then he sees things afresh, sees things as they really are, as if he had awakened from a bad dream. A double subversion![82]

73 'Open Questions' picks up how the photo of the drowned toddler Alan Kurdi[83] changed how the public perceived the refugee crisis, 'changing migrant / cockroaches to human casualties in hours'. As in the psalm, when we see things or people in a new way, our wrong ideas are subverted. 'What doors / can open through a body on a reef.' Poetry preserves an idea or an image[84] which other media may lose as they pass on to another day's news.

Psalm 88 Submission may be subversive

This psalm is darker than even the seven penitential psalms.[85] The writer is shut in, isolated, in the depths of the Pit, under the wrath of a God who has hidden his face.[86] The subversive thing about the psalm is this: he keeps praying, probably because he sees God, not bad luck, as responsible for his plight.[87] And God is still 'God of my salvation' (v. 1)

I based *88 'The Torture of the Pit'* upon the story of Christovao Ferreira, the Jesuit who apostasised to save his Japanese fellow believers from torture.[88] Ferreira had lost even the grain of hope expressed in the psalm in a 'God of salvation' – at least the salvation from torture of his fellows. So he subverted his own faith, made total submission in order to save them.

It is of course a story at odds with Jewish tradition, which commends the mother who witnessed the martyrdom of her seven sons, who are tortured and killed by Antiochus Epiphanes for refusing to bow down to idols.[89] It is controversial to subvert something regarded as noble and nation-building.

Now come the individual poems on the Psalms of Book 5, a tapestry with the long Psalm 119, then the Psalms of Ascent (120 – 134) as centrepiece. Book 5 poems continue to reflect the 'Temple and Tartan' themes of the book, but with more of an emphasis on praise and celebration, since Book 5 is where David 'lays down his crown' in favour of God as supreme ruler.

Part 3 WEAVING IT ALL TOGETHER

8 A Tapestry of Synthesis

Temple and tartan, as object and metaphor, combine the visible with what lies beyond, the immanent and the transcendent. Travel between the two is constantly taking place in the active mind, and a healthy society will prompt this dialogue through religion and the arts. For the poet (and the worship leader, for that matter), a continuing task is to use words which help this journey in the mind. Old words as well as new – I think the modern craze for 'new forms' in art and poetry may have misunderstood the way we relate to the transcendent.[90]

Poem 25 'A New Lexicon' is actually speaking not so much of new words, but learning to see the old words in new ways by connecting life with God, however long it takes (the transition from youth to age is slowed down by using the form of a pantoum). 'Break and make are man and wife / they share a house in every street', and the poem asks God to 'play the heartstrings of success and defeat' and (eventually) 'make music in my empty soul' as I 'wear the hurt' and 'bear the wrong'. Transcribed for Scotland, that means accepting that any mindful 'drive through' (to independence, or any other social and political change) will mean accepting and dealing with pain, and forgiveness.

The Psalms challenge us to recover moral categories like sin and penance. Penance – not as the work done to ensure forgiveness (which was struck down at the Scottish Reformation), but as a sign and recognition of error and injustice. Another word might need to be invented, like 'kinfast' (which combines the idea of 'going without' and 'solidarity'). Intelligent practice of such penance, 'kinfasting', as a recognition of the pain of injustice and the need to put things right, is for leaders to model voluntarily, not impose on others. An example is the decision by Kenneth Kaunda – who made a pilgrimage to the Church of Scotland offices in Edinburgh to thank them for the part they played in Zambian independence – not to eat meat until his people could all do the same.[91]

This would give a new and positive meaning to Psalm 71:7, 'I have been a portent to many', but it would also be a sign of the cost of putting things right, as recognised by the cost of ransom in Psalm 49:8. And since *God* is the one who ransoms us (49:15), God shows this kind of costly leadership. It includes restorative justice (72:1-4).

Concepts like 'tartan' and 'temple' help us hold together immanence and transcendence through metaphor, 'temple' through both universalising and localising the presence of God,[92] tartan in a simpler way through setting these concepts at right angles as they are woven together.

Clerk Maxwell, celebrated in *Poem 111 'Lord of all Being'*, chose a tartan ribbon to demonstrate colour photography,[93] probably for the obvious reason that tartan flaunts colours – but tartan is also a symbol of Scotland, and used here as a metaphor for the axes of immanence and transcendence, for the human and the divine. The other metaphor, temple, tells us more: human and divine are not simply lines of thought that cross at right angles, for 'temple' in the first century Jewish world of thought speaks of the overlap of heaven and earth.

Psalm 110 is accepted by Jews and Christians as a 'messianic psalm' (though their understanding of 'Messiah' differs). *Poem 110 'Priest and King'* thinks that 'God might find some human way / to live this messianic psalm / to work from altar and from throne / explain them both in harmony'. And this harmony carries the metaphor of temple, since 'God's temple feet are on the march'.

This is why the poet Stewart Henderson in a deceptively simple poem, 'Birthday Card', writes:

> I wish you Temple true,
> and all of deep content,
> I wish you royal rare,
> a lasting covenant.[94]

Explanation must be practical as well as intellectual, hence the importance of metaphors in literature and models in science.[95] Psalm 19 'explains' the book of nature and the book of scripture in dynamic metaphor. For Christians later, the person of Christ would be a heuristic metaphor for holding together the life of earth and the experience of God, but this harmony is present already in many of the psalms, whether it is in prayer for the king (Psalm 20), the ups and downs of life (Psalm 23 and the snakes and ladders of *Poem 23*), or the integration of life and faith (Psalm 26, though my *Poem 26* questions whether David himself achieved this).

When 'God gives Moses temple time' in *114 'Exodus'*, this allows Dante to find his feet, and blur the line 'between the polysemous squares / of old interpretation, adding rhyme / to link the Exodus to all of us'. The old becomes new. Our imagination draws us forward.[96] In the *'Space Temple'* of *118*, this 'tartan Lord' allows us back on the magic carpet, travelling space and time.

Tartan

Tartan is a stage where different threads of culture and history play together, and the metaphor has been extended to embrace the synaesthesia of art, music and poetry, as well as the relation of human and divine – *a place of crossing*, which is likely to be a friendly metaphor for Christians at least. The headings of the five books of poems all hint at some kind of 'crossing', and tapestry is in a sense the generic of tartan.

2021 was the centenary of George Mackay Brown's birth. Brown was fascinated by tapestry. He wrote a play about Magnus called *The Loom of Light*, which has seven threads 'which make the shroud', and was staged in Kirkwall in 1972. In his novel about Magnus, the saint king reads 'from his Psalter' – this likely means the Old Testament, since he reads passages from Ezekiel and Isaiah, with just one reading from Psalm 23.[97] The book refers to a coat which

> in a mystical way enwraps the whole community. For consider, all the people have contributed to the making of it.

So the coat is a tapestry stiff with jet and golden and scarlet threads, it is a storied garment, one tapestry from throat to ankle, so that a gazer may see the entire fable of the people . . .[98]

The tapestry in Brown's play is woven with good and bad deeds, and the fabric is endangered by bad deeds – threads may come loose.[99] Book 5 Poems are called 'Tapestry', and *146 'Boundaries'* recognises the struggle between good and evil (events like the killing of Magnus by his cousin Hakon), and the tension between faith and politics (out of Psalm 146). Whereas Brown had in mind the killing of Magnus by his cousin Hakon, this poem refers to the killing of the journalist Jamal Khashoggi in 2018.

> Let everyone be clear about their mission . . .
> . . . let not the priest or prophet be a prince . . .
> let not the prince become a cool assassin.

Temple

Temple is an image which links the personal and the universal, as *a place of enquiry*. You might wish to say that the physical temple is real, it can be touched, and we can walk all round it; the universe is real but we can only touch a little bit of it; the mind is real, yet we cannot touch it, even if we do a brain scan. Like all good images, temple stretches our perception of reality.

The first three chapters looked at three threads of the work of a poet: *enquiry, curating, prophecy* – though this chapter has more to say about prophecy. Chapter Four was about music and wonder, with the poet as singer, the thread being *song*; in this chapter we have considered 'dressing', which is akin to curating, but a good name for it is *celebration*, which ties up with the theme of praise in Book 5 of the Psalms. Now, however, we write about weaving these threads together. Historians, exegetes and theologians also do some of this weaving, and not without imagination, but the poet brings imagination more deliberately to bear on the same texts and events and people, which may also stretch how we perceive reality. This is an older model of poetry, lacking the contemporary enthusiasm for free association, and a deliberate retreat from the post-modern view that meaning is simply what a reader creates for herself. But it nonetheless gives imagination a significant role.

We are made in the image of God. George MacDonald understood that to mean: 'The imagination of man is made in the image of the imagination of God' – who of course has imagination as well as everything else we might attribute to the Deity.[100] To locate the image of God not in our rationality but in our imagination is unusual. While it might seem to redress the balance between science and the arts in favour of the latter, it is actually saying something even more radical, that the sciences require imagination as well as the arts (though this was familiar to someone like Einstein).

Prophecy requires imagination, but an imagination which takes the world and its future seriously. Temple and tartan are encouraging and fruitful images for 'prophetic poetry'. You could say that the wonder of the universe and its occupants stimulates our imagination, and that all poets work with this, whether 'the universe' is the physical universe, the universe of human history or simply the universe of one individual mind. Now, we proceed to weave the five threads together under the heads of five poems from Book 5; this will require some imagination from writer and reader – which is as it should be.

9 A Tapestry of Psalms

The Name – 135 'Mosaic'

While the Psalms frequently give God the name Yehovah, or Yahweh (depending how you put it into English), later it was simply called *hashem*, 'the name', out of respect. But here, at the start of the Psalm, we have 'Praise the name of the Lord.'

The opening words of the poem, 'Sandwich psalm', indicate that the content of the psalm is held between two bookends of praise, expressed by 'chosen lifters'. The chosen are the people of Israel, and especially those gathered in his temple courts to praise. Other Bible texts indicate that this choice is not racist in a modern sense, and that any person may be spiritually part of Israel.[101] One text (James 1:17) even embraces the poet, which of course the Psalms themselves do by implication.

With any kind of belief in God, it is impossible that the Creator could less interesting, less varied in character than the poet who owes her gift to God. When the psalmist writes 'Praise the name of the Lord', this deserves, this evokes, this enables a poet to gather every thread of his talent and offer it to God and to the world.

In this *Poem 37*, the Lord's name is 'layered, like lasagne / which ripples from / that holy standing start.' While this does reflect the variety of God's character, it also evokes the complexity of creation as it develops after the big bang, and the ripples in the fabric of space-time from stellar events. The title of the poem is chosen partly because the psalm is in fact a mosaic of texts from the *Torah*, the Prophets and many other psalms;[102] and partly as a pun on the name of Moses, whose life and work is signalled in verses 8-9 of this psalm.

But the poem contains a warning, taken from the psalm, against idolatry – even the 'friendly idols' of the internet, which are as damaging to human life as any dark idol, as any dark angel called up (as with Pharaoh) from a darkened heart. The psalm itself warns us that those who trust idols become like them.

Fresh Start – 114 'Exodus'

Every poet hopes that in some way readers will be changed by her poetry. The Bible story celebrated in Palm 114 is the big change, the exodus from Egypt, when the enslaved Israelites were led out into freedom, a motif which has inspired modern political freedom movements as well as typifying a basic spiritual rescue from sin. This was the psalm which sparked Dante's *Divine Comedy*, which is why his name opens the poem: Dante walks on his hands because he is celebrating the release of captives from Purgatory – in the poem I am perhaps thinking of hell turned upside down and shaken out by the gospel. To be fair to what Dante actually wrote, I added that he is also walking on his knees, in prayer – but still as happy as a dog with four tails – a 'hound hermeneut' with the medieval four ways of interpreting scripture.

The poem describes earth as a 'story board', into which a poet drives 'layers of meaning' like nails. Think of the six threads as six nails, or perhaps six screws, each of which can have a thread attached which winds its way into the ground of our life and thought.

With these poems, as with the Psalms themselves, there is some intertextuality. For example, in this *Poem 114*, 'cliffs are cleft with cataracts'. This is a reference to Psalm 42:7,

> Deep calls to deep at the thunder of your cataracts;
> All your waves and billows have gone over me.

In Psalm 42 the crashing noise of celebration moves to the crashing sound of water breaking over the poet's head. And God is responsible for this, as for everything – one of the layers of meaning the poet is driving home. The Bible story of Exodus, like our own stories, is full of drama, trauma and trouble as well as purpose and play. In the poem, God gives Moses 'temple time' on Mount Sinai, and Moses struggles there with God to avoid the whole plan of Exodus being lost.

The Bible story begins with creation (Genesis 1-11), followed by the call of Abraham, the growth of a people of God, and their descent into slavery in Egypt. The second book, Exodus, celebrates their rescue and journey to a promised land. Neither that journey, nor the life of Israel in that land, proves to be straightforward, and as a result of disobedience Israel ends up in exile. They have to learn to pray, and write lament songs as well as praise songs.

Learning to Live – 141 'Prayer'

Poem 141 calls life a 'trail of tapestry', with a variety of stitches. Flame stitches signal prayer as an offering of incense; cross stitches signal confusion (or perhaps a humble acknowledgement of life's complexity); continental stitches signal growth to something bigger. Bigger in partnership, with God and with other people. We are making a tent, which has 'room for more than one' – and the word 'tent' evokes the tabernacle of the book of Exodus which was a work of many crafts, including tapestry.

T.S. Eliot said that prayer was more than the sound of the voice praying. In common with all monotheist religion, the Psalmists believe that prayer is more than just an individual sorting out her mind – that God actually listens to our prayer, even if God may not answer at the time or in the way we expect. And that prayer is not just personal therapy, it relates to what is going on, what we do and what others do.

In this psalm, prayer is directed against the evil deeds of the wicked (v. 5c). Whether the Masoretic Text or the Septuagint should be taken for v. 5b, the context is clear from v. 4, no feasting with the ungodly; instead, pray against their actions – with the hope (v. 6) that they will come to see how delightful the psalmist's words really were. This is rare in the Psalms (7:9 being another example) – usually prayer is directed simply against the ungodly and wicked.

It would be convenient to think those 'words' refer to the prayer itself, congruent with Proverbs 25:21-22 and the New Testament command to pray for those who treat you badly (Matthew 5:4) – it is more likely that the psalmist is just wanting to escape any bad consequences for himself. But in any case, his hope is to subvert the evil intentions of the wicked.

The first stanza of this poem concerns the fire of praying with love to God,[103] the second stanza about praying with love to others:

Every day cross stitches lose their place and purpose,
need unwinding in a faithful strike of love,
for modern tapestry's a multi-coloured fellow
learning how to pray good in, and evil out.

The 'strike of love' refers in the first instance to v. 5a of the psalm, when the psalmist may need correcting by the righteous - but then to v. 5d, when he strikes the wicked in prayer, one aspect of the more general 'pray good in, and evil out'.

The poem sets this 'strike of love' in the wider context of life as a 'trail of tapestry' with three different kinds of stitch. It is suspicious of the poet's own progress ('fitful craft', 'cross stitches', 'my own gaucheness'), but trusts that such weakness will in turn be subverted by 'some warp threads simulating God'.

Praying good in, and evil out, is an obvious reference to breathing, which is the theme of the final *Poem 150 'Breathing or Breathless'*, offering praise to God from a life of prayer between baby breath and dying breath.

Coping with the Unexpected – 144 'Stuff'

Fashions of biblical understanding change. Back in the 19th and early 20th century, who would have thought that modern scholarship would become again more sympathetic to the idea that David may have written at least some of the psalms linked to his name?[104] Certainly this Psalm 144 feels like a text David would have written, even if a conservative commentator like John Goldingay still thinks it was written by a later leader invoking the spirit of David.[105]

Stuff happens, whether in the world of biblical scholarship or the world of every day. The four stanzas of this poem take some useful rhymes to let us feel the different features of the unexpected. Harold Macmillan is credited this reply to a question about the greatest challenges to a politician: 'Events, dear boy, events!' The psalm puts it even more starkly, 'Their days are like a passing shadow.'

Stanza one invites us to consider the complexity of a 'shape-shifting God', however much that stretches our minds, since this will help us cope with the 'heart-rending stuff' of stanza two. As in the psalm, there is a prayer for deliverance, with stanza three giving thanks for it. But this third stanza takes us back into the temple, and that is where we can see most clearly the significance of the 'stuff' which is happening to us (as in Psalm 73). My guitar is 'multi-stringed', not just as a nod to the variety of instruments used in temple worship, but in recognition of the number of strings in our own hearts.

In stanza four we return to the uncertainty of events, with God waiting for 'a weighted prayer'. While such a prayer will be heavy enough to make some ripples in a loch, the reader is being asked to consider what makes a prayer 'weighty' – perhaps weighty with anxiety, perhaps weighty with trust – but if the Psalms are anything to go by, either kind of content can lead to blessing; and blessing for this psalm is not a spiritual feeling, but an earthly fact – strong families, food in store, security of capital and defence, public happiness. Which is why the final psalm chosen suggests the spiritual is not 'nice and vague' but 'blood and battles'.

The Gist – 136 'End Game'

Black holes are possibly the most energetic, fearsome and mysterious objects in the entire universe. But when one was photographed for the first time it was given the name Powehi, which in Hawaiian culture means 'the adorned fathomless dark creation'. I reference this in the poem, because the psalm celebrates the extraordinary God whose steadfast love is eternal, yet includes what appear to be destructive as well as creative elements, adorning the name of God with unlikely events.

The epigraph to *111 'Lord of all Being'* included a word which in Hebrew means head, sum, meaning, origin, conclusion (*roʾš* or more easily written *rōsh*); it is in some ways an Old Testament equivalent of the Greek *logos*. The title of this poem *136, 'End Game'*, is trying to echo that, with a cosmic framework in which humans appear, late arrivals maybe, 'dwarfed by skies of light and darkness, / yet a twinkle in God's eye'. The poem (like the psalm) is putting several claims against the cold order of a vast universe:

- There is a moral realm of right and wrong

- There is a spiritual realm which invades and pervades the material

- There is a human realm which God favours, and Israel has a particuar place in that

In the New Testament, these three realms cohere in one person, Jesus of Nazareth, and the word *rōsh* would be as fitting for him as the word *logos*. Everything in the universe will be 'gathered up' in Christ (Ephesians 1:10). The Psalms, with their universal reach, prepare for this by claiming that the Creator of the universe has a special love for one nation, Israel, and Christians have seen many things in the life and worship of Israel which help them understand God's purpose for humankind. The New Testament teaches that Jesus was born and lived as a Jew, and cites the Psalms more than any other Old Testament book.

While we have got here by *enquiry, interpretation* and *curating,* and not without *wonder, song* and *dressing,* without the thread of *prophecy* this would dissolve into clever (or not so clever) words. So I will conclude with some contemporary words for Scotland from the tapestry of these poems – but anyone reading this could think of applications for their own nation. There is now no American, Scottish or English exceptionalism, maybe not even any Israeli exceptionalism, though the Jewish people themselves remain a sign to the world.

10 A Tapestry of Scotland

I remember going to see the Great Tapestry of Scotland when it was on show in Cockenzie House. It was the brainchild of Alexander McCall Smith, along with Alistair Moffatt, Andrew Crummy and Dorie Wilkie as the main executors of the vision. In a marvellous sequence of 160 panels it takes us on a journey from the sea before the emergence of the land mass we now call Scotland, right up to the rebirth of a Scottish Parliament. It certainly has in its own way carried out all the roles I have claimed for the poet, and with excellence, although prophecy has been muted: for example, the persecution of witches was included, but the slave trade links of the Glasgow 'Tobacco Lords' were not. The presentation of Scotland up to the present day was largely positive, and understandably so for the purpose of the tapestry.

McCall Smith himself speaks of the ideals of brother- and sisterhood that the panels illustrate, and they do so because the panels themselves were chosen to portray those things more than the strife and disillusionment which have also been part of Scotland's story.[106] Prophecy is a particular earthing of ideals which is different from moralising. While the prophet may indeed declare some things right or wrong, the essence of prophecy is facing the present, and sometimes the future, with a truth which is not derived from opinion, be that public or private. So I want now to reflect on elements of what I wrote which might be prophetic, even though the poems were simply my response to the Psalms, and not a carefully planned programme of prophecy about Scotland.

One caveat. I am not the Brahan Seer. I am not likely to anticipate the extraordinary ways of travel which may supersede the train and the car – if our human race can survive beyond the current millennium. Nor is this a dramatic programme of eschatology as featured in books like Hal Lindsey's *Late Great Planet Earth*. It is a modest exploration of what God may be saying to us in Scotland (and beyond), and like all prophecy it ought to be carefully checked out by others, and will be tested by what actually happens.[107]

In Psalm 139, the writer says that he was 'fearfully and wonderfully made . . . intricately woven in the depths of the earth', which comes out in *139 'Convenient Fiction?'* as 'our stranger selves, the fabled bits that neuroscience only labels', but just as the psalm refuses to see the human being apart from the presence of God, so in the poem, 'temple textures touch my mind'. It is these temple textures that shape, even grind out, the lens for the five words about the present and future of Scotland which follow. I am also grateful to a number of other thinkers whose wisdom has pointed me in certain directions – no prophet works in isolation.

Lines

William Storrar observes that Scotland is a linear nation,[108] with lines connecting various outlooks to Continental Europe and to America:

As a linear nation, our identity crisis has always been a question of where to draw the line; not just in the sense of the physical borderline from the Solway to the Tweed, but far more in the sense of the imaginative line and the coordinate points in human history and society that set the moving boundaries of who and what we are as Scots.[109]

The 'lines' of the Psalms extend from God to the earth, from Israel to all nations, and from the beginning of human history till the end. Psalm 100, which within my lifetime was sung at public occasions in Scotland, specifically extends these lines in space and time. The question is posed to political and business leaders, to artists and writers, 'On what lines will Scotland develop now, after Covid 19?'

Psalm 141 commends prayer 'against wickedness', and the words of the righteous as weapons for correction. It is of course some centuries since the minister of St Giles in Edinburgh, (another) Robert Bruce said publicly, 'May no man minister in this place who does not have the courage to admonish in the name of God.'[110] If I admonish, I do so gently with two comments about the ideal of Scottish independence:

(a) From *Poem 141 'Fire'*, which considers the lines marked by the stitches in a tapestry, I return to the idea of 'continental stitches'. The first stanza considered flame stitches, and the vagaries of prayer. Stanza two considered cross stitches and the clash of good and evil. Stanza three considers continental stitches, with the prophetic edge of Europe in mind, and the open question as to what 'a tent with room for more than one' implies. Some visions of independence glorify continental Europe and denigrate England. This betrays historical ignorance and economic folly. Whatever the consequences of Brexit, Scotland must find a way to build relationships with both, and avoid being pushed into romantic cul-de-sacs, by preserving 'a steely grasp of our own gaucheness'. The poem also qualifies idealism with the reality of wrong stitches.

(b) In 1990, Storrar offered the 'crucified vision of a humble nation'.[111] Proud words about a football team are harmless enough, but proud words about subjects like Scottish education, or worse about Scotland being better off economically without England do not ring true.

My poem which celebrates humility is *111 'Lord of All Being'*. For epigraph it cites the words of Psalm 111:2 which James Clerk Maxwell had inscribed (in Latin) outside the Cavendish Laboratory in Cambridge, this humble Scot 'unsuspecting that he might become / the greatest scientist since Isaac Newton'. Maxwell brought together different 'lines' of research (electricity, magnetism, and light),[112] and the third stanza puns this with the lines in the tartan ribbon used for the first colour photograph in 1861.[113] The sixth stanza celebrates the meaning of *ròs* which has been already explained.

Scotland may be wealthy enough to stand on its own, like other nations of its size, but independence will mean initial suffering, and maybe relative poverty in the longer run, especially if Scots buy into a different approach to wealth and income distribution than the earlier 'trickle-down' theory or the current populist 'drawbridge' approach. This can be borne with redistribution of income, but the middle and wealthy classes will have to share a vision for independence, as they will likely be poorer overall. Also, in the short term, any significant referendum should have a threshold of say 60%, since the winners in a free society will have to rely on the losers coming behind any change, and not sabotaging it (even if some still cut and run). For such cohesion, a cohesive 'wisdom' will be paramount – such as is indicated by stanza five and Psalm 119:160.

The lines between present and future generations have been frayed by at least two factors: the wealth accumulated by the older generation compared with the poverty of housing and job opportunities available to the young; and the failure of the older generation to tackle the challenge of climate change. Psalm 8 valorises infants, and *Poem 8 'Old and Young Newscasters'* wishes that young people might fire arrows which 'pierce the hide of backward leaders', and thus 'cast the majesty of God'.

Lines by themselves are fragile, like the line carried by one brave and thoughtful man off the stricken *Iolaire*. Attached to it, however, was the rope now memorialised in bronze as a symbol of hope.[114] We need lines of rescue, lines of hope, lines of wisdom.

Tribes

In medieval Scotland tribal differences were largely geographical or clan-based; after the Reformation they remained geographical, but were also religious, and increasingly class-based, up to the mid 20th century, when familiar modern and postmodern factors complicated the picture. Scottish politics have also been tribal, but whereas in the later 20th century they were Labour and Tory, with the Catholic Church largely Labour, and Protestants divided, in the 21st century the Scottish National Party has emerged as the dominant tribe, and the religious vote no longer of any significance.

The tripartite division of my childhood, when Scotland was divided between Conservative (and Unionist), Liberals (Home Rule) and Labour has changed dramatically into SNP and Conservative, with Labour and Liberal Democrats in a minority.

And with the emergence of the Alba Party and the growing strength of the Green Party, as well as the existence of a significant nationalist section in the Scottish Labour Party, the independence vote is divided between a number of parties. The Brexit referendum, with the result in Scotland different from England has accelerated these changes. Tribalism is alive, but changing, complicated by the preference of young people for 'issues' over 'parties'.

Tom Nairn was an early nationalist writer, with his book *The Breakup of Britain*.[115] He was brought up in Cellardyke, in a house with a gate straight onto the beach. In a long review of a book by Neal Ascherson, Rory Scothorne examines the tensions between socialism and nationalism in Scotland, and ends by writing, 'When confronted with a gate onto the ocean, [Tom Nairn] imagines it open. The British left has yet to learn to do the same.'[116] What will now happen in Scotland, as the 'tribes' of Labour and SNP continue to change position after years of jostling for power? And what will happen in the national Church, as (like the Psalms) they work through the implications of the 'line of David' being eclipsed?[117] The Church of England has had years of accommodation with smaller religious tribes in England, the Church of Scotland is now having to come to terms with the growth of independent churches and the loss of shared hegemony with the Roman Catholic Church.

> Tom Nairn shares with Carol Ann Duffy[118] the view that 'the pen is mightier than the sword'; in very different ways they have battled for the mind of their generation. *Poem 29 'Mind Map'* recognises an earlier 'battle for the mind' in the formation of Israel, that human thought must be open ('never watertight'), and that humour and non-violence are key weapons for the future of any part of the world, be it Britain or the Middle East. The stepped format with the poetic conceit of 'five steps' reflects the step parallelism of this psalm, which is found also in Canaanite poetry.[119] As the psalm was probably composed to counter the claims of Baal, the Canaanite god of sex and chance, the poem has God 'cut foes down to size' (as Carol Ann Duffy does in her poem 'Queen Kong' about the mythic monster King Kong).

Tribes are a fact of life, as recognised in Acts 17:26 as well as Psalm 122:4. Will they bring the blessing of strength and inspiration, or the curse of 'tribalism'? An immediate question for Scottish political Parties – but a wider question for society. The replacement of rational thought by celebrity culture, the populism of some European and American leaders, the distancing of the academy from the street, leave an intellectual vacuum which is filled by 'intellectual performers' who gather followers on the internet, but such bubbles of attention may not translate into movements that will change society. Until the second half of the 20th century, Scotland had, for example, a strong and thoughtful socialist movement,[120] but Margaret Thatcher's remark to the Church of Scotland General Assembly in 1988 that 'there is no such thing as society' showed a contrary approach which neither Labour nor SNP has yet been able to do much about. It remains to be seen how significant is Boris Johnston's contradiction of her on the BBC News (29/3/20).

Capital

The mission of the Knights Templar was to defend the pilgrims going to Jerusalem, to what had been Solomon's temple. Jerusalem was important, not simply because it was in Israel, but because for Jewish (and Christian) mystics it was the centre of the world.[121] In 28 'Pinnacle or Pit',

> My hands feel their way to the centre:
> sanctuary, the holy hexagon,
> the space with six edges,
> the heart beating something
> old and fierce . . .

This states the importance of the capital, which appears as Zion in many psalms,[122] not least the Psalms of Ascent, or Jerusalem – 'to it the tribes go up' (Psalm 122:4). Poem 122 refers to the 'three monotheist modern tribes' that all acknowledge Jerusalem as a mother city. Collective identity is typically created round a country with a central capital,[123] though Israel has an issue with having Tel Aviv as its commercial capital today, not unlike

Glasgow in Scotland up to the 20th century. The decanting of population from Glasgow, and the rapid growth of Edinburgh in the 21st century, has made Edinburgh more obviously the Scottish capital, although Glasgow fought back with being the European City of Culture in 1990.

Britain shares this problem, with the difference between London and the North of England in the Brexit vote. Back in 1963 a suggestion was floated in *The Economist* that Britain needed a new capital built in, say, Yorkshire, perhaps to be called Elizabetha, but it came to nothing. In Scotland the traditional disconnect of the Highlands and Lowlands continues – Andy Wightman cites a story from James Hunter anent the 1979 devolution referendum, about a Sutherland man who would be voting to keep the status quo: 'In London they don't give a damn about Highlanders, but in Edinburgh they hate us.'[124] Unlike the Royal Society in London, the RSE covers both the sciences and the humanities, but it is the Royal Society of *Edinburgh*, not Glasgow or Aberdeen or Inverness.

Poem 147 'Jerusalem' presents the city as a place of wonder, although 'the thunder / of its past rolls past the present, / makes the future nervous'. Scotland has the thunder of its own past to cope with, but might have the opportunity to 'reinvent *shalom*, / so wounded outcasts name it home'.

The book of Deuteronomy insists that there is only one place for corporate worship,[125] in its attempt to make the capital real and not nominal. This remains an issue for Scotland, given the divide between the Highlands and the Lowlands, as the Highlands and Islands ('Gaeldom') are more closely linked to Glasgow. This will require Edinburgh and Glasgow to bury their traditional rivalries, and to find ways of affirming other regions, whether by a travelling Parliament or other means. Reinventing *shalom* is the work of Government as well as poets and artists, but it needs a framework which makes space for art and religion (as a second Chamber might do).

The poem also speaks of the capital as being a 'city of metaphor and meaning'. It was a place of pilgrimage, such places being celebrated in *120-134 'Song of the Fifteen Steps'*. Edinburgh cannot claim the same meaning as Jerusalem, but Scots could take pilgrimage more seriously in three regards: treat every journey as a privilege restored after corona virus; treat every journey from country to conurbation and back as bearing (if not laden with) metaphor; and make more of traditional places of pilgrimage. May these fifteen psalms 'line the route, / buffeting politics, toughening faith.'

Leaders

Shadowing all these is the question of leadership, both its nature (what will democracy look like in a future Scotland?) and its character (what kind of people will emerge as leaders?). In Book 1, Psalm 15 (linked with David) sets a high standard for leaders. *Poem 15* chooses to focus on hypocrisy, but the psalm itself makes it clear that integrity (which preserves leaders, Psalm 25:21) means at least not feathering your own nest.

The Psalms deal with both the nature and character of leadership, through their dual focus on the earthly king, and God as king.[126] The most poignant example is Psalm 51, which is linked with Nathan's condemnation of David's adultery and murder. Book 2 poems on *Psalms 49-51* note how the charge of murder stained the lives of both Bruce and David, and the final poem on *Psalm 72* insists: 'Without some thread of hope, / the tales of David, Bruce / and everyone expire.'

The later Psalm 118:9 advises trusting the Lord rather than princes, and Psalm 113:7-8 contains the radical idea that God raises the poor from the dust 'to make them sit with princes'. The *Psalm 72 poem* ends by identifying a leader for whom 'the common weal / is all his care, a temple / built of living stones . . .'

Most of the Book 3 poems, concerning migrants, touch on leadership, though largely in Africa, Asia or the Middle East rather than Scotland. Immigrant slavery in England features in *81 'Freed from the Basket'. Poem 82 'Something Good'* is about the Scottish Clearances, about social change, about the failure of leadership – yet like some of the Psalms, its sharpest note is the failure of God. The psalm itself simply calls on God to judge (82:8).

Book 4 poetry, '*The Iolaire*', is about theological and leadership transition, from earlier models to the leadership of God alone, leaving us to spell that out in practice as we 'learn to play our human nature, / sing a dusty hallelujah'. In Book 5, *Poem 146 'Boundaries'*, while written with the October 2018 assassination of the journalist Jamal Khashoggi in mind, looks at the boundaries between religious and political leaders, and the character of politicians. In the past it was preachers who held the feet of politicians to the fire;[127] today it is social media and elections. 2020 celebrated the 700th anniversary of the Declaration of Arbroath; in that letter addressed to Pope John XXII in Avignon, there are seeds of democracy, but in the context of a shared faith. With that shared faith, an idea becomes more important than any individual leader.

Psalm 11 asks, 'If the foundations are destroyed, what can the righteous do?' So *11 'Exam Time'* asks:

> What is 'wicked', since relativity
> shocked us, rocked amoral waves
> through brains as well as time and space?

Relativity in science is of course different from relativity in morals, though poetry can play on the apparent similarity. The modern ambiguity about the word 'wicked' underlines the difficulty in expecting public opinion to judge leaders well in the absence of an agreed basis of morality. Two current issues illustrate this:

(a) The debate about whether people should simply be able to choose their gender, or whether gender is normally trumped by sex,[128] while not framed in God language, shows the difficulty of privileging liberty of choice, since it pits transgendered against feminist,[129] as abortion pits the rights of the woman against the rights of the unborn child. As Nietzsche pointed out, when you remove God, everything becomes simply a power struggle – today often conducted through social media.

(b) The difficulty in separating law and politics in countries where a strong leader is accused of breaking the law. This was illustrated by the tragi-comedy of the trial of Alex Salmond, the hints of conspiracy, the remarks of the defence counsel overheard in a train, the dangerous overlap of law and government, and so on. In open democracies, judgment is shared by judge and jury, and professionals and citizens are involved in this process. Politicians and their allies did not come out of this well.

While the Psalms do not offer solutions to modern dilemmas, they frame human life with the justice of God. It is not simply that God demands justice, *he is just* (righteousness and justice are a single word in Hebrew); and justice is about relationships as well as actions:

> For the Lord is righteous;
> he loves righteous deeds;
> the upright shall behold his face. (Psalm 11:7)

That is why *Poem 11 'Exam Time'* includes 'Gear up the programme / for the gaze of God' – justice is more than a court or exam room procedure, it is relational, and for the economy as well as education.[130] It requires wisdom as well as law.[131]

The 'Prayers of David' in Books 1 – 3 are framed by Psalms 1 and 72, each of which proclaim a judgment which is more than human opinion, but which also relies on leaders to exercise it properly. While Psalms like 72 glorify a monarch like Solomon, other parts of the OT criticise him sharply.[132] Later Psalms like 146 qualify a ruler's authority. The Psalms are unequivocal that rulers are answerable to God (Psalm 2), but also that they cannot be trusted with absolute power (Psalm 146:3). With Britain in the grip of what Rowan Williams calls not simply 'procedural' but 'programmatic secularism',[133] this will be a note sounded by individual prophets unless we have second chambers which properly represent minorities such as BAME and religious interests.

Meanwhile, the task of the poet as prophet (or perhaps the prophet as poet) is to bring to the table an alternative perception of reality. But that requires, if not God, something which today is labelled 'transcendence' – although a reader of the Psalms might think it a poor substitute.

11 A Tapestry of Praise

Believers have sometimes pretended to be sorry for atheists because the latter 'have no one to thank' for the wonder they acknowledge in the universe. While this is of course resented by unbelievers as condescending, *Poem 115 'The Sky's the Limit'* does explore the idea in the course of locking horns with the Jewish writer Yuval Noah Harari. The poem is fairly robust, accusing those who want to upgrade humans to gods of being

> a cast of hermeneutic dentists,
> sparky savants, shrewd interpreters
> of human possibilities
> who never bump their brilliant heads
> on any ceiling, never feel the limits
> which might let us have some hope
> of praising God eternally.

A Makar, or Poet Laureate, is there to dress public occasions with poetry, an old bardic role. This will involve giving praise where it is due, as happened with events like the opening of the Scottish Parliament, or more modestly the Queensferry Crossing. Whether or not a nation has morphed into atheism or agnosticism, the task of the poet is different from that of a worship leader – but if a poet were to feel it impossible to mention God in a poem because it was no longer politically correct, this would be a sad commentary on our times. At the very least, a poet can enjoy celebrating the world around us, the good achievements and behaviour of humankind, and being generous towards whoever or whatever lies beyond the world we can touch and see. Journalists may say that only the bad makes good news copy, but a challenge to the poet is to be able to celebrate the good in such a way that it becomes more interesting than the bad.

Poem 115 is not against science and its exploration of the universe, but in an unexpected nod to the habit of using 'rights' to settle argument it recognises the human rights of death. While Donne ended one poem by saying, 'death thou shalt die', the poem mocks any claim that humans can prevent death. The argument of the poem is that without the limit of death we lose all hope of praising God eternally, locked into a myth of progress and locked out of a real heaven.

> The thrust of this kind of poetry is to keep imagination in touch with reality, in the belief that this will make imagination more rather than less fruitful, even if this is not where much contemporary poetry is at. Actually, this stance of 'critical realism' is shared with mainstream science,[134] and *139 'Convenient Fiction'* is a sestina which explores these boundaries, ending with:
>
> > Is it science, art, to class God's book
> > convenient fiction, tepid temple stuff?
> > God thinks truth stronger, definitely stranger.
>
> Truth is 'stranger', against a literalist view; truth is 'stronger', against an instrumentalist view (that words are just useful fiction, not actually referring to anything true); critical realism is the view that sits between these two, claiming that words may have a true reference which is not literal.[135] Psalm 139 is certainly not 'tepid temple stuff' in its claim that God is everywhere – there is no private space where God is absent.

Imagination is a gift to us all, whether or not we have faith. But just as MacDiarmid insisted on realism ('socialist realism'), because he was so deeply influenced by the realism of a biblical worldview which he could not accept with one part of his mind, so I have tried to write poetry which sets the tartan firmly in the context of the temple, and the temple in the context of the tartan – that is, in line with the biblical ideas described in the book, which link the temple of the imagination to the temples of the body, the worshipping community and the universe. This is of course why thinkers like Solomon (or those who expressed his thoughts later on) never bought into the kind of three-decker universe that the ancients were supposed to believe in,[136] and kept connecting a Creator with his creation. God was far bigger than a temple, but also to be found within it. The universe was not a closed box, and the image of God was not an idol in a temple, but the human being.

However, while Solomon's temple theology in 1 Kings may be prophetic, his prayer began with thanksgiving, and the final five psalms of Book 5 begin and end with 'Praise the Lord'. The overall title of the book of Psalms in Hebrew is 'Praise Songs', which means that under this title the compilers of the Psalter were happy to weave psalms of lament, complaint, teaching and celebration all together into one tapestry. I have tried to do the same with my poetry, without of course claiming the kind of inspiration which even Hugh MacDiarmid ascribed to David (see Chapter Two).

I have not taken sides on which Psalms could be firmly attributed to him. But I have lived long enough to see fashions of interpretation come and go, and I think it is true of historians as much as of scientists that every so often there are paradigm shifts.[137] I have also witnessed the great change in Scotland, as in much of Europe, from a public belief in God to the current public atheism.

While I do not hide the fact that I write poetry as a believer, I am very comfortable that the gift of poetry, like the five books of Psalms, is for everyone, for all of us who live in this extraordinary temple that we call the cosmos, including those who have an affinity with tartan.

Book 5 Poems: Tapestry

107 Homecoming

'East, West: Hame's Best.'

I remember words
stained on the glass
front door panel,
jiggled into memory
as adventurous
feet jumped step,
paused, passed
the opened door,
thumped the hall
as owner occupiers.
For health and home
give thanks to God.

He had a name –
I don't recall it now.
Came from Poland,
not job hunting
but last century,
stranded by war,
lodging in our house,
reminding us
the world is full
of accidents.
For health and home
give thanks to God.

Ron lived with us
a month or two,
his ways a puzzle
to our children,

but explained to
doctors, therapists
and any friend
prepared to hear out
acid nightmares,
tacit dreams.
For health and home
give thanks to God.

She stayed near us
for many years,
on off, off on,
her brilliant brain
still clawing rubbish,
pawing past life,
filing for recovery
from awful things
no pastor spells
out in a poem.
For health and home
give thanks to God.

I remember the God
stained by journeys
of a searching kind,
more or less
unrecognized,
peering through faces
of pained and queer,
all the unlikely
exiles like us
God wants at home.

108 Larks and Crows

'I will awake the dawn.' *v. 2b*

That lark ascending
Classic FM, twittering to fame,
but softer, almost out of sight
and into spending
time with God, a climb within
some rainbow arc of steadfast love.

That psalm full-throated
throws its praise up high for God to catch
from all the longitudes of earth,
wakes a band
to play God's anthems, fire
a rocket through faith's enemies.

That crow complains,
the rasping back row literalist: 'No sign
of God in army uniform,
the game's a bogey.'
Save us Lord, from all our foes
– save us from impatient friends.

109 A Fork in the Mouth

'When who we think we are is suddenly
flying apart, splintered into
acts we hardly recognize . . .'   W.S. Graham

'No one can tame the tongue . . . with it we bless
the Lord and Father, and with it we curse those
who are made in the likeness of God.'   James 3:8-9

Mouths were made for other things
like kissing, pouting, whistling, laughing
playing oboes, moothies, bagpipes,
drinking *uisge beatha*.

But we remember with such pain
the ding-dong words we had with those
who threw their acid speech at us,
and burned our self-esteem.

The words we rolled around our tongues
for those who spoke behind our backs,
the way we justified ourselves
when under their attack.

And worst of all, we thought that God
would take our side in court
and run the wicked out of town
and out of our fair hair.

Well, *let them curse, but you will bless*,
and quieten every angry voice,
the outside hexes, hate and hiss,
the inside shame as well.

110 Priest and King

God's temple feet are on the march.
Essenes are withdrawn, conflicted,
struggle with doctrinal scandals.
Zealots take the simple sense,
read 'shatter kings' as holy writ
to trample on some Roman sandals.

Even kings need sustenance
while on the road: a little sign
that God might find some human way
to live this messianic psalm,
to work from altar and from throne,
explain them both in harmony.

111 Lord of All Being

'Great are the works of the Lord,
studied by all who delight in them.'   Psalm 111:2

'The sum of your word is truth.'   Psalm 119:160

'A towering figure ranked with Newton and
Einstein.'   *John Gunn F.R.S.E.*

Unsuspecting that he might become
the greatest scientist since Isaac Newton,
James Clerk Maxwell studied optics,

oval curves, electro-magnetism,
opened doors for quantum theory,
Albert Einstein's relativity.

Maxwell took a strip of tartan ribbon,
crossed three different lines of research,
made the world's first colour photograph.

Ahead of the game, he feared the Lord,
filled his mind with wisdom, knowledge,
knew his destiny, his definitions,

took such pleasure in the works of God,
carved that verse outside the Cavendish,
but kept his heart and home in Corsock.

Just one Hebrew word for start and finish,
summit, apex, height, the first, the last,
the best, the chief, the front, the sum:

no wonder Maxwell gave God head room
in his study, sang of heavenly glory
flaming out of every sun and star.

112 Wealth and Poverty

'Furnace no. 8 produced a record output, Mr Carnegie!'
'Whit's wrang wi' the ither seven?'

'They have distributed freely; they have given to the poor.' *v. 8*

We know so much about the wealth
and poverty of states, rich men
who pull a country to the right,
leave the green world black and barren,
fighting for its global health.

We analyse resources, climate,
study culture, works of art;
we scrutinise the role of women,
think religion plays a part,
prosperity is not just fate.

So when we read of dynasties,
great families who rule the land,
we grow suspicious, ask our questions,
deconstruct psalms out of hand
that give the wealthy open praise;

we march for change, for revolution,
hijack the *Magnificat*,
until it all goes wrong; meanwhile
some incorrect aristocrat
has made this psalm his very own.

113 Height and Depth

The temple pinnacle had its ironies
for him who fell from heaven's high artistries,

but Jesus stuck to script: 'Don't test the Lord
your God' – who takes the side of those now floored

and lifts them up, without a miracle
except that loving hand which wraps goodwill

around the needy, lets them sit at tables
with the royals, rewrites morbid labels,

raises wretched, dings to earth high heid yins,
pulls the poor from middens, covers sins,

requests a child to hunt the house for yeast,
and passes over fame to grace the least.

From dawn to dusk, from east to west
the name of God is to be blessed.

114 Exodus

'Dante's angel is at the helm of a boat in which more than a hundred spirits are singing Psalm 114.'   *Edward Clarke*

Dante came to meet me, walking on his hands
– and knees – hound hermeneut with four tails,
nose to a trail he feels and understands.

Each tail wagged the dog to the altar rails:
Judah became temple, Israel God's dwelling
place, layers of meaning driven nails

into the story board of earth, spelling
out God's saving purpose, sowing seeds
of greater morning glory, show-and-telling

Bible meanings in these crazy deeds.
Mountains go mad with magma melt,
cliffs are cleft with cataracts, God reads

his play on the stage of Sinai, his belt
tight round his tribe, only let out a notch
when Moses intercedes with heart-felt

cries for those who cannot stay on watch
while God gives Moses temple time.
Dante finds his feet, plays hopscotch

with his Classic friend, stirring the lime
between the polysemous squares
of old interpretation, adding rhyme

to link the Exodus to all of us. He bares
his chest: it's gospel truth, he swears.

115 The Sky's the Limit

'We will now aim to upgrade humans into gods,
turn Homo sapiens into Homo deus.' *Yuval Noah Harari*

We have ideals, not vain idols,
thoughts of sisterhood, of brotherhood,
of green at the equator, ice restored to poles,
a space farm, energy turned ethical,
industrial barons under lock and key
but getting five (or six) a day
like those we duly recognise
as *homo sapiens*, one of worldwide us,
the wise who once made sacrifice to God
but lately have outgrown such baby teeth.

We have ideas, not false idols,
thoughts of manhood, womanhood
outgrowing death by gene control.
Will scientists write poetry,
or bankers play sudoku games?
If we have all the rights to life,
then death has lost its human rights.
Why should the heart stop pumping blood,
why should we lack spare body parts?
Death, thou shalt really die!

We have such idiots, such idols,
clever fools who live inside
their great ideals, their big ideas;
a cast of hermeneutic dentists,
sparky savants, shrewd interpreters
of human possibilities
who never bump their brilliant heads
on any ceiling, never feel the limits
which might let us have some hope
of praising God eternally.

116 Common Cup

At the September 2018 Communion in St Mary's, Haddington, duty elders included Ian Gray MSP and Councillor John McMillan.

Ian finds us bread, the kind of thing
an MSP is voted in to do,
while John behind gives out the wine, he too
enriching public service, entering
our temple courts as one of us, like when
the link of church and state was sacrosanct,
and here the Provost of a Council ranked
no higher than the least of other men
and women. Clasping hands around the cup,
we drink a portion rooted in a psalm
which pulls us back to Passover, then rolls
us on through three millennia, wraps us up
within the love of God, whose pouring arm
can ground and heal and feed all souls.

117 Nae Hairm

Wee psalm, nae hairm intendit.
Jist the scandal o particularitie.

118 Space Temple

'The Lord set me in a broad place.' *v. 5*

I'll bring
my kilt and Alfred Edersheim;
courtesy of Doctor Who
I'll take this psalm and travel time.

I'll walk
through holy, heather-tasselled gates,
see Blake, inspired, at work creating
annotations on his plates.

I'll look
in every cranny of this psalm,
find Luther lost in admiration,
touched by God's heart-cradling arm.

I'll talk
with Gaudi and with Samuelsson
in Barcelona, Reykjavik,
feel the clunk of cornerstone.

I'll join
a liturgy with *cohēn*, *goi*,
and all who fear this tartan Lord,
sing praise with multi-coloured joy.

119 Fair and Square

No tapestry complete without a square
jaw somewhere, to remind tame images
that words do more than chatter,
show how *torah* draws a frame for life
to challenge slipshod needlework,
set out certain things that matter.

No book complete without some ordering
of chapters, sequences of numbers, letters
sailing A to Z, the blacks, the whites,
all shades of tighter *petit point* let loose
upon a canvas sea, like decorated buoys
which mark each passage with eight riding lights.

No symphony complete without a switch
from law to liberty, a swatch of tones,
an itch unwrapped so strings rehearse
its secret. Bless you, ancient makar, shrewd
composer, artist, stitcher: you have left
your needle prints so clear in every verse.

No life complete without God's art and music
hidden in our sober prose, artless, silent,
waiting for the word to waken, say hello,
and introduce a new dimension, dancing
intimacy to the edge of long horizons,
splashing colour on a great allegro.

120 – 134 Song of the Fifteen Steps

Introduction

Fifteen steps, said the Jewish sage,
on the stairs to reach the Women's Court
all the way from the Court of Israel.

Did he plan to reach the eternal feminine,
anticipate the next millennium,
open the gates to women's rights?

Dream on – he grabbed at a handy memo.
Fifteen men on the dead man's chest
offers a gendered Scots reply.

Fifteen cans in triangular pile,
waiting to topple, then get rolling
as soon as the missive hits the stack.

That's the scene for a pilgrim journey,
with fifteen psalms to line the route,
buffeting politics, toughening faith.

Psalm 120

Jews in exile stepping the world,
Rashi in France, the Rambam in Spain
wrenched out of sync by persecution,
wrestled to ground with a holy text,
writing a *Guide for People Perplexed*.

Were you there with Jamie in 1715,
out with Charlie in the '45?
Gutted in Gallipolli in 1915,
desperate for closure in '45,
not quite sure if you're dead or alive?

Scots do grievance all too well,
but so does everyone who feels
a misfit in an alien world
of fear and war, and longs to escape
from the lies, the cuts, the raw-edged rape.

Psalm 121

Pilgrimage, an upland route
footsteps on the Cairngorms,
guided deeper by Nan Shepherd,
rapt, seeing the world in her body,
feeling the coil of an eagle's rise.
Ascent indeed, but someone higher
gives us all our pilot's wings,
guards our going and our coming.

Pilgrimage, not mountaineering,
love the mountain, not the tops.
Hold the vision, ride the thermal
current, gaze on Angel Peak;
salute the exploits, but remember
hills and valleys frame the journey,
while the end is out of sight.

Psalm 122

A 'terraced' psalm (tribes, thrones, *shalom*),
three levels in Jerusalem.

Three monotheist modern tribes,
with rather different pilgrim vibes,

are eyeing judgement on their thrones
that now lie buried with the bones

of ancient history. Complex
may be the politics, effects

of war, attempts at peace. The hope
is balanced on a rocky trope

that Teddy Kollek, Arab Mayor,
chiselled into public prayer:

'Pray for the peace of Jerusalem'
(and every step to build *shalom*
that lives the meaning of this psalm).

Psalm 123

I have seen that look
in the eyes of a collie
aquiver with hope of a walk,
acquainted with body signals,
knowing the master's habits,
happy with a moment hanging
in the mind of the enthroned one.

Crowns so often shield the eyes,
speed up growth of cataract,
curl the lips of a ruler
centralised in Holyrood,
or lodged down in Westminster.

I must try to meet the gaze
of God, who sees through me
and every would-be king or queen.

Psalm 124

Such public psalms do frighten the atheist horses,
ridden rough through films and wikipedia,
strictly barred from *casa et cathedra*
where a nation prayed the British forces
safely out of France, to fight again.
A Red Sea crossing, wrote the Gaelic poet
of Dunkirk, quite unashamed to show it
in such holy context, all those men
delivered from the raging waters; calm
behind the storm which grounded enemy planes,
cloud which gave divine protection. *Chains*
fell off, their hearts were free to shout this psalm.

Better dismount, see 'Warhorse' and '*Equus*';
no wonder atheist horsemen have no use
for faith; they'd unseat Churchill – and the Bruce.

Psalm 125

On skis, I toured the hills around Glenshee
and hit a whiteout – rather, it hit me
like a dose of labyrinthitis, spun
my senses widdershins, the home run
halted, and my body falling upright,
biped spider on a bath of white,
stranded on a flatbed like a ghost
while the universe went left off piste.

Two legs frozen, six dissolved in fear
I waited for the world to reappear
and give a mountain top the sign, all clear.
I guess Mount Zion comes and goes
like that, somewhere above our woes:
it leaves us hoping that the Lord our God
might ski or leg it down, meet us roughshod.

Psalm 126

That game we drew
at Twickenham,
all fifteen players
heroes, legends;
divine catchup,
return from exile.

You did it once,
now do it again,
God of surprises.

Do it for Scotland,
do it for England,
do it for the world,
every person
setting out
on pilgrimage.

Psalm 127

Zsuzsa worked for us at Carberry,
brought a sense of family with her,
fifteen siblings, self and parents
making quite a quiverful:
Hungarian exiles, holding hard
to Calvin, church and culture
deep in Transylvania,
knowing only God the Lord
can build the house of hope,
guard the city from calamity.

Early to bed, early to rise,
she modelled pilgrimage
for ageing worry warriors
who suffer deficits of faith
and family life, wisdom and sleep.

Psalm 128

'A symphony must embrace the world.'   *Gustav Mahler*

Work and family life and Israel,
that hidden light for every nation,
gladness gift wrapped in a psalm
with liminal fear, immanent love.

One table set for more than one
(*it is not good for man to be alone,*
nor prayer and praise to be confined
within a lonely solo instrument
that plays, and sobs, in wilderness).

One octave for the children,
another for the grand-children,
those fifteen different notes
that make a symphony for Israel,
an orchestra of horticulture,
seeded in a thousand lands.

Psalm 129

Just when the going was downhill,
my progress programmed, fifteen easy steps,
I felt the lash, and shuddered to a stop.

I had the wrong map, dragons painted out,
the giants missing. We had all forgotten
history, the thongs and thorns and daggers
hidden by the cloak of Christendom
now whipped off zipped up torsos.

Temple walls and roof collapsed, its rubble
wrecked my all too easy pilgrimage.
No longer shielded from my enemies,
I yelled at them, a withering curse
that curled my lip, padlocked my heart,
and blocked the blessing that alone
might burst the bubble of my hell.

Psalm 130

We know that psychopaths are born, not made,
autism more than adverse child experience,
and the human genome is the modern key
to unlock mysteries of illness and behaviour.

Read this psalm on a wall in Dachau prison.
We indignantly reject the roots of Hitler's blame,
his paranoid conviction, dictat that the Jews
corrupted Aryan purity, must disappear.

Diagnose our pain from human sin?
How out of fashion – yet, we hear a text
that dives beneath our dismal lives
into the depths, to source a pearl
that Jung and others raked the fire for:
Israel as suffering servant, scapegoat,
kept awake, aching for the morning.

Psalm 131

How odd our culture,
out of step with history,
passing laws of progress
in a freedom sweated
out of the hard hands
of barons who submitted
to that double whammy,
Bible and democracy.
What passing privilege
to choose our pilgrimage,
eye the very heights.

When the crash comes
we will be children
holding on to mother,
hoping in the Lord.

Psalm 132

'Obedience has a history.'   *Eugene Peterson*

A bit of history always helps
that half time pep talk, when you've missed
a chance, a goal, and now the wind
is in your face, the going hard.

Obedience has a long track record
in the storied lives of women,
men like David who knew hardship,
failed, yet found God's faithfulness.

Fifteen dark blue threads remember
those who died inside the mountain,
tartan marks those tunnel tigers
resting till the whistle blows

and Zion's lamp lights David's son,
when every life is joined in one
more powerful than Ben Cruachan.

Psalm 133

How blest is one small step together,
fifteen must be heaven. In
between, we make such heavy weather
of our common life, we sin
against each other, Jacob, Esau,
Isaac, Ishmael, Abel, Cain.

We tear our hair, we clutch at straw
to find our way in, out of Europe,
with no proper sense of awe
at Aaron's beard, and every drop
of oil that consecrated him
a priest, a listener, chosen backstop
for our fall, a pseudonym
for you, for me; the question's whether
we can priest our sister, brother.

Psalm 134

When we get there, questions dry
up, silenced by the sounds of heaven;
no more need to puzzle why
the journey felt like being driven
off road, off stage, just off key.

When we find that wider space
than we allowed in our religions,
heaven may seem a stranger place,
a glorious sequence of black swans
on message, and in harmony.

When we meet to praise the Lord,
our fifteen steps of pilgrimage
will thread their way into a cord
that decorates the title page
of holy books of tapestry.

135 Mosaic

Sandwich psalm,
mosaic of texts
for chosen lifters,
the Lord's name
layered, like lasagne
which ripples from
that holy standing start.

Ten strikes, Pharaoh,
and you're out
– with your calves
and your quarters
pierced by the dark angel
you called up
from a hardened heart.

Struck by a lightning God,
unlike us, who
stroke the internet
for friendly idols,
click on 'next'
to fill our tidy
ideological cart.

136 End Game

They caught that massive hole of blackness,
called it by the name Powehi,
darkest source of evolution,
lit up its event horizon,
put it on a world parade.

Could we wrap up all mystery,
the words of God, the human hope
by probing radio telescopes,
this psalm would bite the cosmic dust
that litters outer, inner space.

It brings to heel the dogging voice
which robs religion of its track
in time, and makes the spiritual
nice and vague, not blood and battles,
earthbound tyrants seeing stars.

This *Great Hallel*, this making song
has God committed, and for ever,
in a universal frame
of right and wrong, taking aim
at rulers, saving refugees.

We hole up in the psalmist's end game,
lowly, hanging on the praise chain,
late arrivals in creation,
dwarfed by skies of light and darkness,
yet a twinkle in God's eye.

137 Finding Your Voice

In memory of Astor Piazzolla, composer, 1921-1992

She senses something missing,
a soul space sectioned,
left in Argentina.

This Nadia Boulanger,
teacher playing therapist
to Astor Piazzolla,

gives him tangoed freedom
to deep root his love of Bach
in Argentinian soil.

Crossover takes time,
voices back from exile,
hearts all clear of hate.

138 Hair

'Samson . . . bowed himself with all his might.'   *Judges 16:30 KJV*

Cross stitch creeps into a corner
p.c. stitchers do not visit:
threads twisted in hermeneutic
horror, recognises Samson,

hears him orchestrate the clatter
of a foreign temple as he bows,
strains, claws two alien pillars
as his final act of worship.

At a safe distance,
she wonders who else
lets their hair grow
under the tapestry.

139 Convenient Fiction?

Starting somewhere in my psyche, temple
textures touch my mind. No need to book
a room, no call to speak to any stranger;
free to open suitcase, strut one's stuff,
repack with jewels from the night, some truth
about the soul, some insight, art or science.

So far so good. I call upon Sir Science
for some knowledge of myself. The temple
library is open, and the truth
about my brain is there in many books
on cortex, lobes and neurons, complex stuff
that keeps on getting brainier – and stranger.

Like how we understand our stranger
selves, the fabled bits that neuroscience
only labels, while Dame Art has stuff
galore from centuries before the temple
closed its canon, not to speak of books
and blogs since then that deep mine truth.

All this is introduction. For some truth
that blows the mind, a story even stranger,
meet a searching God, here in the book
of Psalms: a God who flies ahead of science
fiction, fuels quasars, forms a temple
out of space and time, inspires the stuff

of dreams, knows off by heart each book that stuffs
the shelves of planet earth. To tell the truth,
God reads the dark, the darkness found in temples
or in us, when we become a stranger
to ourselves, and flee from art and science
and from human company, to book

ourselves a place apart, no God, no book,
no sense, no you or me. This nightmare stuff
God also knows, through wind and womb, by science,
art and therapy, in nudging truth
to birth, in changing entropy, these stranger
miracles that mark a cosmic temple.

Is it science, art, to class God's book
convenient fiction, tepid temple stuff?
God thinks truth stronger, definitely stranger.

140 Af Bees n Bleizin

They byket about me, like bees; they gaed down   *formed a nest*
like a bleeze o' thorns . . .
'Wha fank me roun' – atowre their crown   *surround me*
may the ill o' their lips be theekit!   *thatched*
Bleezan blauds come abune them . . .'   *blazing blows*
  Saums 118:12 and 140:9-10, owerset frae
  Hebrew intil Scottis bi P. Hately Waddell

'A see ye keep ae bee,'   *a single bee*
quo Jimmie Shand,
whan gien a measly
thrummle-fu o hinnie   *thimble-full* *honey*
i yon scrimpit B n B.   *tight-fisted*

Aiblins snell-gabbit,   *perhaps sarcastic*
bit no sae nippie   *sharp*
as e speeder venim,   *spider poison*
ir the sairpent souch   *venomous timbre*
o a slidderie tung.   *deceitful*

They fun the bees
o Notre Dame tae the fore,   *up on top*
bit soon as peeries,   *fast asleep*
in a ruiftap skep   *hive*
abune the tempil bleize.   *above*

Thae birsled bougars   *scorched rafters*
sen a reiky waff   *smoky smell*
tae kittlie stangers: *sensitive stingers*
'Dover aroun yir quen   *snooze*
or daunger wins awa.'   *till danger passes*

Lat them as be shairp
stang bi sic fell pizzen   *poison*
cuil thir birse,   *rage*
lae flytin tae   *wrangling*
thon sangschaw keeng.   *music competition king*

141 Prayer

'To my God a heart of flame, to my fellows a heart of love,
to myself a heart of steel.'   *St Augustine*

Every day I pray this trail of tapestry a little further on.
Flame stitches zigzag morning and at evening,
an irregular bargello, yellowed with such fitful craft,
but still alight with all the incense of each night.

Every day cross stitches lose their place and purpose,
need unwinding in a faithful strike of love,
for modern tapestry's a multi-coloured fellow
learning how to pray good in, and evil out.

Every day I stretch my stitch to continental,
with a steely grasp of our own gaucheness,
make a tent with room for more than one,
and find some warp threads simulating God.

142 In the Cave

Who is in the cave with David
and his band of desperadoes?
Plato working on his mind
to sort out false from real foes?
Edgar Poe, his pendulum
of fate aswing to frighten those
with brutal claustrophobia?
Or Bruce, a spider at his nose
to model hope and stamina?

Who is in the cave with me,
when life becomes a prison hut,
and prayer goes round and round my head
and wears a clogging, toxic rut?
My enemies within, without
are wily, smooth and strong, they shut
me into dark despair; there's no one left
to help. Oh save me, Lord, just cut
a path into my soul, and rescue me.

Who is in the Scottish cave,
our catacomb of buried past,
clogged up with credit and complaint,
with argument and counterblast?
Those real and phantom figures huddle
with us, watch and pray and fast
till *faith and fortune, time and tide*
may bring us out, to praise at last
a God who wipes the floor inside.

143 In a Corner

'So Absalom stole the hearts of the people of Israel.' *2 Samuel 15:6*

If not Absalom, another rival
crushes me, dissects my character
and pins it to a dirty washing line.

I remember golden days, when I
was young, my team around me, brilliant
and untagged by blood and lust and power.

In this muddy corner, choked by dust,
I cower, throat-sore, thirsty for you,
knowing I have dragged my country here.

For me read every human being, Scot
or not, each called to be a servant prince
and ruler of the road before our feet.

144 Stuff

Mind-bending stuff:
shape-shifting God
flows happily
without a blink
from lightning flash
to people power,
and personalist
trainer, life coach,
gym and spirit
all in one.

Heart-rending stuff:
crook-fingered aliens
shake hands
and never think
of faithfulness.
Deliver us
from ricin, anthrax,
cyber warfare,
family feuds,
from knife and gun.

Soul-mending stuff:
I will pick up
my multi-stringed
guitar, and link
my voice to angels
in the temple
taking shape
around the praise
of song and psalm
in every tongue.

Impending stuff:
this God is waiting
for a weighted prayer,
pitched – kerplink –
into a loch,
when ripples rich
with consequence
bless barn and beast,
upend the wicked,
keep a kingdom young.

145 A to Z

acrostic seems a little lower case for God,
belittles one whose letters only spell a word,
cannot bow before the majesty,
describe the beauty or the glory,
evoke those intimate connections
firing all things seen and unseen,
gilding star and season,
hearth and holy heritage.

I will bless you every day, my God and King,
just as on weekday afternoons, the synagogue
kept psalms like this in service,
line by crisp and careful line,
marrying grace and greatness,
never close to running out
of verbs and other
parts of stunning speech,
questions left behind this craft of wonder

reaching for the sky, complaints left wailing
somewhere in the wake of praise. A
tapestry of miracle is rolling, scrolling
underneath earth's tragedies, adding
value unsuspected without faith. If
Wallace Stevens could invent so many
extra things about a blackbird, how will
you, my God, approach the
zenith of *your* poetry?

146 Boundaries

Let everyone be clear about their mission,
though the bounds be wide as heaven and earth;
let not the prince become a politician.

How blest the man or woman who long since
picked up a call to servant leadership;
let not the priest or prophet be a prince.

Let God be swift to help, in God's own fashion,
free our speech, hold back the evil thought;
let not the prince become a cool assassin.

My soul is shocked, my fragile being winces
at the sight of blood, the sound of lies;
let not the people put their trust in princes.

147 Jerusalem

City of conflict and combustion,
city of international contention;
city of stones and ancient bones;
city of wonder, though the thunder
of its past rolls through the present,
makes the future nervous.

City of fears and separate parts,
city of tears and broken hearts,
city of God, below, above;
city of metaphor and meaning,
city to explore with mind
and map you make your own.

City of song and ancient praise,
city the Lord alone can raise
above the wrangles and the rasp
of rivalry between the faiths
that claim it – reinvent *shalom*,
so wounded outcasts name it home.

148 People of the Light

Let every biochemist praise the Lord,
and every astrophysicist:
you charm afresh these earthly, heavenly bodies,
make John Keats clear Isaac Newton
of his crimes against the light.

The photons from the sun began their journey
deep in fusion at its core,
set out before the birth of *homo sapiens*,
only now are hitting on
the retina behind my eye.

Let every biochemist praise the Lord,
and every astrophysicist:
you open eyes and ears again to wonder
at God's puns, those particles
which also take the form of waves.

Humans voice the praise of all creation,
God within us praising God beyond,
but God as usual goes ahead of us,
his beam soft booming of a boson,
modern music of the spheres.

Let every biochemist praise the Lord,
and every astrophysicist:
like Israel, you're called to be a light
to Gentile ignoramuses –
go re-enchant the universe.

149 Maturity

She walked half round the church, before
the paper plate fell off her head;
the girl relaxed, such halo practice
proving taxing fun; instead,
she settled for a biscuit with her maw.   *mum*

Her brother flashed the plastic sword
his paw had bought at Stirling, tiny   *dad*
two-edged tribute to the Wallace
and the Bruce, a simple sign he
understood and took on board.

So now may Zion's children grow
to sainthood, wisely exegete
their past, to fight for freedom
knowing also how to beat
the sword to hoe, violence veto.

150 Breathing or Breathless

slow breath and quick breath
the long and the short of it

shallow breath, deep breath,
the ins and the outs of it

noisy breath, quiet breath
whisper and shout of it

bag breath and pipe breath
the puff and the teeth of it

buzzard breath, budgie breath
twitter and cry of it

snout breath and muzzle breath
snuffle and growl of it

baby breath, dying breath
first and the last of it

breathing or breathless
a cosmos of praise to it

Notes on Book 5 Poems

109 Epigraph from W.S. Graham, 'The Fifteen Devices', *New Collected Poems*, Faber, London 2004.

111 The final line is a reference to Maxwell's favourite hymn, 'Lord of all being, throned afar.'

114 Epigraph from a conversation on *The Divine Comedy* with Edward Clarke, who has himself published poems on all the Psalms (*A Book of Psalms*, Paraclete Press, Brewster MA, 2020).

115 Epigraph from *Homo Deus: a Brief History of Tomorrow*, Penguin, London 2015, 24.

118 Alfred Edersheim was a Jewish Christian who wrote about the Temple and wanted to take his readers back through time.

126 On 16/3/19 Scotland and England drew 38-38 at Twickenham.

136 Powehi is in Hawaian culture a name meaning 'the adorned fathomless dark creation' and given to a black hole photographed for the first time in 2019. https://www.theguardian.com/science/2019/apr/12/powehi-black-hole-gets-a-name-meaning-the-adorned-fathomless-dark-creation, accessed 11/4/20.

143 The Septuagint adds, 'When his son is pursuing him' to the heading 'A Psalm of David', hence the reference to Absalom.

146 The reference is to the murder of Jamal Khashoggi on 2/10/18.

Notes on Chapter One

1 In 'Final Soliloquy of the Interior Paramour', Wallace Stevens, *The Collected Poems*, Penguin, New York, Second Vintage Edition of 2015, 555.

2 The *Russkii Mir* or 'Russian World' teaching has now been officially condemned by other Orthodox Churches, leaving the Russian Orthodox Church isolated.

3 Athanasius, *On the Incarnation*, ed. and trans. A Religious of C.S.M.V., Mowbray, London 1953, 116.

4 Scholars like David Mitchell still argue that the headings should be taken seriously, and that (for example), the fifteen 'Songs of Ascents' (Psalms 120 – 134) were composed for the dedication of Solomon's temple (*The Song of Ascents*, Campbell Publications, Newton Mearns 2015). Others put them much later.

5 *Answering God*, Harper and Row, San Francisco 1989, 16 and 33.

6 While there are ruined temples of St Peter and St Moluag on the Isle of Lewis (*teampaill* in Gaelic), the word *templum* is found in the Latin Psalms, with *casa* or *domus* used for the humbler church buildings of Ninian and Columba. There is a village of 'Temple' in Midlothian, which claims to be linked to the order of Templars, but generally you find 'church' or 'cathedral' in Britain, not 'temple'.

7 Andrew Painting, *Regeneration*, Birlinn 2021, 129.

8 '*Taorluath* Singling: Over the Hump' in Book 4 poetry.

9 *Grace and Necessity: Reflections on Art and Love*, Continuum, London 2005, 147.

10 Iain Provan, *Convenient Myths*, Baylor University Press, Waco 2013, 99.

11 John Lundquist in 'The Common Temple Ideology of the Ancient Near East' (from The Temple in Antiquity, ed. Truman G. Madsen, Brigham Young University, Provo UT, 1984, 53-76) in L. Michael Morales (ed.), *Cult and Cosmos: Tilting Towards a Temple-Centred Theology*, Peeters, Leuven 2014, 53.

12 C.T.R. Hayward, *The Jewish Temple*, Routledge, London 1996, 51.

13 J.R. Middleton, *The Liberating Image*, Baker, Grand Rapids 2005, 84.

14 Morales 2014, 4.

15 G.K. Beale, *The Temple and the Church's Mission*, IVP, Downers Grove 2004, 25.

16 See Ludwig Köhler, *Hebrew Man*, SCM Press, London 1973, 131.

17 John Walton, *The Lost World of Genesis One*, IVP Downers Grove 2009, 71f.

18   Jon D. Levenson, 'The Temple and the World', Journal of Religion, Vol. 64 no. 3 (July 1984), 288.

19   John Walton, *The Lost World of Adam and Eve*, IVP Downers Grove 2015, 49.

20   Jubilees 8:19, in Beale 2004, 78.

21   Some versions have God being *at* Sinai, but the connection is the same. The Jewish *targum* has the high mount as Sinai, linking Sinai directly with the 'heights' which other psalms call Zion.

22   The language of the Psalms sometimes echoes older language. The Hebrew word *hêkāl* for temple probably comes from Sumerian é.gal meaning big (gal) house (é) and palace in particular. In 2 Chronicles 3:5 *habbayit haggādôl* 'the big room' is used, which in Ugarit myths is used for Baal's heavenly palace, while in biblical poetry it is used for YHWH's heavenly abode (Psalm 11:4, 18:7).

23   Donald Harman Akenson, *Surpassing Wonder*, University of Chicago Press, Montreal 1998, 311, 408-110.

24   Leslie D. Weatherhead, *A Private House of Prayer*, 1958, reissued by Arthur James, London 1985.

25   In the centuries before Jesus, many Israelites named their sons Yeshua in the hope that they might turn out to be the Messiah. How the name Jesus relates to the divine name, and how Jewish commentators thought of Messiah is set out by David Mitchell in a recent book (*Jesus: The Incarnation of the Word*, Campbell Publications 2021 – see for example 221f.). Mitchell is a Hebrew scholar and musicologist, currently Precentor at Brussels Cathedral.

26   Genesis 1:27, Exodus 20:4. See Iain Provan, *Seriously Dangerous Religion*, Baylor University Press, Waco 2014, 80-82. There are a few examples in ANE texts of a man as an image (for example, Enkidu in the *Gilgamesh Epic* is described as a 'double' of Gilgamesh) but they function differently – see Middleton 2005, 94.

27   *'Song of the Fifteen Steps' (Psalm 125)* from Book 5 Poetry.

28   Respectively, *A Book of Psalms*, Paraclete Press, Brewster MA, 2020, and *David's Crown*, Canterbury Press, Norwich 2021.

29   'Alive' in R.S. Thomas, *Collected Poems 1945-1990*, Orion Books, London 2000, 296.

30   Duns Scotus, *De Primo Principio* 4.29, cited by James Torrance in *John Duns Scotus in a Nutshell*, Handsel Press, Edinburgh 1992, 18.

31   Barry Holz, *Back to the Sources: Reading the Classic Jewish Texts*, Touchstone, New York 1992, 17, citing *New Directions in Literary History*, ed. Ralph Cohen, John Hopkins University Press, Baltimore 1974, 125-47.

32   Levenson 1984, 283, citing Mircea Eliade.

33   Levenson 1984, 284, citing Josephus, *The Jewish War* 3, 7:7.

34 Beale 2004, citing Josephus, *Ant.* 3.145, 181; Philo, *Vit. Mos.* 2.71-145, *Quaest. Exod.* 285.

35 Middleton 2005, 83. He adds that given the prophetic critique of the temple, it perhaps should be a contrast.

36 Provan 2014, 32-34.

37 Beale 2004, 183.

38 George Davie, *The Crisis of the Democratic Intellect*, Polygon, Edinburgh 1986, 21.

39 James Cameron, *The First Book of Discipline*, St Andrew Press, Edinburgh 1972, 46.

40 Children of rich and poor alike must be educated – Cameron 1972, 132.

41 T.F. Torrance (ed. and trans.), *The School of Faith*, James Clarke, London 1959, xxviii-xxx.

42 Cameron 1972, 55.

43 James S. McEwen, *The Faith of John Knox*, Lutterworth, London 1961, 40.

44 'Reformed Scotland also expressed . . . the idea of the "democratic intellect"; not because Presbyterianism is pure democracy, for it isn't, but because it expressed the Christian concept of equality in the sight of God' (R.D. Kernohan, *The Realm of Reform*, Handsel Press, Edinburgh 1999, 13).

45 Davie worked this out in two books, *The Democratic Intellect*, Nelson, Edinburgh 1961, and in 1986 *The Crisis of the Democratic Intellect*, in continuity with the 'common sense philosophy' of Thomas Reid (Davie 1986, 186).

46 J.H. Newman, *The Idea of a University*, ed. I.T. Ker, Oxford University Press, Oxford 1976 (based on the 1889 edition, revised by Newman and published in London by Longmans, Green and Co.).

47 Newman 1889, Discourse VII, especially 145, cf. Alastair McIntosh, Healing Nationhood, Curlew Productions, Kelso 2000, 126-7. More recently, Alasdair MacIntyre defended Newman against the charge of being irrelevant to the modern university, and suggested that his more controversial claim ('theology is the key to all knowledge') might also be relevant to the aims of science today ('The Very Idea of a University: Aristotle, Newman and Us', British Journal of Educational Studies 57:4, 347-362).

48 Tessa Ransford, interviewed by Jenny Lindsay – from the 'National Collective', published on https://bellacaledonia.org.uk/2018/10/06/creando-pensamus-interview-with-tessa-ransford/ 6th October 2018.

49 David Daiches, *The Paradox of Scottish Culture*, Oxford University Press, London 1964, 38.

50 Paul H. Scott, *Towards Independence*, Polygon, Edinburgh 1991, 89.

51 Craig Beveridge and Ronald Turnbull, *The Eclipse of Scottish Culture*, Polygon, Edinburgh 1989, 80-1.

52 Davie 1961, 4.

53 Torrance 1959, xl. Cf. Jim Cullen, *The American Dream*, Oxford University Press, London 2003, 52. America was influenced from this Scottish tradition through John Witherspoon.

54 From Joseph Houston, *Thomas Reid in a Nutshell*, Handsel Press, Edinburgh 2000, 12.

55 See T.F. Torrance, *Belief in Science and in Christian Life*, Handsel Press, Edinburgh 1980; Alister McGrath, *A Scientific Theology*, T&T Clark, Edinburgh 2002, 195f.

56 Houston 2000, 17.

57 Davie 1961, 21, 193.

58 Tom Devine broadly accepts Davie's analysis, but suggests that he exaggerates the degree of specialisation which was imposed on Scotland (Tom Devine, *The Scottish Nation*, Penguin, London 2012, 409).

59 Davie 1961, 301.

60 Alan Riach discusses the thread of 'democracy' from The Declaration of Arbroath (Riach, *Scottish Literature: an introduction*, Luath Press, Edinburgh 2022, 110-111).

Notes on Chapter Two

1 A Drunk Man Looks at the Thistle', lines 2638-40.

2 Between 2017 and 2018, the number quintupled in a year, according to *The Guardian*.

3 Jeremy Hooker introducing Tony Conran, *Three Symphonies*, Agenda Editions, Mayfield, East Sussex 2016, 10 (citing a 1997 book by Conran, *Vison and Praying Mantids*).

4 Gordon Donaldson, *The Faith of the Scots*, Batsford, London 1990, 13. He goes on to cite Kenneth Scott Latourette, *A History of the Expansion of Christianity*, Vol. 1, 240.

5 Meg Bateman, Robert Crawford and James McGonigal, *Scottish Religious Poetry*, St Andrew Press, Edinburgh 2000, xviii.

6 1 Samuel 22:6-19. See G.W.S. Barrow, *Robert Bruce and the Community of the Realm of Scotland*, Edinburgh University Press, Edinburgh 2013, 199.

7 1 Samuel 24:1-7; 25:2-35.

8 1 Samuel 23:27-28.

9 2 Samuel 11.

10 Michael Penman, *Robert the Bruce: King of the Scots*, Yale University Press, London 2014, 94.

11 1 Samuel 18:17.

12 2 Samuel 4 and 5.

13 1 Samuel 22:1-4.

14 2 Samuel 13 to 19, 1 Kings 1.

15 G.W.S. Barrow, *Robert Bruce and the Community of the Realm of Scotland*, Edinburgh University Press, Edinburgh 2013, 389, 403.

16 In Psalm 89:27-29 he is the greatest, but by 89:38-45 he is cut down to size. And Amos 6:5 hints that David himself might have had better things to do than sit around making music.

17 In Douglas Gifford and Alan Riach (eds.), *Scotlands: Poets and the Nation*, Carcanet, Manchester 2004, 18.

18 Third most popular after Adam and Simon (with Michael fourth). See John Reuben Davies, 'Old Testament Personal Names in Scotland before the Wars of Independence', in Matthew Hammond (ed.), *Personal Names and Naming Practices in Medieval Scotland*, Boydell, Woodbridge 2019, 187-212.

19 Penman 2014, 155.

20 Davies 2019, 197.

21 A series of 'Stations of the Cross poems' related to the late 20th century struggle of the Fife miners – Grace Note Publications, Crieff 2018.

22 Guite 2021, 8.

23 Elspeth Jaidelska, '"Singing of Psalms of which I could never get enough": Labouring Class Religion and Poetry in the Cambuslang Revival of 1741', Studies in Scottish Literature, 41 (1), 2015, 93.

24 Paul Valéry in *Poetry and Abstract Thought*, cited by Edward Hirsch, *How to Read a Poem*, Houghton Mifflin Harcourt, New York 1999, 115.

25 Malcolm Guite, *Parable and Paradox*, Canterbury Press, Norwich 2016, 10.

26 'The Prophet's Pen', *New Republic* – https://en.wikipedia.org/wiki/David_Rosenberg_(poet), accessed 15/9/19.

27 A.N. Wilson, *The Book of the People*, Atlantic Books, London 2015, 131.

28 Angus Calder, Glen Murray, Alan Riach, *The Rauchle Tongue: Selected Essays, Journalism and Interviews by Hugh MacDiarmid*, Carcanet, Manchester 1998, 562.

29 See for example George and Isabel Henderson, *The Arts of the Picts: Sculpture and Metalwork in Early Medieval Scotland*, Thames and Hudson, London 2004, 130-2, 243-5 etc; David Clarke, Alice Blackwell and Martin Goldberg, *Early Medieval Scotland: Individuals, Communities and Ideas*, National Museums Scotland 2012.

30 Barrow 2013, 294. Walter Bower in *Scotichronicon* 6:363-5 also says that Bruce referred to 'John the Baptist . . . and St Andrew and St Thomas [Becket]' – Michael Penman, 'Sacred Food for the Soul: in search of the Devotions to Saints of Robert Bruce, King of Scotland, 1306-1329', *Speculum* Vol. 88, No. 4 (October 2013), University of Chicago Press, 1048.

31 Penman 2014, 105.

32 Dante Alighieri 2012, *Inferno*, Canto 20, line 116.

33 https://www.scotsman.com/lifestyle-2-15039/scottish-wizard-who-tutored-the-pope-1-466356, accessed 8/9/19.

34 'Medievalists' (Adrian Hastings, *The Construction of Nationhood*, Cambridge University Press, Cambridge 1997, 1) would have no doubt about this, 'Modernists' (Jonathan Hearn, *Rethinking Nationalism*, Palgrave Macmillan, Basingstoke 2006, 85) say it is more obvious from the Reformation era.

35 2 Samuel 23:1, KJV. This may have covered improvising, composing or even making new instruments, depending how *ḥāšbû* in Amos 6:5 is translated.

36 Heaney, Seamus, *The Government of the Tongue*, Faber and Faber, London 1988, 93.

37 John Barbour, *The Bruce*, c. 1376, ed. and trans. James Higgins, Arima, Bury St Edmunds 2013.

38 There are now books available which correct earlier views, but the most detailed material can be accessed through William Scott's website, https://www.elenkus.co.uk.

39 William Storrar, *Scottish Identity*, Handsel Press, Edinburgh 1990, 28.

40 Donald Davie, *The Poet in the Imaginary Museum*, Carcanet, Manchester 1977 (orig. 1950), 45-6.

41 Davie 1977, 53.

42 Atina Nihtinen, 'Scotland's Linguistic Past and Present: Paradoxes and Consequences', *Studia Celtica Fennica* 2, Jan. 2005, 118-121.

43 See for example Kenneth MacLeod, *The Road to the Isles*, Grant and Murray, Edinburgh 1927; Alexander Carmichael, *Carmina Gadelica*, Floris books, Edinburgh 1992; as well as Bateman *et al.* 2000. The decline and 21st century revitalisation of Gaelic is discussed in Wilson McLeod and Michael Newton (eds.), *The Highest Apple: an Anthology of Scottish Gaelic Literature*, Francis Boutle Publishers, London 2019, 546f.

44 Douglas Dunn (ed.), *Faber Book of Twentieth-century Scottish Poetry*, Faber and Faber, London 1992, xviii and xxi. MacDiarmid was not just making poetry, but trying to make a nation anew.

45 See for example a poem on Psalm 1 in David Curzon (ed.), *Modern Poems on the Bible*, Jewish Publication Society, Philadelphia 1994, 271.

46 Deuteronomy 4:20, 1 Kings 8:51. The image is repeated with regard to Jerusalem before the exile in Ezekiel 22:17-22.

47 Deuteronomy 8:1-5.

48 Ezekiel 36:25. After the return from exile there is no mention of idolatry, apart from Zechariah 13:2 which is (like Ezekiel) a promise that idols will be no more.

49 Hugh MacDiarmid, *In Memoriam James Joyce, A Vision of world Language*, William MacLellan, Glasgow 1956, 55.

50 As shown by Roland Prothero, *The Psalms in Human Life*, Thomas Nelson, London 1903, and, for example, by one of his sources, John Ker, *The Psalms in History and Biography*, Andrew Elliot, Edinburgh 1886, Preface.

51   J. Croumbie Brown (ed.), *Centenary Memorial of Rev. John Brown: A Family Record*, Andrew Eliot, Edinburgh 1887.

52   Gifford and Riach 2004, 22-3.

53   Sarah Carpenter in David F. Wright (ed.), *The Bible in Scottish Life and Literature*, St Andrew Press, Edinburgh 1988, 75.

54   Hearn 2006, 13.

55   Neil Oliver, *A History of Scotland*, Weidenfeld and Nicolson, London 2009, 126-7. Scotus broke away from the abstract Boethian definition of the person as an individual substance, and saw the people not as a collection of individuals but as a community – Torrance and Walls 1992, 13. Cf Storrar 1990, 4-5.

56   Oliver 2009, 142; compare the language of the Declaration of Arbroath.

57   In his catalogue of liturgical items from early times till 1560, Stephen Holmes lists two psalters from the 6th-8th centuries, ten from the 11th-13th centuries, and eight from the 15th century alone (Holmes 2011), as well as a large number of breviaries and other items.

58   Day 2005, 312.

59   For example, John 2:19-21, 1 Corinthians 3:16-17, Ephesians 2:21.

60   Discussed in books on political theology such as Jim Wallis, *On God's Side*, Baker, Grand Rapids 2013.

61   For example, Psalms 24:4, 37:11, 41:1, 72 underlying the Beatitudes of Matthew and Luke.

62   I have been unable to trace the origin of this well known quotation, which I first came across in English in George MacLeod, *One Way Left*, Iona Community, Glasgow 1958, vi.

63   The Qumran communities expected messiahs or 'anointed ones' of different kinds, some more kingly, some more priestly, hence the confusion around the person of Jesus, noted e.g. in John 6:14-15. The Babylonian Talmud says that Messiah's arrival will bring back the dynasty of King David, after what the rabbis called 'the pangs of Messiah' (Bavli, Pesahim 54b and Kethuboth 112b, cited in Donald H. Akenson, *Surpassing Wonder*, University of Chicago Press, Montreal 1998, 388).

64   See for example John Howard Yoder, *The Politics of Jesus*, Eerdmans, Grand Rapids 1972.

65   4QFlor I lines 18-19.

66   Susan Gillingham, *Psalms Through the Centuries*, Vol. 2, Wiley-Blackwell, Oxford 2018, 26. There may be isolated examples in other cultures of what Richard Middleton calls 'the democratisation of ideology' (Middleton 2005, 99-100).

67   Via Marx's reading of the NT in the British Library, and Keir Hardie's interpretation of Christianity.

68   See *Poem 20, 'Royal Rule'*.

69   Clarke 2020, 21.

70   Mark Smith, *Psalms: The Divine Journey*, Paulist Press, New York 1987, 14.

71 John Goldingay, *Psalms*, Vol. 1, Baker, Grand Rapids 2006, 419 (he takes a variant reading of v. 9a).

72 Gillingham 2018, 101.

73 For example, 'moves' and 'proves' in two lines of *17 'Eye to Eye'*, stanza six, are each puns: 'The battle moves within / the soul, where God proves all.' Eugene Peterson has a pun in his version of Psalm 57:10, 'Every cloud is a flag to your faithfulness', where 'cloud' has a double meaning in English but not in Hebrew.

74 In Psalm 145 (for which my poem is also alphabetical), *śin* and *šin* are treated as a single *śin*, making up the 22 letters of the Hebrew alphabet. This form is not quite the English acrostic, which usually has the initial letters making up a word sequence instead.

75 Kenneth Bailey, *Poet and Peasant*, Eerdmans, Grand Rapids 1976, 50.

76 Psalm 78 comes close to this genre, Psalms 105-107 to some extent, but Psalm 68 (assuming the psalm is a unity) illustrates it with the arrival of God in the holy place half way through, in verses 17-18.

77 Derick Thomson, 'Everlasting Life' from 'The Ark of the Covenant' in *Creachadh na Clàrsaich* (1982), cited in Ronald Black (ed.), *An Tuil*, Polygon, Edinburgh 1999.

78 Jasper and Prickett (eds.), *The Bible as Literature*, Blackwell, Oxford 1999, 2.

79 The psalm in question is 71:19, noticed by Kevin Hart in *Poetry and Revelation*, Bloomsbury, London 2017, 12.

80 Cited in Gillingham 2018, 229.

81 Figures supplied to the writer by Nielsen Bookdata. See also sales figures in https://www.theguardian.com/books/2019/jan/21/poetry-sales-soar-as-political-millennials-search-for-clarity, accessed 1/3/19.

82 R.K. Middlemas, *The Clydesiders* (London 1965) cited by T.C. Smout, *A Century of the Scottish People*, 1830-1950, Collins, Glasgow and Yale University Press, New Haven 1986, 271.

83 Wright 1988, 100.

84 In Hogg, James, *Private Memoirs and Confessions of a Justified Sinner*, ed. Garside, Edinburgh University Press, Edinburgh 2001, Hogg refers to singing part of the 10th Psalm (102) and part of the 119th psalm (227). In *The Shepherd's Calendar* (Edinburgh University Press 1995) where you might expect some reference to the 23rd Psalm, he only refers to the singing of psalms, and the reading of Ezra. In his poems, we get no further than 'The psalm was read' in 'The First Sermon' (James Hogg, *Selected Poems*, ed. Groves, Scottish Academic Press, Edinburgh 1986, 170), and a reference to 'Salem's harp' in 'The Pilgrims of the Sun'.

85 This is in contrast to 20th century continental European writers like Paul Celan, Paul Claudel, or Anna Kamienska, American writers like Denise

Levertov, Marianne Moore or Gabriel Preil, contemporary American writers like Scott Cairns or Jacqueline Osherow.

86   Bateman *et al*, 2000, 164.

87   In his poem 'Gospel' – Bateman *et al*. 2000.

88   George Campbell Hay cited in Bateman *et al*. 2000. Ironically it is atheistic writers like these two (and MacDiarmid) who refuse to 'escape' from the world who stay close to the OT worldview.

89   *Scottish Religious Poetry 2000*, 'Canticle', 297.

90   Scott Cairns, *Slow Pilgrim*, Paraclete Press, Brewster, Mass. 2015, 231.

91   Michael Symmons Roberts, *Drysalter*, Jonathan Cape, London 2013.

92   *Psalmody*, Eyewear Publishing, London 2016.

93   'Hallin' in Kenneth Steven, *The Spirit of the Hebrides*, St Andrew Press, Edinburgh 2019, 2.

94   John Stuart Blackie, *Lays of the Highlands and Islands*, Walter Scott, London 1888, 101-108.

95   In 'The Wren', A Plain Glass, Drunk Muse Press 2021, 90. Smart has also written a number of unpublished 'Psalm Sonnets 2009-10' on texts including Psalms 86 and 118.

96   'Borve, Lewis' in Black 1999, 611.

97   Historical novelists do of course – Walter Scott frequently (*Heart of Midlothian, Peveril of the Peak*), and today James Robertson (*The Fanatic*).

98   See Maoilios Caimbeul, *Gràs / Grace*, diglot publication, Handsel Press, Edinburgh 2019.

99   Diana Hendry, *Twelve Lilts*, Mariscat Press, Edinburgh 2003.

100   'Psalm 151' riffing on Psalm 51 (Theresa Lola, *In Search of Equilibrium*, Nine Arches Press, Rugby 2019).

101   Allusions to three psalms in 'Sea Leopard'.

102   'Do I hate them with perfect hatred?' by Helena Fornells of Barcelona (on Psalm 139, unpublished).

103   For example, a meditation on Psalm 77, 1st July 2019, (http://www.sanctuaryfirst.org.uk/daily-worship/drawing-well).

104   'The poet does not write what he knows, but what he doesn't know.' Michael and Margaret Snow (ed.), *The Nightfisherman: Selected Letters of W.S. Graham*, Carcanet, Manchester 1999, 14.

105   James K.A. Smith, *The Fall of Interpretation*, Baker, Grand Rapids 2012, 194.

106   1 Corinthians 2:13 in KJV, better translated 'interpreting spiritual things to those who are spiritual' (NRSV).

107   See Iain Provan, *The Reformation and the Right Reading of Scripture*, Baylor University Press, Waco 2017, 592f. for a general discussion of this; or Gale Yee (ed.), *The Hebrew Bible, Feminist and Intersectional Perspectives*, Fortress, Minneapolis 2018.

108 'Letter to my Children' in Toby Martinez de las Rivas, *Black Sun*, Faber, London 2018, 5.

109 Poem 1129 in her *Complete Poems*, Martin Secker, London 1928.

110 John MacQuarrie, 'Burns: Poet, Prophet, Philosopher', *Expository Times* 86, 1975, 112-114.

111 From 'A Drunk Man Looks at the Thistle', in Alan Riach and Michael Grieve (eds.), *Hugh MacDiarmid, Selected Poems*, Carcanet 1992, reissued Penguin, London 1994, line 153.

112 Augustine, *Confessions*, trans. Pusey, Dent. London 1907, 10.24.35. 'Nor have I found anything concerning Thee, but what I have kept in memory . . . Thou residest in my memory, and there do I find Thee.'

113 Rowan Williams, 'Augustine and the Psalms', *Interpretation*, Jan 2004, 23.

114 Frances Yates, *The Art of Memory*, Routledge and Kegan Paul, London 1966, 24.

115 Quintilian, *Institutio Oratoria* 6.6.51, cited in 'Transfiguration: Christology and the roots of figurative exegesis in St Augustine', *Studia Patristica XXXIII*, Peeters, Leuven 1997, 47.

116 Psalms like 42 and 43 as well as Psalm 139.

117 Malcolm Guite, *Faith, Hope and Poetry*, Ashgate, Farnham 2012, 243. 'I have been concerned to demonstrate the essential power of the imagination to bridge the gap between immanence and transcendence.'

Notes on Chapter Three

1 Exodus 17:8-18, and the unpublished New College lectures of Andrew Ross in 1971. See also Erna Oliver, 'Afrikaner spirituality: A complex mixture', https://www.ajol.info/index.php/hts/article/viewFile/148525/138026 accessed 15/10/19, which cites G.H. Calpin, *There are no South Africans*, Thomas Nelson, London 1944, 17: 'The Old Testament stands Bible to the Afrikaner; this nation has been described as the modern counterpart of an Old Testament tribe'.

2 William Hershaw and Les McConnell, *Saul Vaigers*, Grace Note Publications, Crieff 2021.

3 Hershaw 2018.

4 As in Revelation 5:9 (though of course the 'twelve tribes' all shared one language), or Edwin Muir's poem 'Scotland 1941' (Bateman *et al* 2000, 223).

5 Alastair McIntosh, *Healing Nationhood*, Curlew Productions, Kelso 2000, 9-14.

6 www.alastairmcintosh.com/articles/1999_lpani/russia_text.htm accessed 14/10/21.

7 Deuteronomy 7:7, 8:17, 9:4, 26:5-9, Psalm 44:3.

8 Walter Brueggemann, *The Land*, Fortress Press, Philadelphia 1977, 3.

9 McIntosh 2000, 52.

10 Henry George, *Progress and Poverty*, Pantianos 1905, first published 1879.

11   https://landcommission.gov.scot/2017/12/land-commission-to-look-at-potential-for-land-value-taxes-in-scotland. Cf. McIntosh 2000, 98.

12 George 1905, 124.

13 McIntosh 2000, 47. A similar theology is expressed in Psalm 50:9-11. On page 73 he cites George Gretton's entry on 'Feudalism' in *The Laws of Scotland*, Vol. 18, Butterworth, Edinburgh: 'The Crown cannot dispone but only fue [sic] . . . the Crown has no feudal superior, except God alone.'

14 In Scotland, Andy Wightman argues from natural justice (*The Poor had no Lawyers*, Birlinn, Edinburgh 2013), McIntosh argues from Christian principle.

15 From the article by Tom Hubbard on 'Culture' in *Scottish Review* of 11th August 2021.

16 Dante Alighieri 2012, *Purgatory*, Canto 2, lines 43-48 – the psalm is being sung by the spirits leaving.

17 Edwin Morgan, *Collected Poems*, Carcanet, Manchester 1990, 61.

18 Alasdair Mac Mhaighstir Alasdair, *The Birlinn of Clanranald*, 1776, intro. and trans. Alan Riach, Kettilonia, Newtyle 2015.

19 Hastings 1997, 185, 3-4.

20 Although Canon Kenyon Wright of the Scottish Episcopal Church was a leader of the 'Claim of Right' movement, and the Church of Scotland General Assembly consistently backed devolution – but always with the rider 'within the UK'.

21 A reference to communal singing of Psalm 100 at the first Scottish Assembly in 1999. While the psalm, Gay writes, has its own 'claims about origins and esteem', by 2004 at the opening of Holyrood the psalmody was 'safely hidden in Gaelic' (Doug Gay, *Honey from the Lion*, SCM Press, London 2013, 112-3).

22 Gay 2013, xii.

23   https://www.churchofscotland.org.uk/about_us/church_law/church_constitution (accessed 1/11/19).

24 65% in the 2001 Census, 54% in the 2011 Census.

25 In the 2015 General Assembly a motion to change the Third Article was defeated (http://www.churchofscotland.org.uk/__data/assets/pdf_file/0014/3470/ga10_reports_specarticle.pdf, accessed 1/11/19).

26 As shown by the 2011 Census of Religion in Scotland. Non-established churches, whether Roman Catholic or independent, do not have this tension, whether or not the beliefs of their adherents are pluriform.

27 Neal Ascherson, *Games with Shadows*, Century Hutchinson, London 1988, 63.

28 Cf. Daniel 10:20.

29 McIntosh 2000, 16-18, citing Walter Wink, *Unmasking the Powers*, Fortress, Philadelphia 1986, 95-6, and Buber's 1941 essay, 'The Gods of the Nations and God', from *Israel and the World: Essays in a Time of Crisis*, Schocken Books, New York 1948.

30 See David McCrone, *Understanding Scotland*, Routledge 1992, 201-15, or the iconoclastic Momus, *The Book of Scotlands*, Luath Press, Edinburgh 2018, or Sylvia Warner's review of MacDiarmid's *Lucky Poet*: 'a considerable tradition of being two nations' (Alan Bold, *MacDiarmid*, John Murray, London 1988, 390).

31 Ascherson 1988, 64.

32 Gillingham 2008, 11-12. Verse 1 of the psalm complains that the nations have defiled God's holy temple, a central Maccabean concern.

33 Hastings 1997, 3, 186.

34 Luke 6:13 – see N.T. Wright, *Luke for Everyone*, SPCK, London 2001, 50, and more generally J.D.G. Dunn, *New Testament Theology*, Abingdon Press, Nashville 2009, 54.

35 Though the popular story of pilgrimage, Bunyan's *Pilgrim's Progress*, is based on theology and morality, not the OT.

36 Holz 1984, 17.

37 Herbert Butterfield, *Christianity and History*, G. Bell and Sons, London 1949, 72.

38 As discussed by Doug Gay in 'Theological Constructions of Scottish National Identity', in David Fergusson and Mark Elliott (eds.), *The History of Scottish Theology*, Vol. 3, Oxford University Press, London 2019, 288-302.

39 Cameron 1972, 62.

40 Jane Dawson, *John Knox*, Yale University Press, Newhaven 2015, 83.

41 Dawson 2015, 8. In October 1559, when the 'war of the Congregation' was in crisis, Knox was preaching on Psalm 80 in Edinburgh and Stirling: 'O Lord God of hosts, / how long will you be angry with your people's prayers?' (Lord Eustace Percy, *John Knox*, Hodder & Stoughton, London, 1937).

42 J.H.S. Burleigh, *A Church History of Scotland*, Oxford University Press, London 1960, 256.

43 Cameron 1993, 218.

44 Jonathan Hearn, *Rethinking Nationalism*, Palgrave Macmillan, Basingstoke 2006, 86.

45 Hearn 2006, 222, citing Anthony Smith, *Chosen Peoples: Sacred Sources of National Identity*, Oxford University Press, Oxford 2003, 18.

46 Alexander Henderson, *Sermons, Prayers and Pulpit Addresses*, ed. Thomas Martin orig. 1638, John Maclaren, Edinburgh 1867.

47 Spencer 2016; Willie Jennings in Susan Felch (ed.), *The Cambridge Companion to Literature and Religion*, New York 2016, 252.

48 'In the Psalms, the celebration of salvation history, law, divine rule and wisdom all contribute to the shaping of Israel's faith' - David Fergusson in Duncan Forrester and Doug Gay (eds.), *Worship and Liturgy in Context*, SCM Press, London 2009, 67.

49 *Poem 118 'Space Temple'* sees Blake, Luther, Gaudi and Samuelson and their nations in the 'broad place' of Psalm 118.

50 Hearn 2006, 226-7.

51 The clearest statement of this is actually in (the contemporary) Zechariah 14:9.

52 In Gillingham 2008 the author reports widely from Europe and the Middle East, as well as England, but up to 1900 the book has only two short references to Scotland and Scots (Knox, and Robert Burns' version of Psalm 1), though in the last chapter the Catholic priest James Quinn, and scholars Peter Craigie, William Barclay, George Knight and Robert Davidson are mentioned, along with the designer Alec Galloway, and composers James MacMillan and Kenneth Leighton.

53 Scottish nobles had land holdings in England at least as early as the 12th century, and when there was peace between the kingdoms, the church authorities communicated (Michael Lynch, *Scotland, A New History*, Pimlico, London 1991, 91, 93). In 1303 Alexander Bruce (King Robert's brother) graduated from Cambridge and in 1306 he was Dean of Glasgow (Penman 2014, 49).

54 The first Psalter in English authorised for use in Scotland (1564) was begun in England, continued in Geneva, completed in Scotland. Of the eight or nine contributors, three were Scots – Young 1909, 24-31 gives 8, but 9 are given in https://www.churchservicesociety.org/sites/default/files/journals/1938-1939-43-56.pdf, accessed 11/9/19.

55 William Law, *Serious Call to a Devout and Holy Life*, J.M. Dent, London 1906 (orig. 1728), chapter XV.

56 See the entries in Gesenius and Robinson, *Hebrew and English Lexicon of the Old Testament*, ed. S.R. Driver and C.A. Briggs, Oxford University Press, London 1962 – although there remains a scholarly controversy over whether 'nation' is an ancient or a modern concept.

57 Michael Lynch, *Scotland, A New History*, Pimlico, London 1991, 1-39.

58 Dauvit Broun, in Geoffrey Barrow (ed.), *The Declaration of Arbroath*, Society of Antiquaries of Scotland 2003, 3-5.

59 As in the framing Psalm 72.

60 As in Psalms 95 – 99.

61 Cited in Stephen Maxwell, *Arguing for Independence*, Luath Press, Edinburgh 2012, 27.

62 Gay 2013, 77-8.

63 For example, Ezra 10 and Nehemiah 13:23-30, though these actions would have been justified at the time by arguing that the foreign wives worshipped other gods.

64 Goldingay 2007, 637 interprets Psalm 87:4 as a verse of 'consternation to the Israelite immigration officials!' While Psalms like 8, 15, 22, 65, 67, 107 allow that people of all nations will worship Yahweh, who rescues the poor and the needy, other OT passages like 2 Kings 5:17-19 are more generous to non-Israelites.

65 Hastings 1997, 195-6.

66 Roland Prothero, *The Psalms in Human Life*, Thomas Nelson, London 1903, 142.

67 Stephen Holmes in Robert Anderson et al. (eds.), *The Edinburgh History of Education in Scotland*, Edinburgh University Press, Edinburgh 2015, 63. Song Schools existed before the Reformation – Miller Patrick, *Four Centuries of Scottish Psalmody*, OUP London 1949, xx – and later focused on singing psalms in the vernacular.

68 'The Accession of King James I and English Religious Poetry', https://www-jstor-org.ezproxy.lib.gla.ac.uk/stable/pdf/450784.pdf?ab_segments=0%2Fbasic_SYC-4631%2Fcontrol&refreqid=search%3Afa7500ab8bcfb01a2f731aac5315855f, accessed 15/10/19.

69 William Maxwell, *A History of Worship in the Church of Scotland*, Oxford University Press, London 1955, 82-86. The King 'aspired to be head of the Church as Henry VIII had been' (David Searle [ed.], *Preaching without Fear or Favour*, Christian Focus, Fearn 2019, xix).

70 Murray Pittock, *Poetry and Jacobite Politics*, Cambridge University Press, Cambridge 1994, 10.

71 Nelson Bushnell, *William Hamilton of Bangour*, Aberdeen University Press, Aberdeen 1957, 83.

72 Pittock 1994, 143.

73 Allan MacColl, *Land, Faith and the Crofting Community*, Edinburgh University Press, Edinburgh 2006, 83, citing *The Highlander* of 13 Oct 1877, 6.

74 *An Leabhar Mòr: The Great Book of Gaelic*, ed. Malcolm MacLean and Theo Dorgan, Canongate Books, Edinburgh 2002, 138 & 247.

75 David Mitchell, *The Message of the Psalter* (Campbell Publications, Newton Mearns 2017, originally Sheffield Academic Press 1997, 18-40, 298.

76 Psalm 33:1 ties up with 32:11.

77 A *maskil* is a contemplative poem, from its etymology one that is prudent, one that has insight. 'One shout' may have more of the latter than the former.

78 Isaiah 55:11, Jeremiah 16:14-15, and the whole of Psalm 119.

79 A traditional function of prophecy – see 'Foretelling and Forthtelling' in the article on 'Prophecy' in J.D. Douglas (ed.), *Illustrated Bible Dictionary*, IVP, Leicester 1980 – though often 'insight' is stressed rather than 'foresight', see John Bowker (ed.), *Complete Bible Handbook*, Dorling Kindersley, London 1988, 197.

80 Mika Pajunen and Jeremy Penner, (eds.), *Functions of Psalms and Prayers in the late Second Temple Period*, De Gruyter, Berlin 2017, 229.

81 Mitchell 2017 provides an exhaustive discussion of commentaries on the Psalms from early times to the present.

82 George J. Brooke in Pajunen and Penner 2017, 308-9.

83 For example, with Thomas the Rhymer, https://deriv.nls.uk/dcn23/1084/8731/108487319.23.pdf, accessed 20/12/19.

84 See for example the Edinburgh Gifford Lectures of 2011: Peter Harrison, *The Territories of Science and Religion*, University of Chicago Press, London 2015.

85 These are discussed extensively in Chapter Three of Liam Jerrold Fraser, *Mission in Contemporary Scotland*, St Andrew Press, Edinburgh 2021.

86 David Smith, *Stumbling Towards Zion*, Langholm Global Library, Carlisle 2020, 28.

87 Psalms 6, 13, 22, 55, 102, 142 express both lament and hope. Psalm 88 expresses lament alone. Psalms 28, 35, 59, 94, 10, 137 express the anger of those treated unjustly.

Notes on Chapter Four

1 *Only the Lover Sings*, Ignatius Press, San Francisco 1990.

2 John Purser, 'Musical Structures', in *Rannsachadh na Gaidhlig* 8.

3 *Ceol Mor Notation*, East Indies 1983, cited in Purser, 'Musical Structures'.

4 *The Life and Letters of John Muir*, ed. Terry Gifford, Baton Wicks Publications and The Mountaineers, London and Seattle 1996 (originally by the Houghton Mifflin Company, Boston 1924), 112-3.

5 *Meditations of John Muir: Nature's Temple*, ed. Chris Highland, Wilderness Press, Birmingham AL 2001.

6 Published on 5/2/1876.

7 John Muir referring to Psalm 121 in *The Yosemite*, Century, New York 1912, 261-2, cited by Naomi Klein in *This Changes Everything*, Penguin Random House, New York 2015, 184.

8 Highland 2001, 13. In a letter to Catharine Merrill, he writes: 'God flows in grand undivided currents, shoreless and boundless over creeds and forms and all kinds of civilizations and peoples and beasts, saturating all and fountainising all.' (Muir 1996, 167)

9 *The Autobiography of Charles Darwin, 1809-1882*, Norton, New York 1958, 138-139.

10 Francesca Knox and John Took (eds.), *Poetry and Prayer*, Ashgate, Farnham 2015, 25.

11 Holz 1984, 21. See also Alfred Edersheim, *Jesus the Messiah*, Longmans, Green & Co, New York 1917, 659, 692.

12 From his poem, 'On First Looking into Chapman's Homer'.

13 Burleigh 1960, 351.

14 Rudolf Wittkower, *Architectural Principles in the Age of Humanism*, Alec Tiranti, London 1962, 28-30.

15 Gavin Stamp and Sam McKinstry (ed.), *'Greek' Thomson*, EUP, Edinburgh 1994, 68.

16 Gavin Stamp (ed.), *The Light of Truth and Beauty – Lectures of Alexander 'Greek' Thomson 1817-1872*, The Alexander Thomson Society, Glasgow 1999, 3.

17 Stamp 1999, 116.

18 Stamp 1999, 7. Thomson believed the eternal laws of design established by the Creator were the light of the future, which the architect discerned beneath the ancient forms of Egyptian and Greek construction.

19 Stamp 1999, 101: 'The laws of architecture were not invented by man, but merely discovered by him . . . in the councils of eternity, the laws which regulate this art were framed'. Thomson thought much about the Temple of Solomon and the ideal temple of Ezekiel.

20 Stamp 1999, 27: In his lecture of 24th March 1853, Thomson asks, 'What is this universe but a diagram of the mind of God?' He refers to Psalm 8:1b, 5-6, where God has 'not filled the heavens over our heads with glory without giving us also the power to appreciate; consequently imposing on us the duty of exercising that power.'

21 William Storrar, 'As Open as Possible: Presbyterian Modernity in Scotland's Long Nineteenth Century', in Fergusson and Elliot 2019, Vol. 2, 369.

22 Christopher Rowland, 'The Temple in the New Testament', in Day 2005, 478.

23 Robert Crawford, *On Glasgow and Edinburgh*, Harvard University Press, Cambridge MA 2013, 285.

24 Beale 2004, 331 says, 'This heavenly temple comes down completely to envelop the entire cosmos at the end of the age. Revelation 21 portrays the consummated reality of the temple.' While here he glosses over the fact that the temple has become a city (Rev 21:22), his book demonstrates how the ideas of God and of the cosmos are integrated in a temple theology.

25 Susan Gillingham sees more references to the psalms in Herbert, e.g. with 'The Altar' and Psalm 51:16-17 (Gillingham 2018, 311), but Herbert simply writes 'a broken ALTAR' and 'O let thy blessed SACRIFICE be mine'. She is on firmer ground with 'Easter', which has 'Awake, my lute' (Psalm 57:8, Gillingham 2018, 334).

26 David Jasper, *Heaven in Ordinary*, Lutterworth, Cambridge 2018, 89, 94.

27 George Herbert, *Complete Works*, Digireads.com, Milton Keynes 2013, 60 (41 'The Windows').

28 Colm Toibin, *On Elisabeth Bishop*, Princeton University Press, Princeton NJ 2015, 62, cited in Alison Jack, *The Prodigal Son in English and American Literature*, Oxford University Press, Oxford 2019. MacDiarmid held an even stronger view (see 7.1).

29 Jeremy Begbie, *Redeeming Transcendence in the Arts*, Eerdmans, Grand Rapids 2018, 130.

30 John Challis, 'Naming the Light' in Stand 16(2), 31.

31 Cf. T.F. Torrance, *Reality and Scientific Theology*, Scottish Academic Press, Edinburgh 1985, 117.

32 'The imagination becomes a key instrument of finding that which is able to draw us forward from our given state . . .', Ben Quash, *Found Theology: History, Imagination and the Holy Spirit*, Bloomsbury, London 2013, 285 (discussing D.H. Kelsey, *Eccentric Existence: A Theological Anthropology*, Westminster John Knox Press, Louisville KY 2009).

33 John Paul Lederach, *The Moral Imagination*, Oxford University Press, Oxford 2005, 27.

34 Lederach 2005, 27, citing Susan Babbit, *Impossible Dreams*, Westview, Boulder CO 1996, 174 (for Lederach, seeing fresh images that open the way to peace-building).

35 Hart 2017, 195.

36 'The Secret Voice', in Hugh MacDiarmid, *The Revolutionary Art of the Future: Rediscovered Poems*, ed. John Manson *et al.*, Carcanet and the Scottish Poetry Library, Manchester and Edinburgh 2003, 1.

37 Tillich is one of many theologians who have addressed this issue: 'To call God transcendent in this sense does not mean that one must establish a 'superworld' of divine objects. It does mean that, within itself, the finite world points beyond itself. In other words, it is self-transcendent (Paul Tillich, *Systematic Theology*, Vol. 2, SCM Press, London 1957, 8).

38 From 'The Elixer', Herbert 2013, 156.

39 All four poems may be found on Poemhunter.

40 John H. McGlynn, 'Leaves of Palm and Temples of Language' in *Stand*, Vol. 17(1), 2019, 7 - cf Clarke on Psalm 110 (3.5.1).

41 *Illuminations*, Jonathan Cape, London 1970, 69.

42 Heaney 1988, 94-5.

43 Leavitt 1997, 189-90. He even links them both to 'the music of the spheres'.

44 Cited by Christopher Page, *The Christian West and its Singers*, Yale University Press, London 2010, 353-4. 353-4. The issue of how far 'pagan music' can be used in worship crops up in this early Christian writing (page 94), as well as dramatically in the book of Daniel chapter 3.

45 See Purser's English version of the fuller Gaelic article in *Rannsachadh na Gaidhlig* 8, 1-16.

46 Kirsty Gunn, *The Big Music*, Faber and Faber, London 2012, 241.

47 Maoilios Caimbeul, 'Am Pìobaire Dall', *Breac-a'-Mhuiltein*, Coiscéim, Dublin 2007, p.296.

48 Gunn 2012, 196, 442.

49 Seumus MacNeill, *Piobaireachd: Classical Music of the Highland Bagpipe*, cited in Gunn 2012, 284.

50 The piece is synthesised to incorporate the first two verses of Psalm 46 sung in Gaelic, and the band say they aim to create 'space for the praise of God' (Martin Schröder, *Transforming Tradition: Gaelic Psalms in the work of Capercaillie and Runrig*, Rostock University of Music and Drama, 2015, 11).

51 Schröder 2015, 3.

52 Cited in Riach 2022, 128. Riach makes a point of mentioning the 'vocal inter-connections' in Carver's music.

53 Although usually translated 'sparrow' because it is an onomatopoeic tweeting sound; see Goldingay 2007, 590.

54 In 118 'Space Temple' I link art and architecture with poetry, thinking of Blake's *Annotations to Laocoon*, and how he said that the man who is not a musician, an artist or an architect cannot be a Christian – *Complete Poetry and Prose of William Blake*, (ed.) David V. Erdman, Doubleday, New York 1998, 274.

55 Pibroch music sung as vocables in order to memorise it and pass it on. See Francis Collinson, *The Bagpipe*, Routledge & Kegan Paul, London 1975, 157.

56 Norman MacCaig, 'Moment Musical in Assynt', *Collected Poems*, 201, Birlinn, Edinburgh 2010 (originally in *The White Bird*, London 1973).

57 Alan Bold, *MacDiarmid*, John Murray, London 1988, 307. Bold points out that the poem is consciously neoplatonic, not theistic on page 310.

58 'Figheadóir Mise' in Ronald Black (ed.), *An Lasair*, Birlinn, Edinburgh 2001, 200-201.

59 See Gunn 2010, 184, 196.

60 Citing Urszula Jorasz, as mediated by Anna Gruszczynska-Ziólkowska, *Detrás del silencio – La música en la cultura Nasca*, Lima 2013, especially 173-177.

61 Abba Eban, *Heritage: Civilization and the Jews*, Weidenfeld and Nicolson, London 1984, 69.

62 For example, trumpet, lute, harp, tambouring, strings, pipe, cymbals all mentioned in Psalm 150, lyre mentioned as one of the strings in 1 Chronicles 25.

63 *The Passover Haggadah*, Soncino, London 1959, xii, refers to the last hymn of the *seder* being chanted

64 Gerald Abrahams, *The Jewish Mind*, Constable, London 1961, 89.

65 *Oxford Companion to Music*, ed. Percy Scholes, Oxford University Press, London 1938, 737.

66 Mitchell 2015, 159-210.

67 Goldingay 2006, 50.

68 Holz 1984, 21. See also Edersheim 2017, 659, 692. It opens up other lines of enquiry, for example, is it a coincidence that the three 'Torah Psalms' (1, 19, 119) have those numbers?

69 888 also happens to be the numerical value of the Greek letters for Jesus.

70 https://www.thelivingword.org.au/bringing-sons-to-glory/more-watermarks-of-God.php, accessed on 16/11/19. (The video shows the numerical values, and you can simply add them up.)

71 Mitchell 2015, 63-69, 114-121.

72 John Purser, *Scotland's Music*, Mainstream, Edinburgh 2007, 192.

73 Liner notes by John Purser to the Hyperion CD of that Symphony.

74 Page 2010, 2.

75 Page 2010, 42-43.

76 A document dated c.475 CE has '*Psalmista, id est cantor*' (Page 2010, 215).

77 Church of England Archbishops' Commission on Church Music, *In Tune with Heaven*, Hodder, London 1992, 25.

78 Evelyn Underhill, *Worship*, Collins, London 1962 (Fontana edition, originally 1936), 104f.

79 Patrick 1949, xiv.

80 Alec Robertson in J.G. Davies (ed.), *A Dictionary of Liturgy and Worship*, SCM Press, London 1972, 326.

81 According to the Stowe Missal, see William Maxwell, *A History of Worship in the Church of Scotland*, Oxford University Press, London 1955, 16.

82 M. Dilworth and A.E. Nimmo in Nigel Cameron(ed.), *Dictionary of Scottish Church History and Theology*, T&T Clark, Edinburgh 1993, 141.

83 *Life Together*, trans. Doberstein, SCM Press, London 1954, 44.

84 The Revised English Bible uniquely translates *roʿš* in Nehemiah 11:17 as 'precentor' rather than 'leader'.

85 Patrick 1949, 6-7.

86 Jamie Reid-Baxter, Michael Lynch and Patricia Dennison, *Jhone Angus: Monk of Dunfermline and Scottish Reformation Music*, Dunfermline Heritage Community Projects, Dunfermline 2011, 34.

87 Duguid 2016, 219, but note the Wode Psalter.

88 Duguid 2016, 78.

89 An Anglo-Genevan Psalter was published in 1561, and an English Psalter in 1562 (Patrick 1949, 45f.).

90 Reid-Baxter *et al.* 2011, 34. They comment, 'Although [the 1564 Psalter] was succeeded by another Psalter in 1650, the 1564 one is more varied and more interesting'.

91 Reid-Baxter *et al.* 2011, 28. For example, Jhone Angus was 'precentor de Dunfermline' in 1552.

92 Patrick dates it 1562 (Patrick 1949, 56).

93 Christopher Goodman followed Knox to Scotland in 1559, became minister of St Andrews in 1560, and had in his congregation James Stewart, Earl of Moray. Moray decided that the new tunes should be in four part harmony, and commissioned David Peebles of St Andrews to set them, but

told him keep it simple; Peebles was a master polyphonist, and dragged his feet, but Thomas Wode (a skilled copyist) persuaded him to do it, and the result was the Wode Psalter of 1566, using the music of Jhone Angus, David Peebles and Andro Blackhall – Reid-Baxter *et al.* 2011, 34-40.

94   Canon Emsley Nimmo of St Margaret's, Aberdeen, in a personal comment, told me that no psalms were sung till about 1800, as singing would have attracted unfavourable attention.

95   Gordon Donaldson, *The Making of the Scottish Prayer Book of 1637*, Edinburgh University Press, Edinburgh 1954, 7.

96   Donaldson 1954, 13, 28, 112 (the Psalms are spread, in order, between morning and evening prayer).

97   Duguid 2016, 12.

98   For example, in England the 1560-61 Genevan *Forme of Prayers* had a mixed reception, the English preferring the earlier editions and the Scots choosing the later versions (Duguid 2016, 40). The earliest Gaelic Psalter was not published until 1659, and only had 50 psalms (Patrick 1949, 10).

99   See https://www.churchservicesociety.org/sites/default/files/journals/1938-1939-43-56.pdf for details of the 1650 metrical psalter.

100 *Church Hymnary*, fourth edition, published by Canterbury Press.

101 Patrick 1949, chapter 14.

102 Ian Mackenzie, *Tunes of Glory*, Handsel Press, Edinburgh 1993, 146.

103 Modern composers who have used other styles of music for the Psalms include, for example, John Bell (*Psalms of Patience, Protest and Praise*), Rob Mathes (setting words by Micheal O'Siadhail, 'At Night a Song is With Me'), David Mitchell (Psalm 24 for cantor and chorus), Ian White, U2 (with '40, How Long' in 1982); this should be distinguished from, say, Steven Faux (https://stevenfaux.com/psalms-project/), or Stravinsky ('Symphony of Psalms') whose work is synaesthesia, not psalms to be sung.

104 Citing Eric Walter White, *Stravinsky: the Composer and his Works*, University of California Press, Los Angeles and London 1966, 321. https://en.wikipedia.org/wiki/Symphony_of_Psalms, accessed 10/10/19. Stravinsky did use Psalms 39:12-13, 40:1-3 and 150.

105 John Knox sometimes played the fiddle at wedding celebrations.

106 *In Tune with Heaven* 1992, 37. 'Psalms' only feature in two short sections of the report, and the word is not indexed.

107 Jeremy Begbie, *Resounding Truth*, SPCK, London 2008, 21-2.

108 Hence the verse by Kenneth Steven, 'They have all blown away / the ones who knew these hills by name, / who translated the wind, who spoke / the same language as the curlew. (In 'Greshornish', Steven 2019)

109 Purser 2007, 21-22. This is my own observation, that both call to mind sea or moor birds. I am not aware of literature supporting it, apart from the general comments in Purser 2007, 18-19.

NOTES ON CHAPTERS FOUR AND FIVE

110 Allan MacColl, *Land, Faith and the Crofting Community*, Edinburgh University Press, Edinburgh 2006, 70.

111 Francis Collinson, *The Traditional and National Music of Scotland*, Routledge and Kegan Paul, London 1966, 262-3.

112 Collinson 1966, 261. This is presumably why Purser says that 'Gaelic psalm singing . . . developed partly as a result of a conflict between the Gaelic language and the metrical psalms in English' (Purser 2007, 18). Patrick 1949 gives only four lines to Gaelic psalm-singing.

113 Gunn 2012, 195.

114 'Travelling South' in Harry Smart, *A Plain Glass*, Drunk Muse Press 2021, 26.

Notes on Chapter Five

1 From 'Gairmscoile', in *Hugh MacDiarmid: Selected Poems*, Riach and Grieve 1994, 23.

2 Think of the extraordinary number of African Independent Churches who have adopted the name 'Zion' and the ideas behind it, or more widely the imagery of the 'spirituals'.

3 Alan Riach, *Scottish Literature: An Introduction*, Luath Press, Edinburgh 2022, 76.

4 See for example, Nick Spencer, *The Evolution of the West*, SPCK, London 2016. And of course neither Greeks nor Romans argued that 'in Christ there is no longer Jew nor Greek, slave or free, male and female' (Galatians 3:28).

5 John Leavitt (ed.), *Poetry and Prophecy*, University of Michigan Press, Ann Arbor 1997, 3.

6 Knox and Took 2015, 5.

7 This and the following quotation are from Fearghas MacFhionnlaigh, 'The Midge', being the English translation of 'A' Mheanbhchuileag'. Gaelic version first published by Gairm 1980. English first published in *Cencrastus*, Autumn 1982.

8 'Portrait of the Psalmist as an Old Man', Roberts 2013, 16.

9 From 'To the Legend', ed. and trans. Atar Hadari, *Songs from Bialik*, Syracuse University Press, Syracuse 2000, 16.

10 Walter Brueggemann, *The Prophetic Imagination*, SCM Press, London 1978, 13, 67, 110.

11 Riach and Grieve 1994, 9.

12 Alan Riach, *Hugh MacDiarmid, Selected Prose*, Carcanet, Manchester 1992, 285.

13 Psalm 19:1f.

14 Psalm 19:7f.

15 Stanza 3 of 'Symmie and his Bruther' in Laing and Small, *Select Remains of the Ancient Popular and Romance Poetry of Scotland*, Edinburgh 1885, 314 in a paper sent to me by John Purser, which includes a reference in 1538 to a purchase of 'iii elnis of Heland tertane to be hois to the Kingis grace' (*Accounts of the Lord High Treasurer of Scotland VI*, 436).

16 Jonathan Faiers, *Tartan*, Berg, Oxford 2008, 291, citing Walter Benjamin, *The Arcades Project*, Belknap Press, Cambridge MA 1999.

17 Duncan Glen, *Hugh MacDiarmid, Rebel Poet and Prophet*, Drumalban Press, Hemel Hempstead, 1962, 3.

18 The key literary foundation of tartanry is Walter Scott's *Rob Roy*, which establishes the Highland/Lowland divide, according to Hugh Cheape in Brown 2010, 120.

19 Alan Riach in Brown 2010, 117.

20 *105 Crunluath a Mach: Exegete your Story*, in *'The Iolaire'*.

21 Tom Nairn, *The Break-up of Britain*, Verso, London 1981, 162.

22 Beveridge and Turnbull 1989, 13-14. See also 'The Fall and Rise of Tartanry' in McCrone 1992, 180-1.

23 Faiers 2008, 247, and against him Ian Brown in Brown 2010, chapter 6.

24 Brown 2010, 1, citing John Telfer Dunbar, *History of Highland Dress*, Oliver and Boyd, Edinburgh 1962, 97.

25 Although in the 18th century, tartans were often mixed – one portrait has the 'MacDonald boys' wearing four different tartans, and at Culloden, according to one painting, 23 different tartans were worn by 8 Highlanders (Faiers 2008, 42, 44).

26 The Japanese designer Akiko Fukai formulates a 'proposal for a clothing of the future that will transcend ethnic and gender differences', Faiers 2008, 288 citing Martin and Koda, *Orientalism: Visions of the East in Western Dress* (catalogue), 1994, 75.

27 As in the Book 5 poem on Psalm 132.

28 Provan 2017, 503-4, citing John S. Kselman, 'Why Have You Abandoned Me?' in *Art and Meaning: Rhetoric in Biblical Literature* (ed. Clines, Gunn and Hauser), JSOT Press, Sheffield 1982, 172-98.

29 See Oliver 2009, 384-6.

30 See Cheape 2006 for the history, and Brown 2010 for later developments.

31 John MacQuarrie, 'Burns: Poet, Prophet, Philosopher' in the *Evangelical Times* 86, 1975, 112.

32 William Wallace (ed.), *Poetical Works of Robert Burns*, Chambers, Edinburgh 1947, 533. Other poems cited are also from this volume.

33 In one of his letter poems, 14 countries are referenced along with a number of politicians (Wallace 1947, 328).

34 Published by Octopus, London 1979, along with *At The Back of the North Wind* and *The Princess and Curdie*.

35   See the preface to *George MacDonald*, an anthology selected by C.S. Lewis (Collins, London 1955).

36   Devine 2012, 294.

37   Walter Scott, *The Heart of Midlothian*, OUP, London 1912, 43.

38   Bold 1988, 134-5.

39   Bold 1988, 163.

40   Alexander Moffat and Alan Riach, *The Arts of Independence*, Luath Press, Edinburgh 2014, 21.

41   'A Drunk Man' lines 549 and 554.

42   In 'Sonnets for Scotland' (1084) – Edwin Morgan, *Collected Poems*, Carcanet, Manchester 1990, 448.

43   Much of this is based on the book of Liz Lochhead's poems which she sold me at Moniack Mhor in 2015, *The Colour of Black and White*, Polygon, Edinburgh 2003.

44   Jackie Kay, *Bantam*, Picador, London 2017.

45   Karl Barth, *Against the Stream*, ed. Ronald Gregor Smith, SCM Press, London 1954, 151, cf. Frank Jehle, *Ever Against the Stream*, Eerdmans, Grand Rapids 2002, 3, 96.

46   Tom Devine discusses why only France had a revolution in Devine 2012, 196f.

47   In 1820 two weavers were hanged at Stirling in spite of the sympathy of the crowd. Before the execution, they sang part of Psalm 51 – transcription from *The Word on the Street*, a broadsheet held by the Stirling Smith Museum. (Also from Psalm 30 and 103, according to other sources.)

48   See Smout 1986, 263-271.

49   As in the writing of Jock the Peasant and Sir David Lyndsay in the early 15th century – arguably giving us 'an embryonic ideal of democratic egalitarianism' – Gifford and Riach 2004, xx.

50   The editors of the OT Psalter acknowledge that the Davidic kingship is past. Indeed one reading of the Hebrew text (NRSV margin) allows the 'king' to be identified with God – as in some later Psalms – although the reference to 'his anointed' in verse 6 is clearly to the king unless taken in a messianic sense.

51   Gillingham 2008, 10.

52   John Calvin, *Commentary on the Psalms*, Vol. 1, trans. James Anderson, Amazon 2015, 28.

53   Charles Garside, Jr. in 'The Origins of Calvin's Theology of Music: 1536-1543' (*Transactions of the American Philosophical Society* 69, 4, Philadelphia 1968) in Holladay 1996, 198.

54   W. Stanford Reid in Carl S. Meyer (ed.), *Sixteenth Century Essays and Studies*, St Louis 1971, Vol. 2, 43-44, cited by Holladay 1996, 198.

55   1 Peter 2:9. Revelation 5:10.

56 Exodus 19:6, and the 'messianic' Psalm 110:4.

57 Oliver 2009, 232.

58 Psalm 103:19 (KJV), cited by Oliver 2009, 282.

59 Gillingham 2018, 26. There may be isolated examples in other cultures of what Richard Middleton calls 'the democratisation of ideology' (Middleton 2005, 99-100).

60 Via Marx's reading of the NT in the British Library, and Keir Hardie's interpretation of Christianity.

61 See *Poem 20, 'Royal Rule'*.

62 'A Theory of Scots Letters', Scottish Chapbook 1 no 7 (Feb 1923), 182, cited by Kenneth Buthlay introducing *A Drunk Man Looks at the Thistle*, Scottish Academic Press, Edinburgh 1987, xxiv.

63 David Daiches, *God and the Poets*, orig. Oxford University Press 1984, Zeticula, Kilkerran 2013, 213. In his earlier book, Daiches spoke of 'the co-existence of a belief in individual freedom and extreme intolerance [which] meets us at every turn in Scottish ecclesiastical history' (Daiches 1964, 41).

64 Lesley Duncan, *Images not Icons*, Kennedy & Boyd, Glasgow 2010, 97.

65 Buthlay 1987, xxvi.

66 Faiers 2008, 15.

67 MacDiarmid in 'Talking with Five Thousand People in Edinburgh', *The Hugh MacDiarmid Anthology: Poems in Scots and in English*, Routledge & Kegan Paul, London 1972, 250.

68 Alan Riach, *Hugh MacDiarmid's Epic Poetry*, Edinburgh University Press, Edinburgh 1991, 12.

69 In the disarming act of 1746, operating till 1782 – Brown 2010, 6, as well as Cheape cited in footnote 7 above.

70 Devine 2012, 31f. Devine argues that the Union was crucial to the economic benefits which in turn swayed Scottish opinion in the end (page 59), while Neil Davidson, *Discovering the Scottish Revolution 1692-1746*, Pluto Press, London 2003, argues that the defeat of the Jacobites was more important.

71 Brown 2010, 66-71.

72 Bold 1988, 344 and Brown 2010, 117.

73 Faiers 2008, 175.

74 W.H. Bellinger jr., *A Hermeneutic of Curiosity*, Mercer University Press, Macon GA 1995, 6.

75 Paul Ricoeur, *The Symbolism of Evil*, Beacon Press, Boston 1967, 349, cited in Provan 2017, 549.

76 Les Murray, 'Poetry and Religion' in *The Daylight Moon*, Carcanet, Manchester 1988, 51.

77 Cf. Psalm 107:10, 25 and Robert Davidson, *The Vitality of Worship*, Handsel Press, Edinburgh 1998, 356.

78 G.A.F. Knight, *Theology in Pictures*, Handsel Press, Edinburgh 1981, xii.

79   Hogg 2001.

80   From Sheena Blackhall, 'Millennium Blues', in *Millennium Blues*, Hammerfield Publishing, Aberdeen 1999.

81   Modern versions like the NRSV emend the text, without good reason, to read 'God is good to the upright' – see for example Davidson 1998, 232.

82   Hugh Pyper notes how Psalm 73 subverts 37, but does not go so far as citing the double subversion (*The Unchained Bible*, Bloomsbury, London 2012, 22).

83   Aylan, but his family ask for him to be known as Alan.

84   Cf. the function of the poet in 5.1.

85   6, 32, 38, 51,102, 130, 143.

86   For a theological analysis of the meaning of 'Pit', see Karl Barth, *Church Dogmatics* 3/2, T&T Clark, Edinburgh 1960, 590.

87   While this psalm is not attributed to David, David illustrates the attitude of believing Israelites in 2 Samuel 24:14, when he has to choose between three punishments: one involving nature, one involving enemies, one involving a plague strike from God. He chooses the third, because God can change his mind (as God does, before the people of Jerusalem die along with others).

88   Shusaku Endu, *Silence*, Peter Owen, London 1969.

89   See 2 Maccabees 7.

90   Tillich is one of many theologians who have addressed this issue: 'To call God transcendent in this sense does not mean that one must establish a 'superworld' of divine objects. It does mean that, within itself, the finite world points beyond itself. In other words, it is self-transcendent (Paul Tillich, *Systematic Theology*, Vol. 2, SCM Press, London 1957 and 1978, 7).

91   Kenneth Kaunda, *Letters to my Children*, Longman, London 1973, 37.

92   Tom Wright speaks of the 'prayer of unknowing' by the genuine human being at the heart of the cosmic temple (N.T. Wright, *History and Eschatology*, SPCK, London 2019, 263). Ian Barbour discusses how God can transcend space and time at the same time as being immanent, in *Myths, Models and Paradigms*, SCM Press, London 1974, 138-9.

93   In 1861 he produced the earliest colour photograph, an image of a tartan ribbon, by having it photographed three times through red, blue, and yellow filters, then recombining the images into one colour composite (http://www.historyofinformation.com/detail.php?id=3666, accessed 27/1/20).

94   Stewart Henderson, *Especially, now . . .*, Plover Books, London 2020.

95   Barbour 1974, 42.

96   Quash 2013, 285.

97   George Mackay Brown, *Magnus*, Birlinn, Edinburgh 2008 (originally Hogarth Press 1973), 44-5.

98   Brown 2008, 93.

99   Brown 2008, 94.

100 John McIntyre, *Faith, Theology and Imagination*, Handsel, Edinburgh 1987, 14.

101 See for example, John 1:4, Romans 11:11, James 1:17.

102 Goldingay 2008, 577-8.

103 See the reference in 4.2.1.

104 You can trace this even in the more open-ended translation of the Hebrew *lᵉdawid* as 'of David' in the NIV and NRSV, compared to 'for David' in the NEB and REV.

105 Goldingay 2008, 683.

106 *The Great Tapestry of Scotland*, Birlinn, Edinburgh 2013, v-vi.

107 Deuteronomy 18:22 and 1 Thessalonians 5:21.

108 Storrar 1990, 227-8, having described the medieval vision of a free nation, the Reformed vision of a godly nation, and the Secular vision of a moral nation.

109 Storrar 1990, 235.

110 Searle 2019, 513.

111 Storrar 1990, 251.

112 https://en.wikipedia.org/wiki/James_Clerk_Maxwell.

113 Faiers 2008, 229.

114 Alastair McIntosh, *Riders on the Storm*, Birlinn, Edinburgh 2020, 191. See stanzas 1 and 2 of *Crunluath a Mach* in *The Iolaire*.

115 Verso, London 1981.

116 'From the Outer Edge', review of Neal Ascherson, 'Tom Nairn, Painting Nationalism Red?', *Democratic Left Scotland*, Feb. 2018, in the *London Review of Books*, 6th December 2018, 38.

117 The *Poem on Psalm 132* (the psalm has the exclusive claim for David in v. 18) touches on this, as the 15 men who died within Ben Cruachan were not all members of the Church of Scotland.

118 Writers may be thought to share this view by choice of occupation – or read 'The Literature Act', Carol Ann Duffy, *Collected Poems*, Pan MacMillan, London 2015, 174.

119 Goldingay 2006, 413.

120 T.C. Smout wrote that Scotland had lost the 'vibrant popular political culture it enjoyed from the 1830s to the 1920s' (Smout 1986, 275).

121 'The land of Israel is the centre of the world; Jerusalem is the centre of the land; the Holy Temple is the centre of Jerusalem . . .' (Midrash Tanhuma. *Kedoshim* 10, cited at the start of Simon Sebag Montefiore, *Jerusalem*, Weidenfeld & Nicolson, London 2011).

122 In Psalm 128:5 it is clearly the capital, the place from which people are blessed.

123 Pajunen and Penner 2017, 288.

124 Andy Wightman, *The Poor had no Lawyers*, Birlinn, Edinburgh 2013, 57.

125 Deuteronomy 12:13-14.

126 For the significance of the cry *Yhwh mālak* to Israel, see Oliver O'Donovan, *The Desire of the Nations*, Cambridge University Press, Cambridge 1996, 32f.

127 As in the sermons of Robert Bruce in Edinburgh St Giles concerning the behaviour of James VI, not least at the time of the murder of the Earl of Moray in 1592 (see Searle 2019, xvi). The Iraq War is a more recent occasion.

128 The use of 'normally' allows for gender dysphoria, but the point here is not to take sides on the issue, but to illustrate the difficulty of agreeing on moral issues using only the concept of 'rights'.

129 As Nietzsche pointed out, when you remove God, everything is a power struggle.

130 In the modern world, there are limits to what a single nation can do, so this is one motive for Scotland to seek control over its own economy, not for prosperity but for economic justice – but justice is indivisible, a matter of attitude and behaviour; it can be enabled, but not imposed, by good leadership. See also Andrew Hartropp, *God's Good Economy*, IVP, London 2019.

131 The purpose of Torah (and wisdom in the Psalms) is not to prescribe law but to describe wisdom (see Walton and Walton, *The Lost World of the Torah*, IVP, Downers Grove IL, 2019).

132 Deuteronomy 17:16-17; 1 Kings 11.

133 Rowan Williams, *Faith in the Public Square*, Bloomsbury, London 2012, 40.

134 Alister McGrath, Reality (Vol. 2 of *A Scientific Theology*, T&T Clark, Edinburgh 2002), 125.

135 McGrath 2002, 195f.

136 See 1 Kings 8:27. This point is well made in Wright 2019, 159.

137 Thomas Kuhn's *Structure of Scientific Revolutions* brought this to public attention.

Acknowledgments

Nearly all Bible quotations are from the *New Revised Standard Version Bible*, copyright © 1989 the Division of Christian Education of the National Council of the Churches of Christ in the United States of America. Used by permission. All rights reserved.

One Bible quotation is taken from *The Message*, copyright © 1993, 2002, 2018 by Eugene H. Peterson. Used by permission of NavPress. All rights reserved. Represented by Tyndale House Publishers, Inc.

Thanks are extended to the following individuals and Publishers, who reserve all rights:

Atlantic Books Ltd for permission to quote from *The Book of the People*, by A.N. Wilson.

Batsford Books for permission to quote from *The Faith of the Scots*, by Gordon Donaldson.

Birlinn Ltd for permission to quote from *A Drunk Man Looks at the Thistle*, by Hugh MacDiarmid; from the anthologies *An Lasair* and *An Tuil*; from *Magnus*, by George Mackay Brown; and from *The Poems of Norman MacCaig*.

Boydell and Brewer Ltd for permission to quote from John Reuben Davies' article in *Personal Names and Naming Practices in Medieval Scotland*.

Cambridge University Press for permission to quote from *Poetry and Jacobite Politics*, by Murray Pittock.

Canterbury Press for permission to quote from *Parable and Paradox*, © Malcolm Guite 2016 (rights@hymnsam.co.uk).

Carcanet Press, Manchester for permission to quote from *Collected Poems* by Edwin Morgan; *Hugh MacDiarmid, Selected Poems*, by Alan Riach and Michael Grieve; *Hugh MacDiarmid, Selected Prose*, by Alan Riach; *The Rauchle Tongue: Selected Essays, Journalism and Interviews by Hugh MacDiarmid*, by Angus Calder, Glen Murray and Alan Riach; *The Daylight Moon*, by Les Murray (UK rights); *The Revolutionary Art of the Future*, by Hugh MacDiarmid;

Tom Hubbard for permission to quote from 'The Hoose of Licht', his praise-poem to Patrick Geddes.

Fearghas MacFhionnlaigh for permission to quote from the English version of his poem 'An Tuagh'.

Harry Smart for permission to quote from his poem 'The Wren'.

Icon Books Ltd for permission to quote from *The Autobiography of Charles Darwin*.

Inter-Varsity Press Ltd for permission to quote from *Run with the Horses*, by Eugene Peterson.

John Wiley and Sons Ltd for permission to quote from *Psalms Through the Centuries*, by Susan Gillingham.

Maoilios Caimbeul for permission to quote from his poem 'Am Piobaire Dall'.

Margaret Connolly for remaining world rights for *The Daylight Moon*, by Les Murray.

SCM Press for permission to quote from *The Prophetic Imagination*, © Walter Brueggemann 1978 (rights@hymnsam.co.uk).

Some further acknowledgements will be found in the Notes on the Psalms at the end of each poetry chapter.

Bibliography

Abrahams, Gerald, *The Jewish Mind*, Constable, London 1961.

Adomnan, *Life of Columba*, 8th century, trans. Alan Orr Anderson, ed. Marjorie Ogilvie Anderson, Thomas Nelson, Edinburgh 1961.

Ailred and Jocelyn, *Two Celtic Saints, the Lives of Ninian and Kentigern*, reprint by Llanerch Enterprises, ISBN 0947992294.

Akenson, Donald Harman, *Surpassing Wonder*, University of Chicago Press, Montreal 1998.

Alasdair, Alasdair Mac Mhaighstir, *The Birlinn of Clanranald*, 1776, intro. and trans. Alan Riach, Kettilonia, Newtyle 2015.

Alighieri, Dante, *The Divine Comedy*, ed. Robin Kirkpatrick, Penguin, London 2012.

Alter, Robert, *The Book of Psalms*, Norton, London 2007.

Anderson, Robert *et al.* (eds.), *The Edinburgh History of Education in Scotland*, Edinburgh University Press, Edinburgh 2015.

Apichella, Maria, *Psalmody*, Eyewear Publishing, London 2016.

Ascherson, Neal, *Games with Shadows*, Century Hutchinson, London 1988.

Ascherson, Neal, *Tom Nairn, Painting Nationalism Red?* Democratic Left Scotland, Feb. 2018, in the *London Review of Books*, 6th December 2018.

Athanasius, *On the Incarnation of the Word*, c. 318 C.E., ed. and trans. A Religious of C.S.M.V., Mowbray, London 1953.

Augustine, *Confessions*, late 4th century, trans. E.B. Pusey, Dent, London 1907 (1970 edn.).

Babbit, Susan, *Impossible Dreams*, Westview, Boulder CO 1996.

Bailey, Kenneth, *Poet and Peasant*, Eerdmans, Grand Rapids 1983.

Barbour, Ian, *Myths, Models and Paradigms*, SCM Press, London 1974.

Barbour, John, *The Bruce*, c. 1376, ed. and trans. James Higgins, Arima, Bury St Edmunds 2013.

Barrow, G.W.S., *Robert Bruce and the Community of the Realm of Scotland*, Edinburgh University Press, Edinburgh 2013.

Barrow, G.W.S. (ed.), *The Declaration of Arbroath*, Society of Antiquaries of Scotland, Edinburgh 2003.

Barth, Karl, *Against the Stream*, ed. Ronald Gregor Smith, SCM Press, London 1954.

Barth, Karl, *Church Dogmatics* 3/2, T&T Clark, Edinburgh 1960.

Bateman, Meg, Crawford, Robert and McGonigal, James, *Scottish Religious Poetry*, St Andrew Press, Edinburgh 2000.

Beale, G.K., *The Temple and the Church's Mission*, IVP, Downers Grove 2004.

Begbie, Jeremy, *Redeeming Transcendence in the Arts*, Eerdmans, Grand Rapids 2018.

Begbie, Jeremy, *Resounding Truth*, SPCK, London 2008.

Bell, John L., *Psalms of Patience, Protest and Praise*, Iona Community 1993.

Bellinger, W.H., jr, *A Hermeneutic of Curiosity*, Mercer University Press, Macon GA, 1995.

Benjamin, Walter, *Illuminations*, Jonathan Cape, London 1970.

Beveridge, Craig and Turnbull, Ronald, *The Eclipse of Scottish Culture*, Polygon, Edinburgh 1989.

Black, Ronald (ed.), *An Lasair*, Birlinn, Edinburgh 2001.

Black, Ronald (ed.), *An Tuil*, Polygon, Edinburgh 1999.

Blackhall, Sheena, *Millennium Blues*, Hammerfield Publishing, Aberdeen 1999.

Blackie, John Stuart, *Lays of the Highlands and Islands*, Walter Scott, London 1888.

Bold, Alan, *MacDiarmid*, John Murray, London 1988.

Bonhoeffer, Dietrich *Life Together*, trans. Doberstein, SCM Press, London 1954.

Boutelle, Ann, *Thistle and Rose*, Bucknell University Press, Lewisberg 1980.

Bowker, John (ed.), *Complete Bible Handbook*, Dorling Kindersley, London 1988.

Briggs, Richard S., Campbell, Stephen and Rohlfing, Richard (eds.), *New Song: Biblical Hebrew Poetry as Jewish and Christian Scripture*, Lexham Press, Bellingham WA, forthcoming.

Brown, J. Croumbie (ed.), *Centenary Memorial of Rev. John Brown: A Family Record*, Andrew Eliot, Edinburgh 1887.

Brown, George Mackay, *Magnus*, Birlinn, Edinburgh 2008.

Brown, J. Croumbie (ed.), *Centenary Memorial of Rev. John Brown: A Family Record*, Andrew Eliot, Edinburgh 1887.

Brown, William P. (ed.), *The Oxford Handbook of Psalms*, Oxford University Press, New York 2014.

Brueggemann, Walter, *Praying the Psalms*, St Mary's Press, Winona, MN 1993.

Brueggemann, Walter, *The Land*, Fortress Press, Philadelphia 1977.

Brueggemann, Walter, *The Prophetic Imagination*, SCM Press, London 1978.

Buber, Martin, *Israel and the World: Essays in a Time of Crisis*, Schocken Books, New York 1948.

Burleigh, John, *A Church History of Scotland*, Oxford University Press, London 1960.

Bushnell, Nelson, *William Hamilton of Bangour*, Aberdeen University Press, Aberdeen 1957.

Buthlay, Kenneth (ed.), *A Drunk Man Looks at the Thistle*, Scottish Academic Press, Edinburgh 1987.

Butterfield, Herbert, *Christianity and History*, G. Bell and Sons, London 1949.

Caimbeul, Maoilios, 'Am Pìobaire Dall', *Breac-a'-Mhuiltein*, Coiscéim, Dublin 2007.

Caimbeul, Maoilios, *Gràs/Grace,* Handsel Press, Edinburgh 2019.

Cairns, Scott, *Slow Pilgrim, Collected Poems*, Paraclete Press, Brewster MA, 2015.

Calder, Angus, Murray, Glen, and Riach, Alan, *The Rauchle Tongue: Selected Essays, Journalism and Interviews by Hugh MacDiarmid*, Vol. 3, Carcanet, Manchester 1998.

Calpin, G.H., *There are no South Africans*, Thomas Nelson, London 1944.

Calvin, John, *Commentary on the Psalms*, Vol. 1, trans. James Anderson, Amazon 2015.

Cameron, James, *The First Book of Discipline*, St Andrew Press, Edinburgh 1972.

Cameron, Nigel (ed.), *Dictionary of Scottish Church History and Theology*, T&T Clark, Edinburgh 1993.

Carmichael, Alexander, *Carmina Gadelica*, Floris books, Edinburgh 1992.

Carr, Nicholas, *The Shallows*, Atlantic Book, London 2010.

Caskie, Donald, *The Tartan Pimpernel*, Oldbourne Book Co., London 1957.

Challis, John, 'Naming the Light' in *Stand* 16(2).

Childs, Brevard, *Introduction to the Old Testament as Scripture*, SCM Press, London 1979.

Claire, Horatio, *The Icebreaker*, Chatto and Windus, London 2017.

Clarke, David, Blackwell, Alice, Goldberg, Martin, *Early Medieval Scotland: Individuals, Communities and Ideas*, National Museums Scotland 2012.

Clarke, Edward, *A Book of Psalms*, Paraclete Press, Brewster MA 2020.

Clines, Gunn and Hauser, ed., *Art and Meaning: Rhetoric in Biblical Literature*, JSOT Press, Sheffield 1982.

Cohen, Ralph (ed.), *New Directions in Literary History*, John Hopkins University Press, Baltimore 1974.

Colgrave, Bertram, and Mynors, R.A.B., *Bede's Ecclesiastical History of the English People*, Clarendon Press, Oxford 1969.

Collinson, Francis, *The Bagpipe*, Routledge & Kegan Paul, London 1975.

Collinson, Francis, *The Traditional and National Music of Scotland*, Routledge and Kegan Paul, London 1966.

Conran, Tony, *Three Symphonies*, Agenda Editions, Mayfield, East Sussex 2016.

Crawford, Robert, *On Glasgow and Edinburgh*, Harvard University Press, Cambridge MA 2013.

Cullen, Jim, *The American Dream*, Oxford University Press, London 2003.

Curzon, David (ed.), *Modern Poems on the Bible*, Jewish Publication Society, Philadelphia 1994.

Daiches, David, *God and the Poets*, orig. Oxford University Press 1984, Zeticula, Kilkerran 2013.

Daiches, David, *The Paradox of Scottish Culture*, Oxford University Press, London 1964.

Davidson, Neil, *Discovering the Scottish Revolution 1692-1746*, Pluto Press, London 2003.

Davidson, Robert, *The Vitality of Worship*, Handsel Press, Edinburgh 1998.

Davie, Donald, *The Poet in the Imaginary Museum*, Carcanet, Manchester 1977 (orig. 1950).

Davie, George, *The Crisis of the Democratic Intellect*, Polygon, Edinburgh 1986.

Davie, George, *The Democratic Intellect*, Thomas Nelson, Edinburgh 1961.

Davies, J.G. (ed.), *A Dictionary of Liturgy and Worship*, SCM Press, London 1972.

Davies, John Reuben, 'Old Testament Personal Names in Scotland before the Wars of Independence', in Hammond (below).

Davitt, Michael and MacDonald, Ian (eds.), *Sruth na Maoile*, Canongate, Edinburgh 1993.

Dawson, Jane, *John Knox*, Yale University Press, Newhaven 2015.

Day, John (ed.), *Temple and Worship in Biblical Israel*, T&T Clark, London 2005.

de las Rivas, Toby Martinez, *Black Sun*, Faber, London 2018.

Devine, Tom, *The Scottish Nation*, Penguin, London 2012.

Dickinson, Emily, *Complete Poems*, Martin Secker, London 1928.

Dickinson, William Croft (ed.), *John Knox's History of the Reformation in Scotland*, Vol. 2, Nelson, Edinburgh 1949.

Donaldson, Gordon, *The Faith of the Scots*, Batsford, London 1990.

Donaldson, Gordon, *The Making of the Scottish Prayer Book of 1637*, Edinburgh University Press, Edinburgh 1954.

Douglas, J.D. (ed.), *Illustrated Bible Dictionary*, IVP, Leicester 1980.

Duffy, Carol Ann, *Collected Poems*, Pan MacMillan, London 2015.

Dunbar, John Telfer, *History of Highland Dress*, Oliver and Boyd, Edinburgh 1962.

Duncan, Lesley, *Images not Icons*, Kennedy & Boyd, Glasgow 2010.

Dunn, Douglas (ed.), *Faber Book of Twentieth-century Scottish Poetry*, Faber and Faber, London 1992.

Dunn, J.G.D., *New Testament Theology*, Abingdon Press, Nashville 2009.

Eban, Abba, *Heritage: Civilization and the Jews*, Weidenfeld and Nicolson, London 1984.

Eco, Umberto, *The Role of the Reader: Explorations in the Semiotics of Texts*, Indiana University Press, Bloomington 1979.

Edersheim, Alfred, *Jesus the Messiah*, Longmans, Green & Co, New York 1917.

Endu, Shusaku, *Silence*, Peter Owen, London 1969.

Erdman, David V. (ed.), *Complete Poetry and Prose of William Blake*, Doubleday, New York 1998.

Faiers, Jonathan *Tartan*, Berg, Oxford 2008.

Felch, Susan (ed.), *Cambridge Companion to Literature and Religion*, Cambridge University Press, New York 2016.

Fergusson, David and Elliott, Mark (eds.), *The History of Scottish Theology*, Vols. 1-3, Oxford University Press, Oxford 2019.

Fish, Stanley, *Is There a Text in This Class?* Harvard University Press, Cambridge MS 1980.

Forrester, Duncan and Gay, Doug (eds.), *Worship and Liturgy in Context*, SCM Press, London 2009.

Fraser, Liam Jerrold, *Mission in Contemporary Scotland*, St Andrew Press, Edinburgh 2021.

Frye, Northrop, *The Great Code: the Bible and Literature*, Routledge and Kegan Paul, London 1982.

Fuller, Steve, *Kuhn vs. Popper*, Columbia University Press, New York 2004.

Gay, Doug, *Honey from the Lion*, SCM Press, London 2013.

George, Henry, *Progress and Poverty*, Pantianos 1905.

Gifford, Douglas and Riach, Alan (eds.), *Scotlands: Poets and the Nation*, Carcanet, Manchester 2004.

Gifford, Terry (ed.), *John Muir, His Life and Letters and Other Writings*, Baton Wicks Publications, Seattle 1996 (originally by the Houghton Mifflin Company, Boston 1924).

Gillingham, Susan, *Psalms Through the Centuries*, Vol. 1, Blackwell, Oxford 2008; Vol. 2, Wiley-Blackwell, Oxford 2018.

Glen, Duncan, *Hugh MacDiarmid, Rebel Poet and Prophet*, Drumalban Press, Hemel Hempstead, 1962.

Goldingay, John, *Psalms*, Vols. 1-3, Baker, Grand Rapids 2006-8.

Graham, Roderick, *John Knox – Democrat*, Robert Hale, London 2001.

Graham, W.S., *New Collected Poems*, Faber, London 2004.

Grogan, Geoffrey, *Psalms*, Eerdmans, Grand Rapids 2008.

Guite, Malcolm, *David's Crown*, Canterbury Press, Norwich 2021.

Guite, Malcolm, *Faith, Hope and Poetry*, Ashgate, Farnham 2012.

Guite, Malcolm, *Parable and Paradox*, Canterbury Press, Norwich 2016.

Gunn, Kirsty, *The Big Music*, Faber and Faber, London 2012.

Hadari, Atar, *Songs from Bialik*, Syracuse University Press, Syracuse 2000.

Halik, Thomas, *I Want you to Be*, Notre Dame University Press, Illinois 2016.

Hammond, Matthew (ed.), *Personal Names and Naming Practices in Medieval Scotland*, Boydell, Woodbridge 2019.

Harari, Yuval Noah, *Homo Deus: a Brief History of Tomorrow*, Penguin, London 2015.

Harper, Sally (ed.), *Our Awin Scottis Use*, Universities of Glasgow and Aberdeen, Glasgow, 2000.

Hart, Kevin, *Poetry and Revelation*, Bloomsbury, London 2017.

Hartropp, Andrew, *God's Good Economy*, IVP, London 2019.

Hastings, Adrian, *The Construction of Nationhood*, Cambridge University Press, Cambridge 1997.

Hayward, C.T.R., *The Jewish Temple*, Routledge, London 1996.

Heaney, Seamus, *Seamus Heaney, 100 poems*, Faber and Faber, London 2018.

Heaney, Seamus, *The Government of the Tongue*, Faber and Faber, London 1988.

Hearn, Jonathan, *Rethinking Nationalism*, Palgrave Macmillan, Basingstoke 2006.

Henderson, Alexander, *Sermons, Prayers and Pulpit Addresses*, ed. Thomas Martin orig. 1638, John Maclaren, Edinburgh 1867.

Henderson, George and Isabel, *The Arts of the Picts: Sculpture and Metalwork in Early Medieval Scotland*, Thames and Hudson, London 2004.

Henderson, Stewart, *Especially, now . . .*, Plover Books, London 2020.

Hendry, Diana, *Twelve Lilts*, Mariscat Press, Edinburgh 2003.

Herbert, George, *Complete Works*, Digireads.com, Milton Keynes 2013.

Hershaw, William and McConnell, Les, *Saul Vaigers*, Grace Note Publications, Crieff 2021.

Hershaw, William and McConnell, Les, *The Sair Road,* Grace Note Publications, Crieff 2018.

Highland, Chris (ed.), *Meditations of John Muir: Nature's Temple*, Wilderness Press, Birmingham AL 2001.

Hirsch, Edward, *How to Read a Poem*, Houghton Mifflin Harcourt, New York 1999.

Hogg, James, *Private Memoirs and Confessions of a Justified Sinner*, ed. Garside, Edinburgh University Press, Edinburgh 2001.

Hogg, James, *Selected Poems*, ed. Groves, Scottish Academic Press 1986.

Holladay W.L., *The Psalms through 3000 Years,* Fortress, Minneapolis, 1996.

Holmes, Stephen Mark, 'Catalogue of Liturgical Books and Fragments in Scotland before 1560', *The Innes Review* 62.2 (2011), 127-212, Edinburgh University Press, DOI: 10.3366/inr.2011.0016.

Holz, Barry (ed.), *Back to the Sources: Reading the Classic Jewish Texts*, Touchstone, New York 1984.

Houston, Joseph, *Thomas Reid in a Nutshell*, Handsel Press, Edinburgh 2000.

Jack, Alison, *The Prodigal Son in English and American Literature*, Oxford University Press, Oxford 2019.

Jaidelska, Elspeth, '"Singing of Psalms of which I could never get enough": Labouring Class Religion and Poetry in the Cambuslang Revival of 1741', *Studies in Scottish Literature*, 41 (1), 2015.

Jaki, Stanley, *Praying the Psalms*, Eerdmans, Grand Rapids 2001.

Jasper, David and Prickett, Stephen (eds.), *The Bible and Literature*, Blackwell, Oxford 1999.

Jasper, David, *Heaven in Ordinary*, Lutterworth, Cambridge 2018.

Jehle, Frank, *Ever Against the Stream*, Eerdmans, Grand Rapids 2002.

Johnston, Philip and Firth, David (eds.), *Interpreting the Psalms*, Apollos, Leicester 2005.

Kaunda, Kenneth, *Letters to my Children*, Longman, London 1973.

Kay, Jackie, *Bantam*, Picador, London 2017.

Kelsey, D.H., *Eccentric Existence: A Theological Anthropology*, Westminster John Knox Press, Louisville KY 2009

Ker, John, *The Psalms in History and Biography*, Andrew Elliot, Edinburgh 1886.

Kernohan, R.D., *The Realm of Reform*, Handsel Press, Edinburgh 1999.

Kingsley, Patrick, *The New Odyssey*, Faber & Faber, London 2016.

Klein, Naomi, *This Changes Everything*, Penguin Random House, New York 2015.

Knight, Christopher, *The God of Nature*, Fortress, Minneapolis 2007.

Knight, G.A.F., *Theology in Pictures*, Handsel Press, Edinburgh 1981.

Knox, Francesca and Took, John (eds.), *Poetry and Prayer*, Ashgate, Farnham 2015.

Köhler, Ludwig, *Hebrew Man*, SCM Press, London 1973.

Kuhn, Thomas, *The Structure of Scientific Revolutions*, University of Chicago Press, Chicago 1962.

Laing and Small, *Select Remains of the Ancient Popular and Romance Poetry of Scotland*, Edinburgh 1885.

Lamb, J.A., *The Psalms in Christian Worship*, Faith Press, London 1962.

Latourette, Kenneth, *A History of the Expansion of Christianity*, Vol. 1, Paternoster, Exeter 1971.

Law, William, *Serious Call to a Devout and Holy Life*, J.M. Dent, London 1906 (orig. 1728).

Leavitt, John (ed.), *Poetry and Prophecy*, University of Michigan Press, Ann Arbor 1997.

Lederach, John Paul, *The Moral Imagination*, Oxford University Press, New York 2005.

Levenson, Jon D., 'The Temple and the World', *Journal of Religion*, Vol. 64 no. 3 (July 1984).

Lewis, C.S. (ed.), *George MacDonald, an Anthology*, Collins, London 1955.

Lewis, C.S., *They Asked for a Paper*, Geoffrey Bles, London 1962.

Lochhead, Liz, *The Colour of Black and White*, Polygon, Edinburgh 2003.

Lola, Theresa, *In Search of Equilibrium*, Nine Arches Press, Rugby 2019.

Lynch, Michael, *Scotland, A New History*, Pimlico, London 1991.

MacCaig, Norman, *Collected Poems*, Birlinn, Edinburgh 2010.

MacColl, Allan, *Land, Faith and the Crofting Community*, Edinburgh University Press, Edinburgh 2006.

MacDiarmid, Hugh, *Selected Poems* – see under Riach and Grieve below.

MacDiarmid, Hugh, *In Memoriam James Joyce, A Vision of World Language*, William MacLellan, Glasgow 1956.

MacDiarmid, Hugh, *The Revolutionary Art of the Future: Rediscovered Poems*, ed. John Manson *et al.*, Carcanet and the Scottish Poetry Library, Manchester and Edinburgh 2003.

MacDonald, George, *At The Back of the North Wind, The Princess and the Goblin, The Princess and Curdie*, Octopus, London 1979.

MacFhionnlaigh, Fearghas, 'The Midge', *Cencrastus*, Autumn 1982 (Gaelic 'A' Mheanbhchuileag', *Gairm, 1980*).

MacIntyre, Alasdair, 'The Very Idea of a University: Aristotle, Newman and Us', *British Journal of Educational Studies* 57:4.

Mackenzie, Ian, *Tunes of Glory*, Handsel Press, Edinburgh 1993.

MacLean, Colin and Veitch, Kenneth (eds.), *Scottish Life and Society: a Compendium of Scottish Ethnology*, Vol. 12, John Donald, Edinburgh 2006.

MacLeod, George, *One Way Left*, Iona Community, Glasgow 1958.

MacLeod, Kenneth, *The Road to the Isles*, Grant and Murray, Edinburgh 1927.

MacQuarrie, John, 'Burns: Poet, Prophet, Philosopher', *Expository Times* 86, 1975.

Martin and Koda, *Orientalism: Visions of the East in Western Dress* (catalogue), 1994.

Martin, Hugh (ed.), *Selected Letters of Samuel Rutherfurd*, SCM Press, London 1957.

Maxwell, Stephen, *Arguing for Independence*, Luath Press, Edinburgh 2012.

Maxwell, William, *A History of Worship in the Church of Scotland*, Oxford University Press, London 1955.

McCrone, David, *Understanding Scotland: the Sociology of a Stateless Nation*, Routledge, London 1992.

McEwen, James S., *The Faith of John Knox*, Lutterworth, London 1961.

McGlynn, John H., 'Leaves of Palm and Temples of Language', *Stand* 17(1), 2019.

McGrath, Alister, *Reality* (Vol. 2 of *A Scientific Theology*), T&T Clark, Edinburgh 2002.

McIntosh, Alastair, *Healing Nationhood*, Curlew Productions, Kelso 2000.

McIntosh, Alastair, *Riders on the Storm*, Birlinn, Edinburgh 2020.

McIntyre, John, *Faith, Theology and Imagination*, Handsel, Edinburgh 1987.

McLeod, Wilson and Newton, Michael (eds.), *The Highest Apple: an Anthology of Scottish Gaelic Literature*, Francis Boutle Publishers, London 2019.

Meek, Donald, *The Quest for Celtic Christianity*, Handsel Press, Edinburgh 2000.

Middleton, J.R., *The Liberating Image*, Baker, Grand Rapids 2005.

Mitchell, David, *Jesus: the Incarnation of the Word*, Campbell Publications 2021.

Mitchell, David, *The Message of the Psalter*, Sheffield Academic Press, Sheffield 1997 (reprinted Campbell Publications, Newton Mearns 2017).

Mitchell, David, *The Song of Ascents*, Campbell Publications, Newton Mearns 2015.

Moffat, Alexander, and Riach, Alan, *The Arts of Independence*, Luath Press, Edinburgh 2014.

Momus, *The Book of Scotlands*, Luath Press, Edinburgh 2018.

Montefiore, Simon Sebag, *Jerusalem*, Weidenfeld & Nicolson, London 2011.

Morales, L. Michael (ed.), *Cult and Cosmos: Tilting Towards a Temple-Centred Theology*, Peeters, Leuven 2014.

Morgan, Edwin, *Collected Poems*, Carcanet, Manchester 1990.

Murray, Les, *The Daylight Moon*, Carcanet, Manchester 1988.

Nairn, Tom, *The Break-up of Britain*, Verso, London 1981.

Newman, J.H., *The Idea of a University*, ed. I.T. Ker, Oxford University Press, Oxford 1976.

Niebuhr, Reinhold, *Moral Man and Immoral Society*, SCM Press, London 1963.

Nihtinen, Atina, 'Scotland's Linguistic Past and Present: Paradoxes and Consequences', Studia *Celtica Fennica* 2, Jan. 2005.

O'Donovan, Oliver, *The Desire of the Nations*, Cambridge University Press, Cambridge 1996.

Oliver, Neil, *A History of Scotland*, Weidenfeld and Nicolson, London 2009.

Page, Christopher, *The Christian West and its Singers*, Yale University Press, London 2010.

Painting, Andrew, *Regeneration*, Birlinn 2021.

Pajunen, Mika and Penner, Jeremy (eds.), *Functions of Psalms and Prayers in the late Second Temple Period*, De Gruyter, Berlin 2017.

Patrick, Miller, *Four Centuries of Scottish Psalmody*, Oxford University Press, Oxford 1949.

Penman, Michael, *Robert the Bruce: King of the Scots*, Yale University Press, London 2014.

Penman, Michael, 'Sacred Food for the Soul: in search of the Devotions to Saints of Robert Bruce, King of Scotland, 1306-1329', *Speculum* Vol. 88, No. 4 (October 2013), University of Chicago Press.

Percy, Lord Eustace, *John Knox*, Hodder & Stoughton, London, 1937.

Peterson, Eugene, *Answering God*, Harper & Row, San Francisco 1989.

Peterson, Eugene, *Where Your Treasure Is*, Eerdmans, Grand Rapids 1993.

Pieper, Joseph, *Only the Lover Sings,* Ignatius Press, San Francisco 1990.

Pittock, Murray, *Poetry and Jacobite Politics*, Cambridge University Press, Cambridge 1994.

Prothero, Roland, *The Psalms in Human Life*, Thomas Nelson, London 1903.

Provan, Iain, *Convenient Myths*, Baylor University Press, Waco 2013.

Provan, Iain, *Seriously Dangerous Religion*, Baylor University Press, Waco 2014.

Provan, Iain, *The Reformation and the Right Reading of Scripture*, Baylor University Press, Waco 2017.

Purser, John, *Rannsachadh na Gaidhlig 8*, Edinburgh University Press.

Purser, John, *Scotland's Music*, Mainstream, Edinburgh 1992 and 2007.

Pyper, Hugh, *The Unchained Bible*, Bloomsbury, London 2012.

Quash, Ben, *Found Theology: History, Imagination and the Holy Spirit*, Bloomsbury, London 2013.

Quintilian, *Institutio Oratoria* 6.6.51, cited in 'Transfiguration: Christology and the roots of figurative exegesis in St Augustine', *Studia Patristica XXXIII*, Peeters, Leuven 1997.

Reid-Baxter, Jamie *et al.*, *Jhone Angus: Monk of Dunfermline and Scottish Reformation Music*, Dunfermline Heritage Community Projects, Dunfermline 2011.

Riach, Alan, *Hugh MacDiarmid, Selected Prose*, Carcanet, Manchester 1992.

Riach, Alan, *Hugh MacDiarmid's Epic Poetry*, Edinburgh University Press, Edinburgh 1991.

Riach, Alan, *Scottish Literature: an introduction*, Luath Press, Edinburgh 2022.

Riach, Alan and Grieve, Michael (eds.), *Hugh MacDiarmid, Selected Poems*, Carcanet 1992, reissued Penguin, London 1994.

Ricoeur, Paul, *Essays on Biblical Interpretation*, ed. Lewis Mudge, SPCK, London 1981.

Ricoeur, Paul, *Memory, History, Forgetting*, University of Chicago Press, Chicago 2004.

Ricoeur, Paul, *The Symbolism of Evil*, Beacon Press, Boston 1967.

Ridley, Jasper, *John Knox*, Clarendon Press, Oxford 1968.

Ritchie, Bruce, *Columba: the Faith of an Island Soldier*, Christian Focus, Fearn 2019.

Roberts, Michael Symmons, *Drysalter*, Jonathan Cape, London 2013.

Sacks, Jonathan, *Covenant and Conversation*, Maggid, Jerusalem 2009.

Scholes, Percy (ed.), *Oxford Companion to Music*, Oxford University Press, London 1938.

Schröder, Martin, *Transforming Tradition: Gaelic Psalms in the work of Capercaillie and Runrig*, Rostock University of Music & Drama, 2015.

Scott, Paul H., *Towards Independence*, Polygon, Edinburgh 1991.

Scott, Walter, *The Heart of Midlothian*, Oxford University Press, London 1912.

Searle, David (ed.), *Preaching without Fear or Favour*, Christian Focus, Fearn 2019.

Smart, Harry, *A Plain Glass*, Drunk Muse Press 2021.

Smith, Anthony, *Chosen Peoples: Sacred Sources of National Identity*, Oxford University Press, Oxford 2003.

Smith, David, *Stumbling Towards Zion*, Langholm Global Library, Carlisle 2020.

Smith, Iain Crichton, *New Collected Poems*, Carcanet, Manchester 1992.

Smith, J.K.A., *The Fall of Interpretation*, Baker, Grand Rapids 2012.

Smith, Mark, *Psalms: the Divine Journey*, Paulist Press, New York 1987.

Smout, T.C., *A Century of the Scottish People*, 1830-1950, Collins, Glasgow and Yale University Press, New Haven 1986.

Snow, Michael & Margaret (eds.), *The Nightfisherman: Selected Letters of W S Graham*, Carcanet, Manchester 1999.

Spencer, Nick, *The Evolution of the West*, SPCK, London 2016.

Stamp, Gavin (ed.), *The Light of Truth and Beauty – Lectures of Alexander 'Greek' Thomson 1817-1872*, The Alexander Thomson Society, Glasgow 1999.

Stamp, Gavin, and McKinstry, Sam (ed.), *'Greek' Thomson*, Edinburgh University Press, Edinburgh 1994.

Steven, Kenneth, *The Spirit of the Hebrides*, St Andrew Press 2019.

Stevens, Wallace, *The Collected Poems*, Penguin, New York, Second Vintage Edition of 2015.

Storrar, William, *Scottish Identity*, Handsel Press, Edinburgh 1990.

Thomason, C.S., *Ceol Mor Notation*, East Indies 1893 and East Ardsley 1975.

Tillich, Paul, *Systematic Theology*, Vol. 2, SCM Press, London 1957, 1978.

Toibin, Colm, *On Elisabeth Bishop*, Princeton University Press, Princeton NJ 2015.

Torrance, James, and Walls, Roland, *John Duns Scotus in a Nutshell*, Handsel Press, Edinburgh 1992.

Torrance, T.F. (ed.), *Belief in Science and in Christian Life*, Handsel, Edinburgh 1980.

Torrance, T.F., *Reality and Scientific Theology*, Scottish Academic Press, Edinburgh 1985.

Torrance, T.F. (ed. and trans.), *The School of Faith*, James Clarke, London 1959.

Underhill, Evelyn, *Worship*, Collins, London 1962 (Fontana edition, originally 1936).

Volf, Miroslav, *Exclusion and Embrace*, Abingdon Press, Nashville 1996.

Wallace, William (ed.), Poetical Works of Robert Burns, Chambers, Edinburgh 1947.

Wallis, Jim, *On God's Side*, Baker, Grand Rapids 2013.

Walton, John, *The Lost World of Adam and Eve*, IVP Downers Grove IL 2015.

Walton, John, *The Lost World of Genesis One*, IVP Downers Grove IL 2009.

Walton and Walton, *The Lost World of the Torah*, IVP, Downers Grove IL 2019.

Warren, F.E., *The Liturgy and Ritual of the Celtic Church*, Boydell Press, Suffolk 1987.

Weatherhead, Leslie D., *A Private House of Prayer*, 1958, reissued by Arthur James, London 1985.

White, Eric Walter, *Stravinsky: the Composer and his Works*, University of California Press, Los Angeles and London 1966.

Wightman, Andy, *The Poor had no Lawyers*, Birlinn, Edinburgh 2013.

Williams, Rowan, 'Augustine and the Psalms', *Interpretation*, Jan 2004.

Williams, Rowan, *Faith in the Public Square*, Bloomsbury, London 2012.

Williams, Rowan, *Grace and Necessity: Reflections on Art and Love*, Continuum, London 2005.

Wilson, A.N., *The Book of the People*, Atlantic Books, London 2015.

Wilson, Gerald H., *NIV Application Commentary*, Vol. 1, Zondervan, Grand Rapids 2002.

Wink, Walter, *Unmasking the Powers*, Fortress, Philadelphia 1986.

Wittkower, Rudolf, *Architectural Principles in the Age of Humanism*, Alec Tiranti, London 1962.

Woolsey, Andrew, *Duncan Campbell: a Biography*, Hodder and the Faith Mission, London 1974.

Wright, David F. (ed.), *The Bible in Scottish Life and Literature*, St Andrew Press, Edinburgh 1988.

Wright, N.T., *History and Eschatology*, London 2019.

Wright, N.T., *Luke for Everyone*, SPCK, London 2001.

Yates, Frances, *The Art of Memory*, Routledge and Kegan Paul, London 1966.

Yee, Gale (ed.), *The Hebrew Bible, Feminist and Intersectional Perspectives*, Fortress, Minneapolis 2018.

Yoder, John Howard, *The Politics of Jesus*, Eerdmans, Grand Rapids 1972.

Yousafzai, Malala, *I am Malala*, Weidenfeld & Nicolson, London 2013.

In Tune with Heaven, (Church of England Archbishops' Commission on Church Music), Hodder, London 1992.

The Autobiography of Charles Darwin, 1809-1882, Norton, New York 1958.

The Great Tapestry of Scotland, Birlinn, Edinburgh 2013.

The Hugh MacDiarmid Anthology: Poems in Scots and in English, Routledge & Kegan Paul, London 1972.

The Passover Haggadah, Soncino, London 1959.